Other Books by Author:

Twin Soul Separation

The Face
of the Father

JOAN CLARKE

BALBOA.
PRESS

A DIVISION OF HAY HOUSE

Balboa Press books may be ordered through booksellers or by contacting:

Balboa Press
A Division of Hay House
1663 Liberty Drive
Bloomington, IN 47403
www.balboapress.com
1-(877) 407-4847

Because of the dynamic nature of the Internet, any web addresses or links contained in this book may have changed since publication and may no longer be valid. The views expressed in this work are solely those of the author and do not necessarily reflect the views of the publisher, and the publisher hereby disclaims any responsibility for them.

The author of this book does not dispense medical advice or prescribe the use of any technique as a form of treatment for physical, emotional, or medical problems without the advice of a physician, either directly or indirectly. The intent of the author is only to offer information of a general nature to help you in your quest for emotional and spiritual well-being. In the event you use any of the information in this book for yourself, which is your constitutional right, the author and the publisher assume no responsibility for your actions.

Any people depicted in stock imagery provided by Thinkstock are models, and such images are being used for illustrative purposes only.
Certain stock imagery © Thinkstock.

Printed in the United States of America

ISBN: 978-1-4525-6613-9 (sc)
ISBN: 978-1-4525-6615-3 (hc)
ISBN: 978-1-4525-6614-6 (e)

Library of Congress Control Number: 2012924152

Balboa Press rev. date: 2/21/2013

Dedicated to the Association of Research & Enlightenment (A.R.E.) and to all seekers of the truth worldwide.

ACKNOWLEDGMENTS

On behalf of my beloved, deceased sister, Joan Clarke, author of <u>The Face of The Father</u>, I would like to acknowledge the following individuals, whose help and support have made this book a reality.

The author was thankful to God for blessing her with His desire for her to write this book. She had encouragement from numerous friends and family, too many to list.

My friend and colleague, John Mullins, a life member of the A.R.E., read and reread this book in its entirety. He was able to find with his razor sharp mind many paragraphs which needed rearranging to make the material flow better. His devotion to this cause was outstanding; thank you, dear heart.

The two reviewers, Charlotte LeHecka and Cecelia Anderson, were both tireless and loyal readers of the manuscript. Thank you for giving your professional opinions.

We appreciate so much Claire Gardner, Archivist from the Edgar Cayce Foundation (ECF)/Association of Research & Enlightenment (A.R.E.), who reviewed the Edgar Cayce Reading quotations for accuracy and content within the unpublished manuscript. Her support and encouragement to go forth to publish was like a breath of fresh air coming down on us from on high.

Last, but not least, is my younger sister, Jane Marsh, who has supported this work from the beginning. She promised Joan she would be responsible for getting this book published. Indeed, Jane has worked nonstop seeking and finding just the right publisher for this work. Once found, the work started all over again to sift through all the numerous other chores that go along with her many consultations with those in charge of publishing.

Hats off to you, Jane!

Judy Clarke, Editor

SOURCE OF THE EDGAR CAYCE
WORK AND READINGS

Edgar Cayce was a Christian mystic.

He was born knowing God.

He played with fairies and the "little folk" as a lonely child on the family farm. His relationship with his grandfather continued on even after the grandfather had passed away.

In a vision as a child, he was promised he'd have the opportunity to help others. He had the ability to sleep on his books and retain a photographic memory of every page in the book.

Edgar Cayce was a Christ centered man.

He had a personal relationship with Jesus Christ.

He read the Bible. He believed in prayer. He taught Sunday school. He was psychic. He had visions and dreams.

He was able to go into a profoundly deep state of meditation which others call a self induced hypnotic - like trance.

From this higher state of consciousness he was able to give information on any given topic or answer any question. This ability has been termed a "Reading."

Cayce was able to commune with other subconscious Minds which was his main method of obtaining physical Readings.

He was able to go to the Hall of Records and read from an individual's Book of Life or the Akashic Records.

This was how he obtained most of the Life Readings.

The purpose of the Readings was always constructive and meant to be helpful. Information was never given that would give one individual advantage over another, but only "to magnify the virtues and minimize the faults."

At times, Michael the Archangel spoke.

There were some incidents of communication with the deceased. Although the Readings themselves discouraged spiritualism, there were exceptions for closure or peace about a loved one who had passed on through "God's other door."

The MAIN source of the Readings is from the Christ Spirit. It is stated that they are the work of the "Master of Masters," the "Prince of Peace," the "Lord of Lords," the "King of Kings," and/or from the "Throne of Grace itself."
The Readings warned not to seek council from any other masters or lower sources than Christ Himself.

Reading #281-19:
...As has been the warning to all, so encompass self with the thoughts of the Christ Consciousness that only that which may come from the THRONE itself may BE the Source of that which will guide or direct thee in thy seeking.

Reading #1650-1:
Upon time and space are written the thoughts, the deeds, the activities of an entity has been oft called, the record of God's Book of Remembrance.

Reading #294-7 (294 is Edgar Cayce's Reading number):
Keep the physical fit that the world may know that through this individual, (Edgar Cayce), the manifestations are of the Prince of Peace.

Reading #254-76:
Count it joy, then, even as He, that ye are called by Him in service— in a LOVING service—to thy fellow man; For through this lowly, weak, unworthy channel, (Edgar Cayce), has He chosen to speak, for the purposes of this soul have been to do Good unto his brethren.

Reading #294-1:
Edgar Cayce's Mind is amenable to suggestion, the same as all other subconscious Minds, but in addition thereto, it has the

Power to interpret to the objective Mind of others what it acquires from the subconscious Mind of other individuals of the same kind. The subconscious Mind forgets nothing. The conscious Mind receives the impression from without and transfers all thought to the subconscious, where it remains even though the conscious be destroyed. The subconscious Mind of Edgar Cayce is in direct communication with all other subconscious Minds, and is capable of interpreting through his objective Mind and
imparting impressions received to other objective Minds, gathering in this way all knowledge possessed by millions of other subconscious Minds.

Reading #254-60:
Q: Who is giving this information?
A: As it is a universality of purpose so from those of the general or universal or Cosmic Forces, are ministering that being given in this present interest.

Reading #900-22:
When the Body, Edgar Cayce, in the psychic or subconscious condition, is able then to reach all subconscious Minds when directed to such subconscious minds by suggestion, whether in the material world or in the spiritual world...

Reading #254-83:
Q: To what extent are the Masters of the Great White Brotherhood directing the activities of Edgar Cayce? Who are the Masters directly in charge?
A: MESSENGERS from the higher forces that may manifest from the Throne of Grace itself.
Q: Who are the masters directly in charge? Is St. Germain –
A: (Interrupting) Those that are directed by the Lord of Lords, the King of Kings, HIM that came that ye might be One with the Father.

Reading #254-92:

Less and less of personality, more and more of God and Christ in the dealings with the fellow man.

Ye have an organization then with a physical being, with a mental being, with a spiritual concept. And only that which is not merely idealistic but in keeping with God's, Christ's precepts, Jesus' anointings may be that which may grow and become as a LIVING thing in the experience, in the bodies, in the Minds; yea, to the very awareness of the souls of men whom such a group, such an organization would serve.

...Let each phase of the work present not only mentally but spiritually that there is a grounding in TRUTH as set forth in the Christ-Consciousness as exemplified by Jesus, as has been proclaimed by many of the Saints of old.

Reading #262-6:

Whosoever WILL has a part, or parcel, in HIS work.

He that has CALLED TO thee! If one heeds not, or hears not the invitation, then one has only missed an opportunity and it must all be done over again.

PROLOGUE

It was in 1979 as I was coming down the stairway when I paused on the landing and glanced at my reflection in the mirror. It wasn't my physical self looking back at me, but I recognized the image as my higher self.
Every time I catch a glimpse of my soul self, I know something important is about to happen to me in Spirit.

I heard a voice say, "Write the Face of The Father."
It wasn't the voice of my higher self, but it was the voice of Christ or His Holy Spirit that was leading me. I did not have to ponder the meaning as I KNEW it meant that God wanted me to present the reflection of Himself in Jesus, using the Edgar Cayce Readings.

Later, I was on my way to the A.R.E. to do research and a most exciting thing happened that day. I found a Reading containing the exact words that I had heard. Reading #1567-2 states, "He, the Son, was in the earth-earthy even as we...yet is of the Godhead. Hence, the Mind is both material and spiritual and taketh hold on that which is its environ, its want in our experiences. Then Mind, as HE, was the Word – and dwelt among men and we beheld Him as 'The Face of The Father.'"

Somehow, I did not feel qualified to undertake such a serious task. I have been collecting Readings for this project for many years but now am concerned about how much time I have left in this Life on Earth. Although I am not an intellectual or a Bible scholar, I do have a good insight into the Readings.

I have never encountered in other literature some of the creation memories that have been opened to me. The Edgar Cayce Readings contain many of the same revelations that I was given and have helped to clarify my experiences. And I feel certain that I am not the only one who has had these thoughts. I am not well versed in the many ancient manuscripts and religious viewpoints that exist. I used the King James version of the Bible for scriptures that relate to the Readings. I have taken the liberty of capitalizing words in the Readings and also in the Bible that relate to the message.

I see the Readings and the Bible as literal and also symbolic in interpretation, so I try to look at both sides to see which one or if both will fit.

The time frame(s) used in the Readings can be confusing and is impossible to be proven and will always be debated by different researchers. It seems that the dates given in the Readings could be related to an esoteric numbering system (which in itself conceals higher truths) rather than calendar dates.
I doubt if any of us sees the time frame in perfect order.

Feel free to object or disagree. We are all of different levels of development and no one will ever see the whole picture exactly the same.
My motive in writing the book is first to obey God's direction along with the hope that someone might come to know Jesus as "The Face of The Father."

TABLE OF CONTENTS

TABLE OF CONTENTS

CHAPTER I

THE NATURE OF GOD

The Edgar Cayce Readings describe God as Spirit, as Mind, as "creative energy." God is the First Cause, which is the energy source of all creation. The characteristics of the spiritual nature of God are Light, Law, Love, Truth, Peace, Harmony, Goodness, Mercy and Individuality. The nature of God is always constructive, purposeful and motivated by Wisdom and Love. The "creative force" of God is Omnipresent, Omnipotent, and Omniscient.

> God, the First Cause, the First Principle,
> the First Movement, IS! That's the beginning!
> That is, that was, that ever shall be!
>   (262-52)

> Truth is the unalterable, unchangeable Law, ever.
> What is Truth? Law! Love. What is Love? What is God?
> Law and Love.
>   (3574-2)

> For the Universal Consciousness IS constructive, not destructive in ANY manner...
>   (792-2)

1

There is very little information about the nature of God BEFORE the creation of Christ as the Only Begotten Son.

Tom Sugrue wrote a detailed account about what God was like before this creation in the philosophy section of There Is A River. It is a very interesting and unique viewpoint which is well worth reading.

> "Man demands a beginning and a boundary, so in the beginning there was a sea of Spirit, and it filled all space. It was static, content, aware of itself, a giant resting on the bosom of its thought, contemplating what it was. Then it moved. It withdrew into itself, until all space was empty, and that which had filled it was shining from its center, a restless, seething Mind. This was the individuality of the Spirit; this was what it discovered itself to be when it awakened; this was God. God desired to express Himself, and He desired companionship. Therefore, He projected from Himself the cosmos and souls. The cosmos was built with the tools which man calls music, arithmetic, and geometry: Harmony, system, and balance. The building blocks were all the same material, which man calls the "Life essence." It was a Power sent out from God, a primary ray, which by changing the length of its wave and rate of its vibration became a pattern of differing forms, substance and movement. This created the Law of Diversity which supplied endless designs for the pattern. God played on this Law of Diversity as a person plays on a piano, producing melodies and arranging them in a "symphony.""

Eula Allen wrote in her book, Before The Beginning:

> "All images were first created in spirit, but God is not a worshipper of images. God is love, and the law of love is giving and sharing. God desired companionship. This outpouring of love was the dividing of Himself to create

this companionship. This companion was none other than His firstborn, the Christ, His first begotten in Spirit, the Word."

Eula Allen said that God had to divide Himself to create Christ. (Tom Sugrue skipped over the creation of Christ as the Only Begotten Son and jumped right into the creation of souls.)

To understand the whole picture, first, it is important to include the creation of Christ, as the Only Begotten Son.

Edgar Cayce in his Bible class said:

"The First Principle was that God moved out of Himself."

This was the FIRST CAUSE.
Why did God desire companionship?
God is Spirit.
The "I Am that I Am."
God is eternal.
God is creative energy.
God is self-sufficient.
God is the First Cause or First Impulse.

My thought is that it might be very boring to be ALL that is or ever will be even if One is Truth and Light and contains infinite energy and Power.
I would not want to be it all. Who wants to be everything?
All that is?
To know only One's self?
Only me?
To be all-alone with only One's self?
There would be a void.
There would be an emptiness.
It would be infinitely deep.

3

Did God have to give up a part of Himself to allow an expression of another being beside Himself?
Did God have to divide Himself?
Was there a SEPARATION of the self?
Did God lose a part of Himself in that division?
Or perhaps, He became more of Himself.

Did the Spirit of God in moving out of Himself create a separate vibration apart from His ALLNESS? Or a separateness IN/OF the ALLNESS?

Is there only One God who by dividing Himself makes of Himself two? Or two in One? Another One in the Oneness?

Stillness becomes motion.
Silence gives birth to sound.
The invisible is made visible.
God remains motionless while seemingly dividing Himself by the motion created in the act of His imaging.
How can this be?

How does One give One's Love or "self,"
if there is no one else to receive it?
A person, a place must exist.
Or be created, "Begotten."

Before the First Creation of the Christ, everything was the same.
The same Oneness.
The only "self."
Selfness.

God desired companionship and expression.

Q: The reason for creation…?

A: God's desire for companionship and expression.
(5749-14)

Love gives without thought of self.
The Cayce Readings tell us that desire as will is a part of creation.
Desire and will are part of the fabric of every soul and they become
as Law.

> Desire, as will, is a portion then of the spiritual self.
> (1597-1)

God desired companionship and gave Himself.
In that outpouring of Love, a Son was born.
The Only Begotten Son.

FIRST CONSCIOUSNESS!

> But in His Love, in what we call infinite Love,
> boundless, the unbounding Grace and Mercy and
> patience and Love and long-suffering, these have
> brought to the Father the thought of the lack of the
> WONDERMENT of, COMPANIONSHIP.
> (262-115)

The thought of companionship, the thought of the lack of a
companion, the wonderment of having a companion to share
all with; that is an amazing concept. The sharing of one's self in
consciousness, communication, and memory as a co-creator.
Companionship is so important to us, and we all treasure the
wonderment of it. Without companionship there is a deep void. I
can understand why God desired companionship.

God created His Firstborn Son from Himself. The Spirit moved and
by moving itself out of itself, a separate vibration was manifested. To
do this required a loss or a division of the self. What that may mean
we cannot comprehend with human Minds.

This concept must be spiritually perceived as a mystical experience
or a knowing that bypasses cognizable reason.

The birth was a replica of Himself in Spirit, born from the Body of God, in the Body of God, of the Body of God. SELF BEGOTTEN!

The Son contains the essence of that which the entire Creator is but having free will to experience separate awareness.
The ability to create and to manifest thoughts, purposes, and dreams into tangible realities.

The Only Begotten Son is Christ.
Christ is Mind.
Christ is consciousness.
Christ is God externalized.
Christ is God crystallized.
Christ is the reflection of God.
Christ is the Spirit of God in action.
Christ is the Light.
Christ is at One with God.
Christ is the Word.
Christ is the Logos.
Christ is the invisible made visible.
Christ is the sound of God.
Christ is God made audible.
Christ is in the Holy Trinity.
Christ is the Holy Trinity.
Christ is the Creator of the universe.
Christ is the Creator of all souls.
Christ is the Creator of all that manifests.
Christ is the name of God.
Christ is the nature of God.
Christ is God.
No man has seen God at any time.
We have only seen the manifestations of Him.
Christ is the mirror that reflects the Father image.

No man hath seen God at any time; the Only Begotten Son, which is in the bosom of the Father, He hath declared Him.

John 1:18

No man, no physical matter, has ever seen GOD at any time; only the MANIFESTATIONS of Him.

(707-1)

Did the Spirit of God have to divide to see "itself?"
Did that which was the deep, dark, void in unconsciousness become conscious, bringing forth Light?

God said, "Let there be Light and there was Light." This was not as an activity from the sun, or Light shed from any radial influence, but it was the ability of consciousness coming into growth from the First Cause.

(2528-2)

In the manifestation of all Power, force, motion, vibration, that which impels, that which detracts, is in its essence of the One force, One source, in its elemental form.

(262-52)

Spirit is the FIRST CAUSE, the essence of creative Power, the source of Light, and the motivating influence of all Life. It is God.

Spirit is the First Cause, the primary beginning, the motivative influence, as God is Spirit.

(262-123)

In the beginning was the Word, and the Word was with God, and the Word was God.

John 1:1

> The First Existence…was in the MIND of the
> Creator…
> (2925-1)

Consciousness came into GROWTH from the First Cause.
The "Begotten" self unfolds itself into Light.

According to the Readings, there are only three creations, which
are "matter", "force", and Mind. Matter, force, and Mind are the
ESSENCE of the nature of the Creator. Matter is substance, which
is Body. Force is creative energy or Spirit. Mind is consciousness,
which is intelligence and memory.

> There was, there is, as we find, only three of the
> creations as is given, matter, force and Mind.
> (3744-5)

MATTER
Matter is supreme substance, form, the Body, which is
OMNIPRESENT. It is ALL present, everywhere at once, limitless
and without beginning or ending. It is timeless. This is the Body or
form in which all creation, the Whole universe is contained. This is
the First Cause which is from everlasting to everlasting. Matter in
some form is necessary for energy and Mind to manifest itself. The
Body (matter) is representative of the Father-Mother or God-Parents.
Matter or Body is the Father aspect of the Holy Trinity.

FORCE
Force is SPIRIT. The ALL mighty, ALL powerful, creative energy
of God. Spirit or force is OMNIPOTENT. Force is representative
of the Holy Spirit or Holy Ghost aspect of the Holy Trinity. It is
the "anointed presence" of God. It is "sacred energy" and "creative
holiness." The essence of this "creative force" is like electricity,
but the energy is always purposeful and creative. The Spirit is not
neutral, it is Goodness, Life, Love, Law.

MIND

Mind is the ALL-knowing, ALL-wise, infinite knowledge and Wisdom of God. Mind is awareness, consciousness, and intelligence and memory.

Mind is OMNISCIENT.

Mind is representative of the Christ, the Light, the Word. Mind is the Son aspect of the Holy Trinity.

It is also the aspect of God that manifests all that is created.

All souls, the universe(s) came from and passed through this Mind.

> God as the Father, Creator, Maker; the Son as the Way, the Mind, the activity, the preserver; the Holy Spirit as the motivative force...
> (2420-1)

According to the Readings, we can best comprehend the nature of God through an understanding of the Holy Trinity.

In the Earth, we function from a three dimensional viewpoint. We ourselves are also of Body, Mind, and Spirit; therefore we need to identify with the threefold aspect of the Trinity to understand God and our own selves.

> What is the Godhead?
> Father, Son and Holy Spirit.
> (3188-1)

> Father-God is as the Body or Whole.
> Mind is as the Christ, which is the Way.
> The Holy Spirit is as the soul, or in material
> interpretation, purposes, hopes, desires.
> (1747-5)

God is the ALL-wise, ALL inclusive, ALL manifesting force in the experience of man.

The Holy Trinity aspect of the Godhead does not in any way indicate that God is plural, but rather stresses the ONENESS of all force.

> Know that the Lord thy God is One, and that the Law of the Lord is perfect...
> (3651-1)

> ...the Lord thy God is One! He is NOT divided but One...
> (1456-1)

> For the Lord, thy God, is One. Don't forget it! He's not multiple...
> (3481-2)

> For ye are made Body, Mind, soul. They each have their part in thy Oneness, or they are One; as Father, Son, and Holy Spirit is One.
> (3051-3)

The Word, the Christ, the Only Begotten Son, God's Spirit made audible moved...
Sounding, "I Am that I Am"...
And portions of Himself, souls, came into being.

All of the other souls (sons/daughters as companions) were created in that movement.
They were sparks of divine Light with the Power of Mind and free will to use their Life force to develop into individual souls.

> ...In the beginning was the Word. The Word was God. The Word was with God. He MOVED! Hence, as He moved, souls – portions of Himself - came into being.
> (263-13)

The eternal, absolute, Father of Light created one and only one Son. The First Born, the Only Begotten Son, the Christ, who is God in manifestation. The Son is not made, He is begotten. Through the Christ all other souls were created and are contained therein.

God the Father and God the Son and God the Holy Spirit or Holy Ghost are co-existent, co–Creators, co-joined in Oneness. All three aspects are co-equal and co-eternal.

There are three individual aspects of God in One person. OR three persons in One collective consciousness and Body. Christ is God's revelation of Himself in expression. God divided Himself propagating the Only Begotten Son, thus becoming the Holy Trinity. Once the Holy Trinity manifested, it is eternal and forever unchangeable.

> Q: Please explain what is meant by the Godhead?

> A: That as from which the impulse flows, or returns to. The beginning-the end-of all.
> (262-12)

I wrote a little story in 1967 about my interpretation of the mystery of the Holy Trinity.
The gist of it condensed is this:

> Once upon a time which was way before time existed, there was a Father who was ALL and everything beautiful, and Good that could ever exist. For since there was no before of His existence, there could be no end of it either. The name of this Father was and still is called Love. For there is no time when He was not. There was only one desire within Him and that was to give all and everything which is beautiful and Good. Since He was all and everything Good, His desire was to give Himself.

11

The Father gave all and everything that He was, and Love moved all and everything beautiful out of Himself. In the Giving there is no thought of self, just the outpouring of the Love which when given separated Himself from Himself.

The Father was complete and therefore, gave Himself completely.

Once He had given everything, which He was, the Gift of Giving was completed.

This complete Gift of Giving became the Only Begotten Son of the Father.

For in the Giving, the Father gave all of Himself that He was and is and will be forever more.

The Only Begotten Son is God's Gift of Love.

The Gift contained the entire Giver, for the Giver was all and everything Good that could ever be given.

There is only One Son for all and everything that can ever be given was given when He was born and there is nothing else to be added for all and everything beautiful was contained in the outpouring of that total Giving. Giving never subtracts, it always adds, thus instead of less the Father became more.

Instead of being the only One, He was now TWO instead of One. Two Ones in the Oneness.

Now and forever more, we have God the Father and God the Son.

God the Father is the Giver, the Body in which all that is beautiful and Good that can ever exist is contained.

The Only Begotten Son is within the bosom of the Father. Like a wheel within a wheel, vibrating, moving, pulsating, overflowing with Life, Love, and energy, He creates thoughts which take shape and which form patterns.

The Son has all the attributes of His Father with the desire to create and the free will to choose His expressions. The Son is the Mind of the Father.

Christ is the First Light of consciousness.

Consciousness is God awakened in Light.

The Son is God in consciousness or God "awareness."

The Christ Mind is the intellect in which everything that is Good and beautiful that can ever be THOUGHT is contained. Now in the Godhead of the Father and the Son, there is also Spirit. The Spirit is the Holy, creative energy of God. It is the essence of God in motion.

Thus, we have the Father who is the Giver and the Body in which all is contained, and then we have the Son, who is the Gift and the Mind in which all consciousness is contained, and we have the Spirit, which is the creative energy and movement of God in action, which is always purposeful and creative in motivation.

The Holy Spirit is the third person in the Holy Trinity of God.

It is the Giving. The threefold nature of God is Body, Mind, and Spirit. The Father, the Son and the Holy Spirit, is Giver, Gift and Giving or Body, Mind and Spirit.

In the beginning was the Word and the Word was with God and the Word was God. The Word is Christ, the Only Begotten Son of the Father. Now the Gift spoke to the Giver, the Son spoke to the Father saying, "Let us make souls in our likeness after our image."

The Son like His Father desired companionship and expression. God the Son, the Christ, the Word, MOVED and as He moved, the Gift of Giving gave of Himself... SOULS... portions of Himself came into being.

The Giver is the Father, the Gift is the Son, and the Giving is the Holy Spirit. Together they are THREE Ones in the Oneness. (End of story)

> For Life is the manifestation of that force ye call God,
> in whatever form it may appear; and is ONE!
> (2505-1)

In the Godhead there is found still the three-dimensional concept, God the Father, God the Son, and God the Holy Spirit.

(1747-5)

Then, the Christ Consciousness is the Holy Spirit, or that as the promise of His presence made aware of His activity in the Earth. The Spirit is as the Christ in action with the Spirit of the Father.

(262-29)

The One God now appears as Three Divine Powers.
We have a "TRINITY of Divine Beings in One God."
God manifests as "Three Powers in One Person."

Three personal aspects or "Three Persons in One Divine Power."
A person is the individual revelation of one's self and identity.
The three Trinity aspects of God are One and indivisible, and they are inseparable.
We can think of them separately to comprehend the functions more clearly but they cannot ever be disjoined.
The Trinity is manifested in time for the purpose of self-unfoldment.
But it is eternally and infinitely conjoined.

Giving thanks unto the Father, which hath made us to be partakers of the inheritance of the Saints in Light.
Who hath delivered us from the Power of darkness, and hath translated us into the Kingdom of His dear Son:
In whom we have redemption through His blood, even the forgiveness of sins:
Who is the image of the invisible God, the Firstborn of every creature:
For by Him were all things created, that are in Heaven, and that are in Earth, visible and invisible, whether they be Thrones, or Dominions, or Principalities,

or Powers: All things were created by Him, and for
Him:
And He is before all things, and by Him all things
consist.
And He is the Head of the Body, the church: Who is
the beginning, the Firstborn from the dead; that in all
things He might have the preeminence.
For it pleased the Father that in Him should all fullness
dwell.

        Colossians 1:12-19

God…hath in these last days spoken to us by His Son,
whom He hath appointed heir of all things, by whom
also He made the worlds; who being the brightness
of His glory, and the express image of His person,
and upholding all things by the Word of His Power,
when He had by Himself purged our sins, sat down
on the right hand of the Majesty on High; being
made so much better than the Angels, as He hath by
INHERITANCE obtained a more excellent name
than they.

        Hebrews 1: 2-4

God alone understands the end from the beginning and the depth
of His purposes.

There is always a mysterious aura about God and we do not have
the right to delve into His secret domain.

There is a realm in which are involved the eternal purposes of God
which are not able to be comprehended by Angels or mortals unless
revealed to them by God. These are sacred areas which may only
be entered through reverent faith and trust and knowing that "the
divine will" of God is always just.

CHAPTER II

CREATION OF SOULS

> All souls are from One...
> ...For all souls were created in the ONE.
> (1770-2)

First we have the Christ, the Word, the invisible God manifested and made visible in the Son.
There is only one God, which appears as Three Divine Powers.
The Son aspect of God is the part of God that manifests in consciousness.
It is through the Christ Consciousness Spirit that all the other souls were created.
God created the Only Begotten Son out of Himself and the Christ created souls, us, out of Himself.

> He, that Christ Consciousness, is that FIRST spoken of in the beginning when God said, "Let there be Light, and there was Light."
> (2879-1)

The Readings give a definition of the Christ Consciousness that most people seem to be able to relate to as a Universal Consciousness of the Father Spirit.

> Q: Should the Christ Consciousness be described as the awareness within each soul, imprinted in pattern on the Mind and waiting to be awakened by the will, of the soul's Oneness with God?
>
> A: Correct. That's the idea exactly!
> (5749-14)

> ...the Universal Consciousness for one sojourning in the Earth.
> (3188-1)

> Or, would that all would learn that He the Christ Consciousness, is the Giver, the Maker, the Creator of the world and all that be therein!
> (696-3)

> In the beginning, celestial beings. We have FIRST the Son, then the other sons or celestial beings that are given their force and Power.
> (262-52)

> What Light was in Him that is Light, that is Life, that is out of darkness? WHITE Light!
> (275-39)

Did Light emerge out of the darkness? Did the deep unconsciousness bring forth consciousness?

In Genesis 1:2, it states that: "...and darkness was upon the face of the deep."

Was God impersonal, vast, beyond comprehension, unknown, unseen, unidentifiable, deep in darkness, as meaning being unmanifested?

> Darkness, that it had separated – that a soul had separated itself from the Light.
> Hence, He called into being Light, that the awareness began.
> (262-56)

God separated Light from darkness, land from the Heavens, dry land was separated from the waters. Before this act of separation, all was dark and formless. The void.

An act of separation is required to create Life.
Must consciousness be separated from unconsciousness to become aware of itself?
Awareness began with Light, which was the First Consciousness.
The First Consciousness is the "White Light of Christ."
All souls as points of Light in Spirit were created in that First Beginning. They were powerful spiritual beings, sons of the Most High God containing an actual portion of the Creator and divisions of Himself.

Each soul (Spirit) contained the attributes and characteristics of the Creator with the free will to choose for itself and to be separate individual beings.
Souls were created in the image of God in Spirit.
This is an image in Spirit of the qualities of God's nature.
The image is not like a picture or a photograph but the image is of the fabric, of the Source itself, with qualities and principles of God in essence. Spirit, Love, "beauty," Harmony, Peace, Mercy, Goodness, Light, Law, "justice," Truth, Wisdom, creativity, curiosity, eternal Life and individuality.

Souls were as Spirit beings created to be companions having access
to all the creative energy needed to become unique expressions of
themselves.

Each soul was intended to be separate in individuality with
free will choices which would allow the soul's own personal
experiences to be different from any other. Yet, each soul is
connected with each other's spark of Light as brothers growing
together in Oneness, as a family.

Souls or sons and daughters of God were not meant to be replicas
or clones of the Creator but were able to form into unique selves
through thought and personal expression and experience. Each
soul has an individual purpose different from any other soul with a
special duty to perform.

No two souls would be identical but each different and individual
with its own unique developments, talents and memories.

> In the beginning, all souls that were as portions of the
> thought of God were given the opportunity for expression,
> as to be companions for that creative force - or God.
> (2420-1)

> Q: When did I first exist as a separate entity?

> A: The First Existence was in the MIND of the
> Creator, as all souls became a part of the creation. As
> to time, this would be in the beginning. When was
> the beginning?
> First Consciousness!
> (2925-1)

> ...and the Gift of God is being conscious of being
> One with Him, yet apart from Him – or One with,
> yet apart from, the Whole.
> (5753-1)

The conditions existing in the spiritual realm of the Creator in the beginning of soul creation given in the Readings is rather vague and fragmented.
The Readings name the birth of these companions, as "souls." But they seemed to have first begun as sparks of Light in infinity.

It seems to be indicated that the newly born souls in Spirit had all the knowledge of the Creator but LACKED the experience required to form into their full potential as individual selves.
Consciousness came into GROWTH from the First Cause means that the full potential was yet to be realized or manifested.
The individual sparks of the Christ Light and Life were as SEEDS containing within it the formula for its potential growth and able to bring uniqueness into its self with free will choices.

> Each soul was in its First Division from the Godhead to be a companion with that force, that influence, that purpose. Hence, the purpose is to GROW in Grace, knowledge, understanding, for the indwelling in that PRESENCE.
> (1861-4)

Each soul had individual consciousness, memory, and Mind with the ability to express itself and to be companionable to the Creator and to the other souls or sons.

> For in the beginning, God said, "Let there be Light." Ye are one of those sparks of Light, with all the ability of creation, with all the knowledge of God.
> (5367-1)

> Each soul is just as each atom, as each corpuscle. For remember, ye are as corpuscles in the Body of God. Each with a duty, a function to perform...
> (3481-2)

> As the sons and daughters of God are personal,
> are individual, with the many attributes that are
> characteristics, personalities or individualities…
> (254-68)

Spirit is the essence of creative Power and energy and the Source of all Light. It is the First Cause.

We that are in the third dimension can only understand the nature of God through the three-fold expression of God in the Holy Trinity as Father, Son, and Holy Ghost or Body, Mind, and Spirit.

There is only one Spirit of God and all manifestations of Life in any plane of consciousness are crystallizations of that Spirit.

> ALL souls are from One.
> …For all souls were created in the One.
> (1770-2)

> Spirit is that portion of the First Cause which finds
> expression in all that is everlasting in the consciousness
> of Mind OR matter.
> (2533-1)

Souls were created in the spiritual image of the Creator with a soul to be MADE through growth and experience in the environments of the realms provided for it to use. They had desire to express themselves and free will as to choose how they would direct their energy.

> The individual entity before coming in Earth's plane
> bears only the Spirit relation to the universal forces,
> with a soul to be MADE, through the environments
> of creation, equal to the created, given the free will as
> to how same shall be developed.
> (900-59)

It is our free will that makes us individuals who are aware of ourselves as separate, unique and one of a kind beings.

21

> For the will of each entity, of each soul, is that which
> individualizes it, that makes it aware of itself…
> (853-9)

The souls began to use their free will as they expressed themselves
in the various realms of consciousness which had been provided for
them by the Creator.

> The soul is complete only in the Law and realm of its
> Creator. And the fact that the soul has a will, the factor
> that makes for the freedom of activity in the various
> realms where consciousness may be experienced in
> that soul-Body, is as true as the "I AM" exists in the
> present.
> (553-1)

Before the Earth and its solar system were created, souls as
sons and daughters of God had experiences in other realms of
consciousness.

> For, the universe was brought into being for the
> purpose of being the dwelling place of the souls of
> God's children.
> (2396-2)

> For, remember, all these planets, stars, universes, were
> MADE for the entity and its associates to rule, and
> not be ruled by them, save as an individual entity gives
> itself to their influence.
> (2830-2)

They had spiritual bodies as vehicles of expression before physical
matter existed.
Souls are as much of a Body in the eternal as in the physical.

> ...for ONLY the Spirit and soul are eternal but they are as much a Body in the eternal realms as the physical Body is a Body in the material realm.
> (5159-2)

Souls had a Body like the Creator. It was a Body of soul consciousness to build and shape and express itself.

> Man in his former state, or natural state, or permanent consciousness, IS soul. Hence in the beginning all were souls of that creation, with the BODY as of the Creator - of the Spirit forces that make manifest in using same in the various phases or experiences of consciousness for the activity.
> (262-89)

Mind is the builder. Spirit is the Life force that energizes the mental pictures imaged by the soul in its discovery of itself. Souls were not meant to create or express in opposition to the plan and nature of the Creator which would cause disruption or create negative influencing. Using free will to express anything that was not centered in Love would cause them to be separated from their spiritual atmosphere and Oneness with God.

In the use and possession of their free will Gift, some souls began to manifest that which was out of God's will and was in rebellion against His Law of Love.

Although souls were free to make individual choices as they desired and imaged, they were still subject to the universal and spiritual Laws already set in motion.

> ...error or separation began before there appeared what we know as the Earth, the Heavens; or before space was manifested.
> (262-115)

23

God is Light and Love and there is no darkness within Him at all. His nature is completely constructive, and always overflowing with Goodness and Love. God's motives are pure kindness, which is full of blessings to all created beings.

> ...God is a God of knowledge...He IS Light, and in Him is no darkness at all.
> (262-96)

How did rebellion enter into God's perfect Heavenly Kingdom?

> ...sin and error is not of God - save through His sons that BROUGHT error, through selfishness, ... by which Angels and Archangels are separate from the fullness of the Father.
> (479-1)

Each soul was still in Spirit as a celestial being testing its free will. To be a companion and to indwell in the presence of God, souls were not expected to manifest qualities that did not exist in God's nature.

Self glorification and selfishness caused disruption of the Harmony, Peace, and Goodness in the Heavenly realms.
God did not prevent souls from manifesting selfishness as He had given them free will. It was their choice.
Breaking of Law results in consequences. For every action there is a reaction. It is an unchangeable spiritual Law.
Law is not punishment; it establishes order and brings enlightenment which corrects mistakes.

God knew that souls must have free will. The Creator wanted them to be free to choose to be companionable. The risk was that souls could also choose NOT to be companionable. Love cannot be forced, it must be given freely.

For without the Gift of free will to the soul, how COULD it become aware of the presence of the all–abiding creative force or energy called God?
(945-1)

...He did not prevent once He had given free will... For, He made the individual entities or souls in the beginning. For, the beginnings of sin, of course, were in seeking expression of themselves outside of the plan or the Way in which God had expressed same. Thus it was the individual, see?
Having given free will, then, - though having the fore- knowledge, though being Omnipotent and Omnipresent – it is only when the soul that is a portion of God CHOOSES that God knows the end thereof.
(5749-14)

...all souls in the beginning were One with the Father. The separation, or turning away, brought evil.
(262-56)

The souls who fell desired that which was not in God's nature or will.

This depends upon the desire. For as creative activities are applied, what ye DESIRE becomes LAW.
(5265-1)

What separated Spirit from its First Cause, or what causes Good and Evil? DESIRE! DESIRE!
Hence desire is the opposite of will. Will and desire, One with the creative forces of Good, brings all its influence in the realm of activity that makes for that which is constructive in the experience of the soul, the Mind, the Body, One with the Spirit of Truth.
(5752-3)

...each soul - in every stage of its consciousness – is as precious in the eyes, in the heart, in the purpose of the God, as the other. For, all are His offspring.
(2771-1)

The Law of the Lord is perfect. It converteth the soul of those who will hearken, who will make daily application of that His Word and His promptings bid them to do.
(262-128)

The Law of the Lord is perfect, converting the soul; the testimony of the Lord is sure, making wise the simple.
Psalm 19:7

...divine Love, in which each and every soul lives and moves and has its being.
(1468-1)

...for corruption may NOT inherit eternal Life, and must be burned up. Know that thy God is a consuming fire, and must purge every one, that ye may enter in. In patience does one overcome.
(262-26)

The more self conscious the soul became, the more aware it became of its own self interests and experiences until it became separated from the Source of the Creator. We were meant to know ourselves and to be at One with the Creator yet separate in individual awareness.

Becoming overly self centered to the point of selfishness and self glorification caused us to lose that Oneness with the Creator.

And, as has been given the warning, there is today set before thee Life and death, Good and Evil, and what

ye CHOOSE with the will of thine own soul – upon
that depends what the growth of the soul will be.
(288-36)

Many religions do not believe in the pre-existence of the soul but
think that we began in the flesh creation in Adam.
According to the Readings, we were all created at the same time in
Spirit eons before Adam was even a thought in God's Mind.
The Bible has some scriptures that indicate that we, as souls, did in
fact exist before Adam.

Where wast thou when I laid the foundations of the
Earth? Declare, if thou hast understanding.
Who hath laid the measures thereof, if thou knowest?
Or who hath stretched the line upon it?
Whereupon are the foundations thereof fastened?
Or who laid the cornerstone thereof; when the
Morning Stars sang together, and ALL the SONS of
God shouted for joy?
Job 38:4-7

God hath not cast away His people which He
foreknew.
Romans 11:2

For whom He did foreknow, He also did predestinate
to be conformed to the image of His Son, that He
might be the Firstborn among many brethren.
Romans 8:29

God gave His newly created companions free will so they could
voluntarily attain their place in Christ as co-creators.
Souls fell in consciousness in the Spirit.

Christ had to set up a Way and a pattern for these lost companions
to be able to return to their original state of being.

Joan Clarke

Christ would give Himself as the Way back home.

The beloved Ones must return to their Creator.

> Know thyself, then, to be as a corpuscle, as a facet, as a
> characteristic, as a Love, in the Body of God.
> (2533-7)

CHAPTER III

THE FALL OF CELESTIAL BEINGS

> The Lord hath prepared His Throne in the Heavens;
> and His Kingdom ruleth over all.
> Bless the Lord, ye His Angels, that excel in strength,
> that do His commandments, hearkening unto the
> voice of His Word.
> Bless ye the Lord, all ye His hosts; ye Ministers of His,
> that do His pleasure.
> Bless the Lord, all His works in all places of His
> Dominion:
> Bless the Lord, O my soul.
> Psalm 103:19-22

BEFORE the creation of the new souls as sons and daughters of
God in the Spirit, there was the fall of Angels in Heaven.

We usually think of Angels as being messengers and Guardians.
Angels are ministering Spirits who are a bridge between Heaven and
Earth representing the divine symbols of God's Love for us.

I have always heard that Angels do not have free will.

Maybe they have a different kind of free will than the sons of God.

Most of us think of an Angel as a supernatural being who mediates between God and man. Angels worship God and choirs of Angels sing His praises before the Throne in Heaven.

Angels minister over all living things in the natural world and in the universe as well. Angels oversee and maintain the functioning of God's vast creations.

Was there a time when there were no Angels?

According to the Bible, Angels were created beings.

They were messengers described as flames of fire.

> And of the Angels He saith, "Who maketh His Angels Spirits, and His Ministers a flame of fire?"
> Hebrews 1:7

Perhaps some of the Angels do not have free will and others do.

Could some of these celestial beings we call Angels have been sons of God and not Angels at all?

OR there could have been a group of Angelic beings who also had free will. Without free will, how could an Angel disobey and rebel?

I think God desires and appreciates sincere communication from all created beings. Therefore, He gives ALL His Angels free will that they may serve Him without any forced allegiance.

Angel means celestial being.

Sons and daughters of God are also celestial beings who were created AFTER the rebellion in Heaven.

There is no mention of them being involved in the "war in Heaven." It is possible that they were not created as yet.

The Cayce Readings and the Bible make a DIFFERENCE between the two types of beings.

Angels are different than SOULS who were created to be companions of God.

An Angel has a different PURPOSE from a soul who is a son/daughter of God. An Angel is composed of a different frequency of Light which is closer to the Creator.

The original rebellion in Heaven consisted of celestial beings that were referred to as Angels.

We are all fascinated by stories of invisible supernatural beings who are involved in a celestial Good-versus-Evil struggle.

All the major religions believe in the existence of Angels.
(Hinduism, Buddhism, Judaism, Islam, Zoroastrianism, and Christianity are just a few.)
The sons of God fell in Spirit as well but it was a different kind of fall and it happened AFTER the fall of the Angels.

There are different types of Angels mentioned in the Readings and in the Bible and other manuscripts that describe a vast realm of Heavenly hierarchies:
Angels, Guardian Angels, Archangels, Seraphim, Cherubim, Hosts, Thrones, Dominions, Principalities, Powers, and Virtues.
Besides the Angels of Light there are Angels of darkness and death.

One lady was told by the Cayce Readings that she was surrounded by Cherubs.

> About the entity's whole experience there are Cherubs, that are more in keeping with the thoughts - or that are an influence for Good...
> (2520-1)

31

The source of the rebellion in Heaven was that some of these created beings as Angels chose to disobey God and to glorify and magnify themselves rather than the Creator.

The Angels and the sons of God both manifested selfishness instead of Love which led to their fall. This is what they have in common. Both the fallen Angels and sons of God were guilty of self glorification and selfishness.
They worshipped the images they created for themselves more than they worshipped the Creator.

Thoughts are DEEDS in the mental world.

> As thoughts are deeds in the mental world, as are the activities of a physical being as related to the associations, the relations, the words, the activity in a material world…
> (752-1)

But thoughts were of a different quality and purpose in the fall of the Angels.

There is an indication in the Cayce material that each of us has an Angel that stands always before the Throne of God and it is indicated that we may be that Angel ourselves as it is the part of our pure soul in Spirit that is still connected to God.

> Doth He, thy Lord, thy God, choose to send messengers, alright; for He does to each soul. Has it not been stated, and is it not an awareness within thee that "Behold thy Angel stands ALWAYS before the Face of the THRONE of the Maker!"
> (2402-2)

...as He has given, "I will not LEAVE thee comfortless"
and "I will give my Angels charge concerning thee"
and "Will ye be my people, I will be your God."
THE FACE OF SELF'S OWN ANGEL IS EVER
BEFORE THE THRONE. COMMUNE OFT
WITH HIM.
(1917-1)

What does that mean to "commune oft with him?"
Is it referring to our own individual Guardian Angel, or our higher self
or the original spark of the divine that is our portion of God, or could
it mean to commune with Him, the Christ in whom we live and
move and have our being? I like to think it means all of the above.

The original creation of the sons and daughters of God in Spirit is
similar to Angels since they are celestial beings.
There are also Readings that state that the Angel always remains an
Angel and that they are like the Laws of the universe.

The Readings indicate that Angels are a different creation from that
of man who was made a little LOWER than the Angels.

...the soul remains ever as One. For it is in the image
of the Creator and has its birthright in Him.
(1243-1)

But man has the ability to be One with God through Christ
becoming even HIGHER than an Angel.
The Angels purpose is to attend God and to minister to the sons/
daughters of God who are companions in Christ.

...He, the Son of Man, became One with the Father.
Man, through the same channel (Jesus Christ), may
reach that perfection, even HIGHER than the Angel,
though he (the Angel) attends the God.
(900-16)

The Edgar Cayce Readings support the Bible account of a "war in Heaven" in which Lucifer or Satan and a third of the Angels were cast out of Heaven.

Some authorities believe that the "war in Heaven" took place when "man" in Adam was created.

These same Bible authorities do not see us as spiritual beings BEFORE the Earth and Adam as the First Flesh Man who was created. They do not have the Cayce concept that we were souls BEFORE the Earth was created.

My opinion has always been that the "war in Heaven" came BEFORE the Earth was created and the Readings also indicate the time frame as pre-Adamic.

Whatever the time-frame, it returns to the same fact in principle that the Angels who rebelled refused to worship the Christ or the Only Begotten Son of God as God.

(Time is not a reality in the Spirit but we need it to measure experiences.)

> And his tail drew the third part of the stars of Heaven, and did cast them to the Earth...
> Revelation 12:4

> And there was "war in heaven": Michael and his Angels fought against the Dragon; and the Dragon fought and his Angels, and prevailed not; neither was their place found any more in Heaven.
> And the great Dragon was cast out, that old Serpent, called the Devil and Satan, which deceiveth the whole world:
> He was cast out into the Earth, and his Angels were cast out with him.
> Revelation 12:7-9

Q: What is meant here by the "war in Heaven" between Michael and the Devil?

A: ...as is understood by those here, there is first- as is
the spiritual concept-the spiritual rebellion, BEFORE
it takes mental or physical form. This warring is
illustrated there by the war between the Lord of the
Way (Archangel Michael) and the Lord of Darkness
(Satan) - or the Lord of Rebellion.
(281-33)

There is the thought that the Angels were jealous or envious because
God loved the Firstborn Son, the Christ in a more personal way
than they.

The Son was able to enter into the depths of God and His purposes
in a deeper way than the Angels.

The Angels could not enter into the infinite Wisdom of God. Some
of the Angels could not understand God's purpose in exalting the Son
and endowing Him with such unlimited Power and command.

The Angels refused to bow to Adam or man as in mankind because
they knew that the Christ Himself would incarnate as man.
Therefore, their refusal to bow or worship man was because man
was a part of the Christ Spirit.

These Angels rebelled against the authority given to the Son.
Christ, the Only Begotten Son had pre-eminence over all the
Angels. The Angels were more like ministering Spirits who were
subservient to God.

A son has a relationship with a father that is deeper and more
personal than that of a servant or even a business partner.

An Angel is not a companion but is rather as a divine servant. The
Angels were not propagated beings.

Christ was the Only Begotten Son.

The Son was given EQUAL status to God. He is the HEIR to the
Throne.

It has been written that some of the Angels refused to bow to the
authority of the Christ. Many Bible authorities state that the Angels
refused to bow to Adam as in mankind as previously mentioned.

35

This is because Adam was the First Flesh Incarnation of the soul who became Jesus and was the Christ.

> (God) hath in these last days spoken unto us by His Son, whom He hath appointed heir of all things, by whom also He made the worlds; who being the brightness of His glory, and the express image of His person, and upholding all things by the Word of His Power, when He had by Himself purged our sins, sat down on the right hand of the Majesty on High; being made so much better than the Angels, as He hath by inheritance obtained a more excellent name than they.
> For unto which of the Angels said He at any time, "Thou art my Son, this day have I Begotten thee?"
> And again, "I will be to Him a Father, and He shall be to me a Son?"
> And again, when He bringeth in the First Begotten into the world, He saith, "And let all the Angels of God worship Him."
> Hebrews 1:2-6

The last verse seems to indicate that Angels were at the birth of the Only Begotten Son and those Angels were commanded by God to "worship Him."

Some Bible scholars believe that this scripture means that the Angels were to worship man because it mentions bringing Him (the Christ Son) into the world as Jesus Christ. The Readings state that the First Begotten Son was created long before the Earth or flesh man was manifested.

Christ, Himself, created the universe and the world called Earth as the Bible testifies; therefore, He had to pre-exist.

> In the beginning was the Word and the Word was with God, and the Word was God.

The same was in the beginning with God.
All things were made by Him; and without Him was
not any thing made that was made.
John 1:1-3

That was the true Light, which lighteth every man
that cometh into the world.
He was in the world, and the world was made by Him,
and the world knew Him not.
John 1:9-10

Most of the Angels do not GROW as souls do, their design and
function was set for eternity at the moment of their creation.
They were created to help guide, maintain and implement God's
will in His manifested realities. Angels attend to God in Heaven.

If the Angels were there BEFORE the Only Begotten Son was created,
then it is understandable that some of them couldn't comprehend
that God had a Son that was made equal and had authority over all
of creation, including them.

The Angel's loyalty was to be to God only but now there was also
the Christ who was God, too.
God the Son.

The Christ, the Word, and Only Begotten Son were One in nature,
character, and purpose with God, the Eternal Father.

Lucifer was the most highly exalted Angel next in honor to God's
Only Son. Lucifer had been in the presence of the Creator and the
glorious Light of the Eternal One had shone especially upon him.
Lucifer who has been called Light Bearer, Son of the Morning, or
Morning Star, was one of the celestial Angelic beings who rebelled
in Heaven.
It is hard to believe that the First Sin and separation from God
happened in Heaven or in Spirit.

Before his rebellion, Lucifer was called the "Anointed Cherub Who Covereth."

The Bible speaks of the great integrity of this perfect being who had the divine confidence of God and who served God faithfully.

Lucifer must have had deep insights into God's purposes to be in such an exalted position.

> Thou wast perfect in thy ways from the day that thou wast created, till iniquity was found in thee.
> Ezekiel: 28:15

Lucifer was made of fire, not clay, and felt superior to man.

Lucifer was the Prince or leader of the revolt in Heaven.

Lucifer considered himself more beautiful than Christ and more God-like.

Lucifer had unique gifts but must have developed an infatuation with his own beauty. Pride in his own glory fed his desire for supremacy. The Prince of Angels was not content to be over the Heavenly host but coveted the glory that had been invested in the Christ Son.

> Thine heart was lifted up because of thy beauty, thou hast corrupted thy Wisdom by reason of thy brightness...
> Ezekiel: 28:17

The Bible and the Readings state that "No man hath seen God at any time."

> No man hath seen God at any time...
> John 1:18

> As it has been indicated and given of old, no man hath seen God at any time.
> (262-119)

No man, no physical matter, has ever seen God at any
time; only the MANIFESTATIONS of Him.
(707-1)

The Angels have seen God; therefore, they must know Him in a
way that we do not. But now, we have seen Jesus Christ who is His
manifested messenger in the Earth.

...God, who gave self in the Son that man might
approach that Throne in a Way that all may be One
with Him...
(31-1)

Lucifer was blinded by his own beauty and chose to QUESTION
the Wisdom of the "divine will."
God's "divine will" is always perfect and beyond questioning.
Lucifer refused to bow to a Christ-Son-Being that he considered
beneath him and inferior.
Why was the Son able to have a depth in relationship that was
denied to Lucifer or other Angels?
Lucifer was able to convince some of the Angels to also question
that God's government might be unfair.

Lucifer and one third of the Angels could not see the Christ in His
FULLNESS but only in His NEWNESS or birth state.

Lucifer and other Angels who sided with him refused to bow to the
Christ as God. The God Son was not seen as God by them.
Lucifer incited the rebellion in Heaven stating that God was unfair
to expect the Angels to worship or bow down to the Only Begotten
Son. They considered themselves superior.
After all, they were there FIRST, before there was a Christ.
By denying the Son they were denying the Eternal God as well.
Thus, the rebellion started that is still unresolved.

God made known to all the Angels that His Son was equal with Himself and that wherever there was the "presence" of the Son, it was as HIS OWN "presence." The Word of the Son was to be obeyed as readily as that of God for the Son is God also.

God, in fact, sat back, as it were, and gave the whole Kingdom of Heaven to the Son to rule. God relinquished all authority to Christ.

> (God) hath in these last days spoken unto us by His Son, whom He hath appointed HEIR of all things, by whom also He made the worlds.
> Hebrews: 1:2

It pleased God that all the fullness of Himself should dwell in the Son. The Oneness of God was now the Oneness of the Holy Trinity. Once the birth of the Only Begotten Son was completed, there was no going back or changing it as it was sealed for eternity. Christ the Son of God was God and could NOT ever be separated as they are One-Self FOREVER. The God-Self. God had become the TRIUNE God and the revelation of it was more than some of the Angels could comprehend.

But instead of trusting God to reveal the mystery to them, they disobeyed and incited a "war in Heaven."

The secret of the rebellion in Heaven seems to be that Lucifer and some of the Angels wanted to be as Christ, Begotten Sons. They did not want to be only Angels.

These Angels wanted the equal status with God that Christ had, and that the other sons of God created in Christ were to have.

There is a biblical account of Lucifer who was once the chief of Angels that states:

> How art thou fallen from Heaven, O Lucifer, Son of the Morning! How art thou cut down to the ground, which didst weaken the nations!
> For thou hast said in thine heart, "I will exalt my Throne above the stars of God:

I will sit also upon the mount of the congregation, in
the sides of the north:
I will ascend above the heights of the clouds; I will be
like the Most High."
Yet thou shall be brought down to Hell, to the sides
of the pit.
                    Isaiah 14:12-15

Lucifer and his Angels wanted to take over leadership of the universe.
Lucifer wanted to be as Christ, the Creator of the universe. After the
"war in Heaven," in which Christ with the Archangel Michael and
his Angels won, Lucifer and the Angels with him were cast out.
Heaven was cleansed of the rebellion.
However, they continued their war and rebellion in the other realms
or dimensions of consciousness, including the Earth when it was
being created.

The Readings state that the Christ is the Maker or Creator and
that the influences of "that Spirit of the Dark Forces" or Lucifer are
allowed (sent) in the Earth for the correction when man or a soul
manifests evil desires.

> Q: Comment on "The Devil and Satan, which
> deceiveth the whole world, he was SENT out into the
> Earth."

> A: Did He not—the Christ, the Maker—say this over
> and over again? That so long as spite, selfishness, evil
> desires, evil communications were manifested, they
> would give the channels through which THAT Spirit
> called Satan, Devil, Lucifer, Evil One, might work?
> Also He has said over and over again that even the
> Devil believes, but trembles—and this is as far as he
> has gone except to try to deceive others.
> (262-119)

It is important to remember that Angels do not die, they are immortal. The Angels existed before Earth was created and before man in flesh was created.

Most of the Angels continue to remain exactly as God intended them to be when they were created.

If we entertain selfish desires and thoughts, we open the door to evil influences, thereby inviting them in.

> Hence that force that rebelled in the unseen forces (or in Spirit) that came into activity, was that influence which has been called Satan, the Devil, the Serpent; they are one. That of REBELLION!
> Hence, when man in any activity rebels against the influences of Good he harkens to the influence of Evil rather than the influence of Good...Evil is rebellion.
> (262-52)

> Know that even as the Powers of evil are loosed for the correcting of many, so are the glories of HIM (Christ) made manifest in the hearts and lives of many.
> (262-30)

Were there Angels before the Only Begotten Son was created?
Some authorities say, yes, some say, no.
I believe that there were Angels before God created the Only Begotten Son even though I know that they are manifested beings. Angels worshipped and praised God BEFORE the Son was begotten.
How can this be if God was in an unconscious state of being in the deep, dark, void contemplating what He is until He manifested Himself into the Light and the Christ?
It is a paradox.

Hebrews 1:6 stated that when the Only Begotten Son was brought into the world, God said, "And let all of the Angels of God worship

Him." There were Angels before Christ that resented Him when He was born. Then other Angels were created after Christ when the other sons of God were being manifested, to minister to them.

> Are they not all ministering Spirits, sent forth to minister for them who shall be heirs of salvation?
> Hebrews 1:14

It seems to be indicated that there may have been Angels before Christ, then more Angels with a different purpose designated afterwards to minister to the souls created in Christ and to oversee the manifested universe(s).

> For He shall give His Angels charge over thee, to keep thee in all thy ways.
> They shall bear thee up in their hands, lest thou dash thy foot against a stone.
> Psalm 91:11-12

> ...for He hath made man a little lower than the Angels, with the ability through his (man's) will to make himself equal with the Father, that MAN may even JUDGE Angels!
> (262-31)

Whether they were Angels or sons, or both, the result of this rebellion in Heaven is that celestial beings were cast out.
But only after there was a "war in Heaven" in which Christ and His Angels won. This battle in Heaven was lead by the Archangel Michael.

A Reading seems to indicate that the Angels came into being when the manifested forms were being created which would mean AFTER the Only Begotten Son was manifested.

> With the bringing into creation the manifested forms, there came that which has been, is, and ever will be, the Spirit realm and its attributes – designated as Angels and Archangels. They are the spiritual manifestations in the Spirit world of those attributes that the developing forces accredit to the One Source…
> (5749-3)

> For, to each entity, each soul, there is ever the ministering Angel before the Throne of Grace, the Throne of God.
> (3357-2)

> But to which of the Angels said He at any time, "Sit on my right hand, until I make thine enemies thy footstool?"
> Are they not all ministering Spirits sent forth to minister for them who shall be heirs of salvation?
> Hebrews 1:13-14

The Christ was manifesting Himself into souls.
All the other sons of God were created in that manifestation.
Angels appeared at this creation.

The creation of Angels is a mystery that we cannot comprehend with human Minds and limited information.

The Angels that existed before the Only Begotten Son were a different type of Angel than those Angels designated later to serve man.
Some of the celestial beings referred to as Angels later could have been souls created in Christ as His younger brothers and sisters.
Could it be possible for an Angel to become a soul?
We do not know when souls were created but it is indicated that they began to individualize when Earth was being created.

There are Angels that are as Laws of the universe and do not change and there are Angels and celestial beings (souls) who can choose to rebel against God and have a different type of free will.

> Q: Are Angels and Archangels synonymous with that which we call Laws of the universe?
>
> A: They are as the Laws of the universe...
> (5749-3)

Man has the ability to be One with God through Christ, even though the Angel attends God and is before Him continually. Therefore, man has a potential in God that the Angel does not have.
This indicates that there are Angels that do not change.

> ...man was made a little lower than the Angels, yet with that Power to become One with God, while the Angel remains the Angel.
> ...He, the Son of Man became One with the Father. Man, through the same channel, may reach that perfection, even higher than the Angel, though he (the Angel) attend the God.
> (900-16)

There are various types of Angels and most of them do not disobey God but are as divine attendants and messengers.

> Behold, I send an Angel before thee, to keep thee in thy Way...
> Exodus 23:20

We do not know if Angels have the same type of free will as a soul. It would seem that Angels would not have any intention of doing otherwise than that for which they were created, which is to serve and glorify God and to be messengers to the sons of God created in the Christ.

An Angel's will and motivation is to perform God's will.

The rebellion in Heaven by Angels causes some teachers to suspect that these celestial beings might have been souls who have free will instead of Angels.

However, even if this could be true, it does not mean that all of us are fallen Angels as some people are teaching.

Of all the souls given Readings by Edgar Cayce, not even one was said to be a fallen Angel. There are Readings for pre-Adamic beings who were souls in Amilius entering as "Thought Form Projections." There are also other beings called "Mixtures" and "Things" who are part "Thought Form" and animal but there is no Reading on file for a fallen Angel who lived as a man.

There are some fallen Angels mentioned by name, like Ariel, who fought with Lucifer in the "war in Heaven."

The original Cayce group was said to be a part of the Christ Spirit projected by Amilius. (A soul incarnation of the Only Begotten Son.)

Edgar Cayce and his companion soul came into being or individual consciousness with a multitude of souls projected by Amilius during the creation of Earth. Edgar Cayce is a good example to use as a soul who was not in existence during the "war in Heaven" and had no part in it.

Edgar Cayce was a soul of Light.

These souls involved in the Cayce work came into the Earth with Amilius and were on a rescue mission to help the fallen souls find the way back to God.

(Some of these fallen beings that entered the Earth to help may have been part of the fallen Angel group.)

The Readings state that Angels came into being when Christ was manifesting portions of Himself in soul creation (us).
The Bible states that God ordered the Angels to worship the Only Begotten Son when He was created indicating that they were present at His birth.
Both concepts could be true.

God may want us to visualize Him and the Heavenly creation individually.
We each have our own personal relationship with God that is different from any other soul. We each visualize Heaven and the Angels as it fits into our personal understanding.
We are all on different levels of consciousness with individual memories of "Before the Foundation of the World."

There are Angels that are as Laws of the universe and do not change. There are beings called Angels that rebelled against God and were cast out of Heaven. There are beings who were sons of God who fell in Spirit.
I see a difference in the creation and the purpose intended for the two types of beings.
I see a difference in time frame for the fall of each type of being.
Christ was newly manifested when the rebellion of Angels happened.
We do not know if souls were even manifested yet.

The "war in Heaven" could have happened BEFORE pieces of Himself (Christ) as souls (us) were projected and manifested.
There are Readings which state the individualization of the souls created to be companions took shape in Earth and its planetary system. (The it's became the I's.)

The "its", now, is the man!
(364-12)

Because of the dispute in Heaven with fallen Angels, and then the fallen souls, we now have two influences.

47

We have Angels and celestial beings of Light and Angels and celestial beings of darkness.
The two influences are that of Truth and that of rebellion.
There are two choices.
The choices are for Good or Evil, Light or darkness, Love or selfishness.
We can choose glorification of self and self-centeredness.
We can choose the glorification of God and Christ centeredness.
Some souls or sons and daughters of God chose to serve God and some Angels and souls chose to serve self.

> Choose thou! For, there is this day set before thee, Life - and death; night and day. Choose thou!
>   (315-3)

> ...what ye choose with the will of thine own soul- upon that depends what the growth of the soul will be.
>   (288-36)

> Hence the two influences that are ever before thee; Good and Evil, Life and death; Choose thou!
>   (262-119)

It is indicated that the majority of those cast out of Heaven, are still in rebellion and some of them are on a mission to ensnare the souls of Light.

> ...I beheld Satan as lightening fall from Heaven.
>   Luke 10:18

> For the Angels of Light only use material things for emblems, while the Angels of death use these as to lures that may carry men's souls away.
>   (1159-1)

Where or to what place, or state of consciousness were the Angels or fallen beings sent when they were cast out of Heaven?

The Bible states that they were sent forth into the Earth.

> He was cast out into the Earth, and his Angels were
> cast out with him.
> Revelation 12:7-9

> And the Angels which kept not their first estate,
> but left their own habitation, He hath reserved in
> everlasting chains under darkness unto the judgment
> of the great day.
> Jude:6

There are many different levels of consciousness in Spirit and in Mind.

> In my Father's house are many mansions...
> John 14:2

There are individuals in the Spirit realms as well as in the Earth whose intentions are evil or who are motivated by selfishness.
They have been given NO POWER over us. We have to invite them into our consciousness by making wrong choices or have selfishly motivated DESIRES to be influenced by them.

> For, every soul has the stamp of its Creator.
> But if that soul does the fruits of evil, the stamp MUST
> become smeared, blurry – and the end is fearful.
> (531-3)

Halaliel is an Angel who offered to direct the Readings but was refused as the Cayce family did not trust the aggressive spiritual influence they felt, so they rejected the offer and chose to continue with the Christ (Jesus) as the director.
This Angel was NOT one of the Lucifer group or a fallen Angel but said to be an Angel of Light who was not the Christ but with the Christ from the beginning. Halaliel was also active in the "WAR in

Heaven" against the fallen Angels who were cast out and Halaliel stood with the Christ and Michael the Archangel.

But the Readings stated later that the RIGHT choice was made in NOT accepting Halaliel. This is also the Angel who gave some of the Earth changes.

> Q: Who is Halaliel, the one who gave us a message on October 15?
>
> A: One in and with those courts Ariel fought when there was the rebellion in Heaven.
> Now, where is Heaven? Where is Ariel, and who was he? A companion of Lucifer or Satan, and one that made for the disputing of the influences in the experiences of Adam in the Garden.
> (262-57)

The Cayce Readings advise not to NAME or seek to know the names of the Angels but rather heed the message of the Angel which is more important than personal identification.

It also says to make sure that the Angel does not deny that Jesus Christ came in the flesh.

> Seek not so much the name as rather the message; and that he doth not deny that He hath come in the flesh...
> (2402-2)

This is a Reading that requires deep study to understand all the implications involved.

> Remember, there is knowledge as may come that is not from above.
> Such knowledge has oft brought confusion...
> (2072-8)

The Christ Consciousness, the Holy Spirit and our Guardian Angels bear witness for each of us in Heaven.

> And the Christ Consciousness, the Holy Spirit AND thy Guardian Angel bear witness in the Spirit.
> (2246-1)

Some of the Angels and Archangels have never been involved in the Earth and its material world.

> There are those consciousnesses or awarenesses that have not participated in nor been a part of the Earth's PHYSICAL consciousness; as the Angels, the Archangels...
> (5755-2)

Lucifer, simply put, represents spiritual rebellion.
Satan represents mental rebellion and then the Devil represents the physical level of the same influence: Rebellion, selfishness and self-glorification, desires not in God's will.
Rebellion is the choice to put "ME" first instead of God or fellow beings first. Lucifer desired a universal Kingdom in which he wielded supreme Power which stirred up a great ambition within himself. He made no attempt to stop his self-exaltation, but gave it full reign.
The evil seed of self glorification took root in him and continued to grow until it produced a harvest of misery and woe for those Angels who followed him.
It has been stated that "pride" was the cause of the rebellion in Heaven. Thus the saying, "Pride goeth before a fall."

> Not a novice, lest being lifted up with PRIDE, he fall into the condemnation of the Devil.
> Timothy 3:6

Paula FitzGerald, who wrote plays based on the Readings said that it was revealed to her that pride is refusing to see yourself in the wrong when you KNOW that you are in the wrong. (Paula wrote three plays based on the Readings: <u>Son of Promise, My Eldest Son,</u> and <u>All My Sons.</u>)

Lucifer must have left his PLACE in the presence of God to work to confuse and convert other Angels to his way of thinking.

God, being pure with only Good intentions, projected the Truth but Lucifer came to be known as the "Father of Lies" because he began to use deception to convince the other Angels that God was unfair. At some point, Lucifer must have realized his error but PRIDE prevented him from admitting his mistake or asking for forgiveness.

The Readings refer to Satan and Lucifer as the same person, or same Angel.

> Who was Ariel? A companion of Lucifer or Satan, and one that made for the disputing...
> (262-57)

There is spiritual wickedness in high places.

The Anti-Christ is that force, influence, group or person who opposes Christ and tries to substitute himself in Christ's place. The Anti-Christ denies the Son and also denies the Father since they are One person.

There are those celestial beings who are STILL in rebellion that exist as beings of darkness who seek to trap and lure souls seeking the Light.

> The thief (Satan) cometh not, but for to steal, and to kill, and to destroy...
> John 10:10

> Remember…many poisonous vines bear beautiful flowers. But what manner of seed? In what way are they constructive? Think on these.
>
> (1947-3)

He that is last bound refers to Lucifer, Satan or the Devil who is the personification of that Anti-Christ Spirit. (See Chapter XI, The Anti-Christ.)

> Be sober, be vigilant; because your adversary the Devil, as a roaring lion, walketh about, seeking whom he may devour.
>
> 1 Peter 5:8

God has not willed that any of the celestial beings perish and has provided a Way of return for all the lost souls and perhaps also for the lost celestial beings and/or Angels who repent.

> …Hell was prepared for Satan and his Angels, yet God has not WILLED that ANY soul should perish.
>
> (900-20)

Most Christian religions do not believe that Lucifer or the fallen Angels can be saved. Most churches believe that the fallen Angels can never be forgiven.

> …there are those who from the first – as he that is last to be bound – had the import to do evil.
>
> (281-34)

They believe that the Lake of Fire is their destiny.

> And the Devil that deceived them was cast into the Lake of Fire and Brimstone…
>
> Revelation 20:10

Few people think that Lucifer, or Satan could be reinstated.
Many others do not see Satan as a person but more as an influence
that is misdirected.
The Readings see Satan as a person as well as an influence.
We make our own Heaven or Hell by our soul choices.

> For, the Heaven and Hell is built by the soul!
> The companionship in God is being One with Him;
> and the Gift of God is being conscious of being One
> with Him, yet APART from Him – or One with, yet
> apart from, the Whole.
> (5753-1)

A personal Savior and a personal Devil is similar to saying that we
make our own Heaven or Hell.

> Evil is rebellion. Good is the Son of Life, of Light, of
> Truth, that came into physical being to demonstrate
> and show and lead the Way for man's ascent to the
> Power of Good over Evil in a material world. There is,
> then, a personal Savior, there is a personal Devil.
> (262-52)

It could also be interpreted to mean Jesus Christ is the Savior and the
Devil or Lucifer is an actual person or Angel as well as an influence.
Lucifer is a fallen Angel who is as a misdirected creative force yet
allowed of God.

> Hence that force which rebelled in the unseen forces,
> (or in Spirit) that came into activity, was that influence
> that has been called Satan, the Devil, the Serpent; they
> are one. That of REBELLION!
> Hence, when man, in any activity rebels against the
> influence of Good he hearkens to the influence of Evil
> rather than the influence of Good.
> (262-52)

We can work with God or we can work against God, which will depend on our free will choices.

> For as each soul is a part of the Whole, individual in itself through the Mind of the creative forces, it is thus—as a soul—a co-worker WITH or AGAINST that First Cause or principle.
> (2113-1)

Indifference can be Evil when we ignore what we know to be Good or right and do nothing about it. We can see another who has needs or problems and be indifferent when we should help them.

> Hence, will is given to man as he comes into this manifested form that we see in material forces, for the choice. As given, "There is set before thee (man) Good and Evil."
> (262-52)

This is one of the ways Karma is created.

> Karma is, then, that that has been in the past builded as INDIFFERENCE to that KNOWN to be right!
> (257-78)

We can allow this force to act through our physical lives whereby it could become a choice for evil.

> For the Law of the Lord is perfect, and whatsoever an entity, an individual sows, that must he reap.
> That as Law cannot be changed. As to whether one meets it in the letter of the Law or in Mercy, in Grace, becomes the choice of the entity.
> (5001-1)

O if souls, bodies, everywhere, would gain that knowledge that the abilities to be sons of God or of the Devil lie within self's own individual will!
(416-2)

Being forewarned, be forearmed, for the WILL – as is the Gift of the Creator to man, made a little lower than the Angels, with the Power of choosing for self as to whether the entity that is given in the Body will be One with the Creator or attempt to set up SELF in that position of AT VARIANCE with that Creator, as seen by HIM who made "WAR in Heaven"-
In this position then, the entity must build for itself. The conditions are set, even as the Lord hath given, "This day I have set before thee Good and Evil. Choose thou whom thy peoples and thy self will serve…"
(1565-1)

…each soul is destined to become a portion again of the First Cause, or back to its Maker.
(987-2)

It seems that Light was called forth so that we could be AWARE of our error and correct the darkness of our mistake.

…He has not willed that any soul shall perish, but from the beginning has prepared a Way of escape! What is the meaning of separation?
Bringing into being the various phases so that the soul may find in manifested forms the consciousness and awareness of separation and (a return to) itself, by that through which it passes in all the various spheres of awareness.
Thus the separation between Light and darkness.

Darkness, that it had separated- that a soul had separated itself from the Light. Hence, He called into being Light and awareness began.

(262-56)

We have all fallen and come short of the glory of God intended for each of us.

Evil can only become a reality in our Life when we rebel and choose that which is not in the Law of Love or by choosing outside of God's will for us.

As we attune our will and Mind to God we will seek to do His will in Mind, Body, and Spirit.

"Not my will but let thy will be done in me," needs to be our constant prayer.

This is why it is so important to DISCERN the difference between what is Good and what is Evil so we can make the correct choices.

If we really know God, we will trust that His will for us is for our best interests. Our true will then will become to do His will in all things.

Who knows us or cares more for us than our own Creator?

Be not overcome with EVIL, but overcome Evil with Good!

(288-27)

Hence that which has been indicated – that Serpent, that Satan, that Power manifested by entities...

THROUGH WILL separated themselves.

Is God's hand short, that there would not be all that each soul would require?

For it is not by the will of God that any soul perishes, but with every temptation, with every trial there is prepared the Way of escape.

God the Father, then, is the Creator – the beginning and the end. In HIM is the understanding, BY and

through those influences that have taken form-in universes-to meet the needs of each soul-that we might find our Way to Him.
(5755-2)

What mark, what essence, what memory will be left by us is our choice to make.

Because we were made for the purpose of being companions with Him, a little lower than the Angels who behold HIS face ever yet, as heirs, as joint heirs with Him who IS the Savior, the Way...
For we CAN, as God, say Yea to this, Nay to that; we CAN order this or the other in our experience, by the very Gifts that have been given or appointed unto our keeping. For we are indeed as laborers, co-laborers in the vineyard of the Lord-
...and we choose each day WHOM we will serve!
And by the records in time and space, as we have moved through the realms of His Kingdom, we have left our mark upon same.
(1567-2)

Hopefully wherever we are, we will seek to make it a better place for others.
Let us not restrict the Mercy of God in our consciousness.
If a fallen soul can be forgiven, why not a fallen Angel?
Forgiveness cannot be given if one refuses to see itself in the wrong or will not admit to a mistake or to the wrong committed so it can be corrected.

Whatever the outcome of this rebellion that began in Heaven, we know that God's decision will be the right one and that it will be just.
The Christ has already won the war but the details are still uncertain.

We do know that some souls will be blotted out of God's "Book of Remembrance."

Why did God allow "sin" to be permitted?
God's infinite Wisdom did not destroy Lucifer or Satan but instead cast him out into a manifested world.
Had God blotted out Lucifer, the inhabitants of the universe would serve God out of fear instead of Love.
All of God's created beings must see the principles of Good and Evil that are involved, so God let them be manifested in full form.
God's Law is perfect and when transgressed against, suffering and death is the penalty.
The justice and Mercy of God and the immutability of His Law must be placed beyond question forever.
The purpose for God creating His Only Begotten Son would be revealed to all the Angels and all the other souls.
It would only be through the Light and Love of the Only Begotten Son that those who were lost could be saved from their offenses.
Christ Himself, the God-Son, would pay for their sins and lead them back to God. Christ would be crowned King of the universe(s) and no one would ever question His authority or identify as God again.
For Christ alone is worthy of all honor and glory and praise.

> I am the Way, the Truth, and the Life: No man cometh
> unto the Father, but by me.
> John 14:6

> For God so loved the world, that He gave his Only
> Begotten Son, that whosoever believeth in Him should
> not perish but have everlasting Life.
> For God sent not His Son into the world to condemn
> the world; but that the world through Him might be
> saved.
> He that believeth on Him is not condemned; but he
> that believeth not is condemned already, because he

hath not believed in the name of the Only Begotten Son of God.

And this is the condemnation, that Light is come into the world, and men loved darkness rather than the Light because their deeds were evil.

For everyone that doeth evil hateth the Light, neither cometh to the Light, lest his deeds should be reproved.

John 3:16-20

Who is the image of the invisible God, the Firstborn of every creature:

For by Him (Christ) were all things created, that are in Heaven, and that are in Earth, visible and invisible, whether they be Thrones, or Dominions, or Principalities, or Powers:

All things were created by Him and for Him:

And He is BEFORE all things, and by Him all things consist.

And He is Head of the Body, the church:

Who is the beginning, the Firstborn from the dead; that in all things He might have the pre-eminence.

For it pleased the Father that in Him should all fullness dwell.

Colossians 1:15-19

That at the name of Jesus every knee should bow, of things in Heaven, and things in Earth and things under the Earth;

and that every tongue should confess that Jesus Christ is Lord, to the glory of God the Father.

Philippians 2:10-11

CHAPTER IV

CREATION OF THE HEAVENS & THE EARTH

Thus realms of systems came into being as vast as the Power of thought in attempting to understand infinity, or to comprehend that there is no space or time.

(5755-2)

When the Heavens and the Earth came into being, this meant the universe as the inhabitants of the Earth know same; yet there are many suns in the universe-those even about which our sun, our Earth revolves; and all are moving toward some place – yet space and time appear to be incomplete.

Then time and space are but one...

For, remember, they, - the sun, the moon, the planets – have their marching orders from the divine, and they move in same.

(5757-1)

For the Earth, upon which the entity resides as a
specific individual in the present is only a portion of a
great solar system, which in turn is a small portion of
other great systems.

(615-1)

For, the Earth is only an atom in the universe of
WORLDS!

(5749-3)

The Readings state that we cannot conceive of the requirements of
the influences needed to meet all the idiosyncrasies of a single soul.

Take what has just been given; that there are
conditions that may meet every idiosyncrasy of the
INDIVIDUAL soul!

(5755-2)

Vast realms were needed for all these forming individualities to
express their own concept of God and creation as they grew into all
that they were created to be.

All souls were made as companions, as a portion of
the Whole. For it is in the image, in the pattern of
the creative forces; and only that as is constructive can
abide in that creative presence.

(1230-1)

Each soul was in its First Division from the Godhead
to be a companion with that force, that influence,
that purpose. Hence the purpose is to grow in Grace,
knowledge, understanding, for the indwelling with
that PRESENCE.

(1861-4)

All the sons of God did not choose to rebel as many were developing and growing into their individual potential that they were created to be.
They had not chosen to use their free will in opposition to the plan for their fulfillment. These souls made choices to serve God and to be co-workers and co-creators.

> ...an entity, Body-Mind was first a soul before it entered into material consciousness.
> (4083-1)

The rebellious souls chose to serve self and work against the nature of God, adding negative influences to God's creation.
God through Christ created the cosmos, planets, stars, and universe(s), all for His celestial children to dwell in and to rule.

> Yet all are the work of His hand, are thine to possess, thine to use - as One with Him.
> (5755-2)

Each soul was a perfect balance of negative and positive forces of female and male combined in One self, which is androgynous.
Therefore, when we speak of the "sons of God," it refers to son and daughter combined, as in one complete soul. Male and female aspects enjoined into One Whole entity. The soul is non-sexual and non-flesh. Its Body is of spiritual matter clothed in Mind.

> It is a fact that the soul is only complete in all of its attributes as a fit companion or associate of the realm from which Spirit first found itself conscious of a will; bringing the soul into passive and active energies we know take form in matter with a positive-negative nucleus about a center.
> (553-1)

> The Spirit wheels in flight,
> Coming down flying high,
> Peacefully winging on pure air,
> Aloft composing Yin and Yang.
> Chu Yuan

Souls retained knowledge of all that they experienced and the memory of their actions.

The sons and daughters of God together as One self kept a close spiritual relationship and companionship with God through Christ.

The same DESIRE for companionship that was in God exists within us as well.

> ...the desire of that companionship innate in that created, as innate in the Creator, that brought companionship into the creation itself.
> (364-5)

All souls make a record of their thoughts and experiences.

Their activities are as energy patterns and emanations that are recorded in God's "Book of Remembrance." This is referred to as the Akashic Record. Each soul has a name and a "Book of Life."

> For Light moves on in time, in space, and upon that skein between same are the records written by each soul in its activity through eternity; through its awareness... not only in matter but in thought, in whatever realm that entity builds for itself in its experience, in its journey, in its activity.
> (815-2)

> Such records of every entity are upon the skein between time and space.
> (688-2)

God's imaged creations began to emerge and from the spiritual pattern in His Mind, thus forming the Earth and its planetary system of Heavenly consciousness.

All things in the material world have an unseen beginning.

> For in the beginning God moved and Mind,
> knowledge, came into being – and the Earth and the
> fullness thereof became the result of same.
> (5000-1)

The material world is a shadow or a reflection of the spiritual
patterns in God's Mind that was manifested by and through the
Christ Consciousness.

> In the beginning, when there was the creating, or the
> calling of individual entities into being we were made
> to be the companions with the Father-God.
> (1567-2)

> The Earth and the universe, as related to man, came into
> being through the MIND-MIND-of the Maker…
> (900-227)

> First that of a mass, which there arose the mist, and
> then the rising of same with Light breaking OVER that
> as it SETTLED itself, as a companion of those in the
> universe, as it began its NATURAL (or now natural)
> rotations… slowly… receding or gathering closer to
> the sun, from which it receives its impetus…
> (364-6)

The Children of God lived in the cosmos as souls in Spirit while the Earth
was being created and before flesh man was created. While the Earth was
being created, souls as celestial beings watched and also participated.

> …among those who first came into the Earth's sphere
> before it became inhabitable to human Life. Only
> then as the vision did the entity (Spirit entity) view
> the Earth's sphere, and in that passed to the other
> spheres about the Earth.
> (228-2)

>...dwellers upon the moon preceded the abilities (expressed in a form known as matter in the Earth.)
>(264-31)

All of God's creations followed fixed Laws that were set in motion and which still exist today.

>...for man was created a little bit higher than all the rest of the Whole universe, and is capable of harnessing, directing, enforcing, the Laws of the universe.
>(5-2)

>The Earth's sphere, with the first creation in the Mind of the Creator, has kept its same creative energy, for God is the same yesterday, today and forever...
>(900-340)

Individual consciousness is formed by experience and memories.
Memories and experiences not compatible with the Spirit of Truth have to be reviewed and changed as they have formed patterns that are not lawful or worthy of a companion.
This is where the Law of Karma or of cause and effect comes into functioning in a soul's Life. We must meet previous thoughts and actions. What goes out of us comes back to us again.
Errors must be corrected. We have opportunities to change our mistakes and to break old patterns by establishing new ones that are pleasing to God.

>If the experiences are ever used for self-indulgence, self-aggrandizement, self-exaltation, each entity does so to its OWN undoing, or creates for self that as has been called KARMA – and must be met!
>(1224-1)

What we do to others we also do to ourselves.
What goes out of us in thoughts and deeds will eventually return to us again. "What goes around, comes around."

It is true because it is the Law.

> Learn the LAW: that ye reap what ye sow!
> The manner in which ye measure to others, it will be
> measured to thee again!
> That is an unchangeable Law!
> Then, live the Law; be the Law, as respecting such.
> (2185-1)

LAW IS THE IMPERSONAL ASPECT OF GOD.

> He IS impersonal; but so VERY personal!
> It is not that ye deal only with IMPERSONAL - it is
> WITHIN and WITHOUT.
> (1158-12)

> For, the Earth is a causation world, for the Earth, cause
> and effect are as the natural Law.
> (3645-1)

Misapplication of spiritual Laws caused the separation of some souls and/or celestial beings from God.
The material world would allow the lost souls to learn to manifest the correct principles and awareness that would lead them back to God.

The restrictions of time and space LIMIT manifestations.
Time also confines and limits the use of free will.

> "Let there be Light", then, was that consciousness
> that TIME began to be a factor in the experience
> of those creatures that had entangled themselves in
> matter; and became what we know as the Influences
> in a material plane.
> (262-115)

> The entity or soul, in any given period in time of manifestation in space, may use those attributes of that phase of its consciousness in whatever realm it moves, according to the dictates of that which impels it – through its will.
> (815-7)

In the third dimension, experiences are divided into units.
Time is a way of measuring experience.
In the subconscious forces the measure of time and space disappear.
The Readings indicate that time is a factor in the whole planetary system of Earth. However, time is not yet complete.

> Time is not yet complete, time is not yet at hand, why?
> The LAWS are set, Love can only remove same.
> (5326-1)

Individual choices we make will affect and change the future.
Our thoughts and deeds are recorded upon the skein between time and space in whatever realm in which we have experience.

Thoughts are tangible things (deeds) which can become as a form of solid matter. The Readings state that thoughts can become miracles or crimes.

The souls desired images in thought would take time and space to become hardened or crystallized.

Their thought creations would become more visible to themselves in a time, space, and patience dimension. They would know to be careful of what they thought, desired or dreamed as thoughts will manifest and become hardened visualizations or creations that will have to be met.

Since there is no time as we know it in the "higher dimensions," it is not possible to conceptualize a time frame for all these various events that occurred. We use time in the Earth to measure our experiences. The

Readings do indicate that there is space and time in our solar system but also state that time does not exist in the subconscious forces.

It is like a wheel within a wheel, each turning in opposite directions. The view changes according to where the spokes of your point of awareness are focused in the wheel. It is similar in thought to a parallel world.

Real time is more of an "eternal now" in which all events which we know as past, present, and future are contained in the ever-present now. The past, present, and the future exist simultaneously, like parallel worlds. But the future is not sealed.
It is being projected by our present thoughts, desires and actions.
YET time is not complete as choices are still being made which will alter the outcome of the future.
Upon time and space are written the activities, thoughts, and deeds of each soul throughout all his environments whether in or out of the Earth's atmosphere or in other dimensional realms.

> ...in the spheres about the Earth, space and time...
> (3508-1)

Therefore, time must be continuing in that INTER-BETWEEN as we continue on our journey back to the Father.
It is difficult for us to conceive of time not being the same reality in other realms when it is so important in our dimension.

> ...Hence, LIGHT forces pass much faster, but the records are upon the esoteric, or etheric, or Akashic forces, as they go along upon the wheels of time, the wings of time, or in WHATEVER dimension we may signify as a matter of its momentum or movement.
> ...they are the records upon the wings or the wheel of time itself. Time as that as of space-as inter-between. That inter-between, that which is, that of which, that from one object to another when in matter is of the same nature, or what that is is what the other is...

69

>...as is termed in man's terminology as DIMENSIONS of space, or DIMENSIONS that give it, whatever may be the solid, liquid, gas, or what ITS FORM or dimension!
>(364-6)

Spirit is Law, government, order, Harmony, and justice.
Law is perfection.
Justice is that force that seeks to correct imperfection.
The Law is not a respecter of persons and is impersonal.
When in the Earth, if you throw a ball into the air, the gravitational pull will bring it back down, no matter who throws it up. It's a Law.
Christ is the Law and all Law is subject unto Him.

The physical Laws can be superceded if one's will is centered in and One with the Creator.
Jesus became the Master of natural Law while in the Earth by manifesting the Christ Consciousness. (Examples are: Walking on water, the Resurrection, and the Ascension into Heaven.)

>There are, as were set in the beginning, as far as the concern is of this physical Earth plane, those rules or Laws in the relative force of those that govern the Earth, and the beings of the Earth plane, and also that same Law governs the planets, stars, constellations, groups, that constitutes the sphere, the space, in which the planet moves. These are of the One force.
>(3744-5)

The fall of many of the companions had already happened in Spirit before the Earth was created.

>Sin—the separation—that as caused the separation of souls from the universal consciousness – came not in the sphere of materiality first, but in that of Spirit.
>(1602-3)

...an entity, Body-Mind was first a soul BEFORE it entered into material consciousness.

(4083-1)

The creation of the Earth and its planetary system in the spiritual-material plane is an opportunity for souls to become aware of their error and separation from God. Many souls have become oblivious to the purpose for which they are created. They are lost souls, who are no longer able to be true companions of God.

> For the Spirit of God moved and that which is in matter came into being, for the opportunities of...
> His sons, His daughters. These are ever spoken of as One.
> (262-114)

> For, the universe was brought into being for the purpose of being the dwelling place of the souls of God's children.
> (2396-2)

> ...all souls became a part of the creation.
> (2925-1)

> Desire brought the Earth and the Heavens into being from an All-Wise Creator.
> (276-3)

In the spheres about the Earth, time and space do exist. It may be a different time than we experience in the third dimension.
A form of time exists in our planetary system because it is connected to Earth in consciousness and functions as one Whole unit.

> God moved, the Spirit came into activity.
> In the moving it brought Light, and then chaos.

> In this Light came creation of that which in the Earth
> came to be matter; in the spheres about the Earth,
> space, and time; and in patience it has evolved through
> those activities until there are the Heavens and all the
> constellations, the stars, the universe as it is known…
> (3508-1)

The purpose of material creation has to be completed before time will be erased.

Time ceases to exist as we know it in the subconscious forces but time will continue until we have been perfected and returned to God.

All souls have planetary sojourns and they influence these realms as the planetary environments also influence each entity.

> For, as long as an entity is within the confines of that
> termed the Earth's and the sons of the Earth's solar
> system, the developments are within the sojourns of
> the entity from sphere to sphere…
> (441-1)

> …in the Earth's environ or Earth's orbit are PLACES
> or conditions or spheres of abode for those particular
> classified environs of a soul, is not only reasonable but
> a practical thing…
> (553-1)

> Time and space are occupied or are peopled with the
> elements or spheres, that become activities for souls
> or entities in their journey through TIME and space;
> seeking that home not built with hands but with the
> thoughts and with the deeds and with the manners
> in which we have dealt with our fellow souls, or our
> fellow beings.

> Hence we find these as PLACES or as spheres—or as planets; sojournings in that environ...
> (1597-1)

The Earth and flesh bodies are as a school for the testing portion of the universal vibration.

> Thus a soul is in the Earth, in the material manifestations, as in a school of experience.
> For, no soul gains knowledge or understanding save through experience.
> (2608-1)

> Then, in the many stages of development, throughout the universal, or in the great system of the universal forces, and each stage of development made manifest through flesh, which is the testing portion of the universal vibration.
> (900-16)

> When an individual incarnates in the Earth, he has POSSIBLY passed through all the various spheres, either once, twice, MANY times...
> (311-2)

The Edgar Cayce Readings agree with the concept of creation found in the Bible in the Book of Genesis but enlarges the concepts and details.

The Bible is more than just a literal book inspired by God and the historic record of a group of people. The Bible is also filled with mystical symbolism, which provides a deeper spiritual meaning.

The Readings state that the Bible is the history of a "soul group" that was created before Earth began. Then with the creation of mankind in Adam, they as individuals actually lived and many of them were reborn and had Readings. The Bible is literal and it is also symbolic in parts, and it must be spiritually understood to know which passages are literal and which are symbolic or both.

The Bible is like a metaphor for each soul seeking the Light to see its own passage through various Lifetimes of experience on its long journey for enlightenment and the return to God.

It is symbolic of our own personal story. The Bible reminds us of our own experiences and awakens memories of our past and helps to reveal the pattern of the Christ needed for us to return to God.

The people in the Bible also represent various states of awareness or consciousness.

(For example, Abraham means faith, Israel means seeker of Truth.)

The Book of Genesis reveals the spiritual creation and opens us to the memory of our spiritual past from "Before the Foundation of the World."

Jesus the Christ is not only the subject of the Bible but the author as well, according to the Readings.

> He is not merely the subject of the Book. He is the author in the greater part, having given to man the Mind and the purpose for its having been put in print.
> (5322-1)

> But study to know thy relationship to thy Creator.
> No better handbook may be used than the Scripture itself.
> (1966-1)

> The nearest true version (of the Bible) is that ye apply of whatever version ye read, in your Life.
> (2072-14)

> Read it to be Wise. Study it to understand.
> LIVE it to know that Christ walks through same with thee.
> (262-60)

The "First Beginning" in Genesis refers to the spiritual creation of the Only Begotten Son as Christ. God manifests Himself into Light. When Cayce was asked which passages to read in the Bible, he said,

> "the creation of man in the first three chapters..."
> (1173-8)

> And God said, "Let there be Light."
> And there was Light.
> Genesis 1:3

> ...the first of everything that may be visible,
> in Earth, in Heaven, in space, is of that Light
> -IS that Light!
> (2533-8)

Many eons of experience exist between the creation of Christ with the other souls or sons of God and the physical creation of mankind in Adam. Adam as man/mankind in flesh was only created to meet the needs of conditions existing in the Earth at a MUCH later period.

The creation of man in the Bible and in the Readings is a threefold creation.
There are the spiritual, the mental and the physical creations.
First is the creation of the Christ and then the other soul companions of God in the Christ Spirit, which is the spiritual creation.
All the sons and daughters as "One Spirit entity" or group soul were created in the same beginning.

Each soul in the group contained within it the POTENTIAL of being individualized portions of His (Christ's) very self.

> For, as a corpuscle in the Body of God, ye are free-willed
> and thus a co-creator with God.
> (3003-1)

Then the Angels and other manifested beings were created, whose purpose was to minister to the souls created in Christ.
The Angels were also to assist and to maintain the realms of realities coming into manifestation according to God's will and image throughout the universe(s).

Next we have the mental or consciousness levels of being.
This is the activity in Mind of the expressions of the Christ and His younger brothers and sisters in Him (souls/us).

Christ moved, the other sparks of Light as souls moved into expressions of themselves in the Heavenly realms of awareness.

Souls were using free will to express and experience their images. This was for the growth needed to develop into the individual self that was projected by Christ.
Souls had separated from the constructive plan and purpose intended for their full development and son-ship and Oneness with God.
They were expected to assist in the creation of matter, not become personally entangled in it.

Many of these souls entered the Earth before it was habitable to human Life as "Thought Form Beings" where they had experiences.
This was an illegal, forced entry, which was not ordained of God.
God had not created a form for souls to inhabit in the Earth.

> ...souls projected themselves into matter, and thus brought that conscious awareness of themselves entertaining the ability of creating without those forces of the Spirit of Truth.
> (5755-2)

It was not originally intended that the souls would inhabit physical bodies, which came later, only to meet the needs of existing conditions.

It was only in the material plane with its co-existing planetary system or mental-spiritual levels of consciousness that the fallen souls could become aware of their mistakes and misuse of their creative force.

> ...by becoming aware in a material world IS-or was-the ONLY manner or Way through which spiritual forces might become aware of their separation from the spiritual atmosphere, the spiritual surroundings, of the Maker.
> (262-56)

> For that which has a beginning must have an ending. Hence rebellion and hate and selfishness must be wiped away, and WITH IT will go sorrow and tears and sadness. For ONLY Good shall rule.
> (262-114)

Each entity created is a part of the whole creation and part of all of the universe. All the many realms that exist are part of our experience.

The other planets in the Earth's solar system rule the destiny of all matter that was created in the various dimensions.

> In the beginning, as our own planet, Earth, was set in motion, the placing of other planets began the ruling of the destiny of all matter as created, just as the division of waters was and is ruled by the moon in its path about the Earth; just so as in the higher creation, as it began, is ruled by the action of the planets about the Earth.
> (254-2)

The planets are environments of various levels of consciousness which are available to souls for growth and development.

The solar system of which the Earth is a part is only a portion of the Whole. For as indicated in the number of planets about the Earth, they are of one and the same - and they are relative one to another.

It is the cycle of the Whole system that is finished, see?
(5749-14)

In the beginning God created the Heavens and the Earth.

How? The MIND of God MOVED and MATTER, form, came into being.
(262-78)

Matter, then would be the offspring of energy and not the parent, as is often thought.
(195-70)

First there was the consciousness of Light then that Light was followed by chaos or darkness and confusion. Chaos is the state which resulted when the Spirit entities misused their birthright Gift of free will.

The darkness or void is also used to describe the state of unconsciousness before it manifested into personal individual awareness.

Chaos includes the fallen Angels as well. The fallen celestial beings were cast into the material world of consciousness, which includes this Whole planetary or Heavenly realm as one unit, or world for experience.

In the beginning when chaos existed in the creating of the Earth, the Spirit of God moved over the face of same and out of chaos came the world- with its beauty in natural form, or in nature.

As the Spirit of God once moved to bring Peace and Harmony out of chaos, so must the Spirit move over the Earth...
(3976-8)

There were other realms of matter in higher dimensions.
God created the Heavens as well as the Earth.

There are many levels of consciousness besides our solar system
(many mansions/universes or states of consciousness.)

There are at least twelve dimensions of consciousness in our
planetary system.
In the Spirit, awareness can be stretched to experience eleven, twelve
and twenty-two dimensions, the Readings state. Therefore, we have
the possibility of experiencing twenty-two dimensions of Mind.

> Learn the lesson of the interpreting of the dimensions
> of the Earth, or that the three-dimensions in the Mind
> may be seven, and in Spirit, eleven and twelve and
> twenty-two.
> (5149-1)

The Earth and its planetary system are all interconnected.
It is ONE Whole UNIT or cycle of varied mental/spiritual
ENVIRONMENTS, for the soul to develop and express and to
grow into its perfect function in the Body of God.

Souls are to experience these realms in consciousness in their mental
- spiritual bodies of awareness. These planetary levels of Mind
represent actual PLACES or mental conditions to indwell.

> Thus we find that the sojourns about the Earth, during
> the interims between Earthly sojourns, are called the
> astrological aspects.
> Not that an entity may have manifested physically on
> such planets, but in that consciousness which is the
> consciousness of that environ. And these have been
> accredited with certain potential influences in the
> MENTAL aspect of an entity.
> (2144-1)

Thus as the soul passes from the aspects about the material environs, or the Earth, we find the astrological aspects are represented as stages of consciousness; given names that represent planets or centers or CRYSTALIZED activity.

Not that flesh and blood, as known in the Earth, dwell therein; but in the consciousness, with the FORM and manner as befits the environ.

(1650-1)

Earth represents the third dimension.
The third dimension is "time, space, and patience."
It is through time, space, and patience that a soul may become aware of the infinite.

For each phase of time, each phase of space, is dependent as one atom upon another. And there is no vacuum, for this, as may be indicated in the universe, is an impossibility with God.

(3161-1)

The Earth and its solar system were created in God's perfect Harmony and order.

For, when thou beholdest the glory of the Father in the Earth, how ORDERLY are His glories! Hast thou watched the sun in its orbit? How ORDERLY are those places of the habitation of the souls of men…

(440-14)

Each Spirit entity was created with a purpose to perform. The soul has a function in the Body of Christ, which is the universal Mind. Each planetary influence vibrates at a different rate of vibration. As an entity enters that planetary influence, it can change the entity for the better (as it is an environment of the Universal Consciousness), depending on the will of the entity allowing the influence.

> An entity entering that influence enters that vibration;
> not necessary that he change, but it is the Grace of
> God that he may!
> (281-55)

The various planets represent different vibrations that can be
ABSORBED by the soul while in its planetary environment.
Venus represents Love and the fourth dimension. The Body form of
Venus is similar to that of Earth but on a higher frequency.
Venus is like the "higher self" of Earth.

> For each soul in its advent into this Earth solar system,
> and becoming an indweller in the realm of materiality,
> becomes subject to the Laws and the attributes of this
> present solar system, with the influences from the sun,
> from the sun's planetary companions in this present
> solar experience.
> (510-1)

The companions of the sun are the other planets in Earth's solar
system. Each planet represents a state of consciousness for experience
and growth in the mental-spiritual planes.
There is NO flesh and blood Life on these planets but all are
inhabited.

> Not as a physical Body as known in the Earth, but as
> a Body adaptable to the environs of Jupiter; for there's
> Life there, as there is in Saturn, Sun, Moon, Venus,
> Mercury, Uranus, Neptune, Mars; all have their
> form...the elements about same are inhabited, if you
> choose, by those of their own peculiar environment.
> (630-2)

For man is not made for this world alone.
(4082-1)

Many souls are indwelling in these planetary environments and have experiences. This is not a PHYSICAL or human experience but an environment to develop the mental/spiritual Mind and build higher consciousness.

Remember that in the Earth, the soul is only using a small part of its higher level of consciousness and this is very limited from what the soul can experience in other realms.

These planetary influences are experienced as intuitive forces when we are in the Earth. If we listen to these influences, then act upon the intuitive forces received, we can express a higher dimension of awareness while we are in the Earth.

> For it is not strange that music, color, vibration, are all a part of the planets, just as the planets are a part-and a pattern-of the Whole universe.
> (5755-1)

Tom Sugrue in <u>There Is A River</u> wrote that music is one of the building blocks God used to create the universe.
It is comforting to think of music and color existing in all dimensions.

We are all as individual musicians in God's infinite cosmic orchestra, sounding out our unique tunes that blend in with the Harmony of the Whole concert being performed throughout time.
Each individual soul song is important to the Whole symphony.

> That the soul – a portion, an expression of God's desire for companionship – might find expression, the souls of men and women came into being; that there might be that which would make each soul, then, as a fit companion for that realm.
> There is the necessity of fitting itself through the experiences of all phases and realms of existence, then; that it, the soul, may not cause disruption in the

> realm of beauty, Harmony, strength of divinity in its
> companionships with that creative force.
> (805-4)

The Earth and its solar system, which are as companion planets that
include the sun and moon, were created as a unit or cycle of varied
realms of consciousness through which the sons of God would
express and experience and develop in Spirit.
The planets are referred to as environments.

> ...each soul manifests in other dimensions through
> sojourns in the environs about the Earth.
> (2462-2)

The planetary dimensions contain at least twelve different pure
states of awareness. The Readings discussed only eight of them
which affect us now.
The soul needs to experience all realms of creation to be able
to function in Harmony and beauty as a companion with the
Creator.

When Earth became a dwelling place for physical matter, God
created plants, land, water, minerals, then the animals first in His
Mind, then LATER they were manifested or they became animated
in matter.

> When the Earth became a dwelling place for matter,
> when gases formed into those things that man sees in
> nature and in activity about him, then matter began
> its ascent in the various forms of physical evolution –
> in the MIND of God!
> (262-99)

> Let it be remembered, or not confused, that the Earth
> was peopled by ANIMALS before peopled by man!
> (364-6)

Joan Clarke

While the Earth was being created, spiritual beings as souls projected themselves into matter to experience the various elements and the five physical senses in the animal Kingdoms.

> Hence we find the evolution of the soul... as is manifest in the material world, took place BEFORE man's appearance, the evolution of the soul in the Mind of the Creator, not in the material world.
> (900-19)

The Earth was not intended to be a place of habitation in flesh for the sons of God. It was peopled with animals, with land, and plants, minerals, rivers, lakes and mountains and the elements of fire, air, and water and Earth.

God had NOT created any form worthy of His souls to inhabit in the third dimensional world of matter nor was permission given to invade it.

But some souls became fascinated with and DESIRED to experience animal, vegetable or mineral matter.
We have no idea as to God's original purpose in creating the animals.
The companions interfered in the animal Kingdoms and altered them. It may take until we are all returned back to God or either blotted out of His "Book of Remembrance" for God's original purpose with the animals to be fulfilled.

The souls who entered this sphere had to project Thought Form images of themselves into the material they desired to experience. Being co-creators as part of their nature, they could draw upon the creative force within themselves to translate their mental pictures into the desired materialization.

They could also draw and assemble matter into their Thought Form bodies by infusing their spiritual essence into matter to create the mental images desired. In this way, their spiritual – mental bodies were externalized and became visible in the Earth.

The results were hybrid beings composed of Spirit, Mind, and also physical matter of all the various elements in the Earth.

At first they could enter into an animal or a plant or mineral and leave with their spiritual (Astral) bodies intact. They could move into an animal and co-join with it and then leave and still be free to be themselves. This act was similar to what we might term "possession" (which is when a disincarnate entity FORCES itself into a human person's Body to experience physical sensations or to take control of that vessel.)

Eventually, the souls got trapped in their own hybrid creations and were unable to move back out of matter into the spiritual realms.

These combinations of Spirit and matter became hardened, or crystallized into the image created. They got stuck in the form they were experiencing, which solidified.

The REAL problem is that once they got stuck, they were no longer functioning as celestial beings.

Their creations were no longer creations that were separate from their soul identity.

Once stuck, the soul was cut off from its higher functioning as a celestial being of God. They had amnesia and loss of identity. The physical world became more real than the spiritual.

Their higher consciousness became limited to this dimension and planetary system.

Many souls had become so entangled in the animal Kingdom, that what is thought to be the mythological half human and half animal beings, was actually a reality at that time. Beings formed from animal parts, commingled with human - like parts, were the first inhabitants of the Earth.

Many beings had the physiognomy of man but had animal tails, scales, hooves, or parts of plants, trees and minerals. For example, there were the centaur, the satyr, the mermaid, the Styx, and the unicorn.

...those who were PHYSICALLY entangled in the animal Kingdom with appendages, with cloven-hooves, with four legs, with portions of trees, with tails, with scales, with those various things that Thought Forms (or evil) had so indulged in as to separate the purpose of God's creation of man as man-not as animal but as man.

And the animal seeks only gratifying of self, the preservation of Life, the satisfying of appetites.

With INFINITY injected in same brought the many confused activities or thoughts that we know NOW as APPETITES.

(2072-8)

Because of their spiritual influence and ability to create, they changed the material substance and the material also altered them. It was like a mixture of the soul's Astral or Spirit Body with the animal or plant Body of Earth.

INFINITY, the soul force of celestial beings, was injected into living animals who were in manifestation or forming into what they were created to be. This powerful spiritual influence altered God's creation changing it into a different being.

Some people believe that some of the animals would have evolved into a level of awareness whereby they could be granted a type of soul status as younger brothers and sisters.

It still could be a possibility, due to our Love and devotion to certain pets.

Do animals go to Heaven or into higher realms of consciousness?

Would Heaven be happy without our beloved pets?

Many children who have Near Death Experiences are greeted by animals and pets when they have a death encounter.

I think God loves the animals more dearly than we do.

This group of souls was out of God's will and in rebellion and they were enticing other souls to enter Into their mischief and join in their self indulgences and self centered practices.

> ...beings...able to push out of themselves in that direction in which its development took shape in thought -much in the way and manner as the amoeba would in the waters of a stagnant bay, or lake, in the present.
> (364-3)

> ...when souls sought or found manifestation in materiality by the Projection of themselves into matter -
> ...as became Thought Forms—and when they had so ENTICED the companions or souls of the Creator...
> (257-201)

The celestial beings of Light who were still functioning in Harmony with their spiritual identity affected the material Life being created constructively, while those celestial beings who had fallen in Spirit manifested negative influences because they were not in the Spirit of Truth.

> ...souls projected themselves into matter, and thus brought that conscious awareness of themselves entertaining the ability of creating without those forces of the Spirit of Truth.
> (5755-2)

Some of the negative results of their activity are still visible in nature as cannibalistic influences in animals, in the plants as poison ivy, thorns on the roses, and stinging insects, ticks and mosquitoes and other pests.

Souls became intermingled in an immersion with animals and nature until it grew out of them and many were trapped within these distorted creations.

The original Thought Forms were sort of like ghost shapes of Lighted smoke. When they got trapped in an animal and solidified, their offspring were formed as half celestial being and half animal. This is how the "Mixtures" came about.

A soul could become an animal if he wanted to do so.
Souls and animals lived together as brothers and partook of each other's consciousness.
They shared souls in a sense but animals do not have the soul qualities or free will or the super-conscious Mind of celestial beings.
They did not eat each other, as plants were the food of them both.
However, a time came later when there was blood shed and who knows who was killing or eating whom.
There were animals who were trapped souls and then the ones who were just plain animals.
Taking the Life of an animal with a soul of One of God's sons inside would have been a terrible mistake. The thought of eating the flesh that a soul inhabited is cannibalism even if it was part animal.
Remember the animals were the only beings who actually belonged on the Earth and who were created to be here at this time. The higher celestial beings were the INVADERS.
The desire to BE as Gods was more Powerful than the desire to glorify God. They set themselves up as Gods over the different Kingdoms developing on the Earth. This is the same sin that happened with Lucifer and the fallen Angels.
I think that souls must have overly identified with God's Light within them to the point of thinking themselves God.
After all, they were parts of God containing the same creative abilities as the Creator. This is a trespass against God.

> What caused the First Influences in the Earth that brought selfishness? The desire to be as Gods, in that rebellion became the order of the mental forces in the soul; and sin entered.
>
> (5753-1)

They became narcissistic and filled with so much self-Love that they forgot their Love of God and ceased to be companions.

Even though they were able to enter in and out of animal beings and in and out of their own created Thought Forms, they had Spirit bodies.

There were also various types of monsters, prehistoric huge animals, and human giants.

> Some brought about monstrosities, as those of its association with beasts of various characters. Hence those of the Styx, satyr and the like; those of the sea, or mermaid; those of the unicorn, and those of the various forms-these Projections of what? The abilities in the PSYCHIC forces (psychic meaning, then, of the mental and the soul...)
>
> (364-10)

The animals had voice communications but the celestial beings used "thought transferences" at first. They also began to use words to express their images as well.

Birds and other animals use various sounds or calls that have meaning to them. Birds sing to attract mates.

Each species of bird has different songs. One of the primary reasons for bird songs is to establish the existence of boundaries. It is within the existence of this territory that a pair of birds will raise their young, so it must be jealously guarded from rivals as it will provide protection and food for both parents and their young until the breeding season is over. Singing lets other birds of the same species

know that a family is in residence and intruders are not welcome. Other species of birds are tolerated as they have different feeding and nesting requirements.
Besides the various bird songs, there are different bird calls that have their meanings.

Can we possibly imagine what it is like to be what a mineral is? What is the consciousness of a mineral?

> As those that sought forms of minerals – and being able to be that the mineral was...
> (364-10)

Think of all the different kinds of minerals that exist.
People throughout the past ages have worn various stones and metals to stimulate a higher level of psychic functioning and sensitivity. Even today gems are considered precious and of great value (gold, silver, diamonds, rubies, emeralds, lapis, the pearl, turquoise, etc.)

According to the Readings, various stones have vibrational properties that can induce well being, stability, increase longevity, and help attune the Body and Mind to its spiritual Source.

> (Properties of gold when assimilated vibrationally)
> ...for these feed directly to the tissue of the brain itself and when given properly - silver and gold may almost lengthen Life to its double, of its present endurance.
> (120-5)

The most ideal Body was the physical Body created by God for Adam at a later period as in the Five Races.

> In the matter of form, first there were those as Projections from that about the animal Kingdom; for the THOUGHT bodies gradually took FORM, and the various COMBINATIONS of the various

forces that called or classified themselves as Gods,
or rulers over - whether herds or fowls, or fishes, etc.
(Projections)
In PART (of) that (animal) Kingdom and (in) PART
of that as gradually EVOLVED into a physiognomy
much in the form of the present day may...
These took on MANY sizes as to stature, from the
midget to the giants - for there were giants in the
Earth in those days, men as tall as ten to twelve feet...
and well proportioned throughout.
The ones that became the most USEFUL were those
as would be classified (or called in the present) as the
IDEAL stature, that was of both male and female (as
those separations had been begun); and the most ideal
was in that period when He (Adam) appeared as five
in One – see?
(364-11)

The animal and man-like combinations that existed before Adam
was created were a sort of combination of the animal or plant Body
and similar to the Body of man as was later created.
This was a PHYSICAL entanglement as well as a "Thought
Form."
The animals were of flesh and blood.
Why was there a resemblance since man was not as yet created?

The spiritual Body or Astral Body of the soul must have been similar
and was perhaps used as the pattern for the Body of Adam.

Anyone who has ever seen an Angel knows that they have heads
with faces and eyes and arms and although they may be fashioned
out of Light instead of flesh, they resemble us somewhat, or we
resemble them in form.
Our celestial bodies are like those of the Angels. The celestial
Body-image was manifested through the animal Body and it too
solidified.

There were several different types of Body forms experimented with throughout this long ago period of time.

These early Life forms were called "Root Races" by the Cayce Readings but he did not list a lot of sub-Root-Races that other sources do. The Cayce viewpoint is different. The First Root Races were in Lemuria and then later in Atlantis. The Fourth Root Race we have now was completed in the Ra period of Egypt.

Souls were attempting to disentangle themselves from their associations with the animal Kingdoms.

> ...there was the first appearance of those that were as separate entities or souls disentangling themselves from material or that we know as ANIMAL associations.
> For the Projections of these had come from those influences that were termed LEMURE, or LEMURIAN, or the land of MU.
> (877-10)

Lemuria became a highly developed civilization which lasted well into the Atlantean era.
Lemuria was a strange period in civilization.
They were able to be in a Body or out of a Body and act upon it or to influence materiality. The bodies in Mu were not so closely knit in matter as those of today as this was BEFORE the perfect Body form.
These Thought Form bodies were spiritual entities, some of whom were mixed in with animal flesh and other physical elements like plants and minerals.

> Before this we find the entity was in that land that has been termed Zu, or Lemuria, or Mu. This was before the sojourn of peoples in perfect Body form; rather when they may be said to have been able to through those developments of the period be in the

Body or out of the Body and ACT upon materiality. In the Spirit or in the flesh these made those things, those influences that brought destruction; for the atmospheric pressure in the Earth in the period was quite different from that experienced by the physical beings of today.
(436-2)

Evidently Mmuum was named after sounds or "calls" used at the time. This was before the Body form was perfected.

...the entity was in that land that has been termed Zu, or Lemuria or Mu.
This was before the sojourn of peoples in perfect Body form...
The entity was named Mmuum, or rather those calls that make easy the mysteries of words as related to sounds...
(436-2)

The experiences in Mu were the determining factor in the Body type that started out as a Thought Form but materialized into that which became man.

Before that the entity was in the land now thought of or termed La, or Mu - Lamu.
Those experiences then made for the determining between the Thought Forms and those that materialized into what became man.
(1387-1)

The entity then was among the household of Aja in the name Amelelia, and acted as the Priestess to those in the Temple of LIGHT, that made for the guiding of those things pertaining to the motivative influences...in the present as those who oversaw the

> communications between the various lands—as of
> Om, Mu, the hierarchy land in that NOW known as
> the United States, in that particular portion of Arizona
> and Nevada that are as a portion of that Brotherhood
> of those peoples from Mu.
> (812-1)

These first soul Projections that were entangled in matter were from the early period of Lemuria or the land of Mu, once in the South Pacific but now submerged.
Lemuria became a high level of civilization in many ways.

These "Mixed" creatures had offspring or descendants, which resulted in further confusion and additional problems.

The offspring of a soul trapped in an animal resulted in being one of the "Mixtures."
The appendages (feathers, paws, tails, beaks, claws, scales, hooves) of the "Mixtures" were very difficult to get rid of as they still existed after Lemuria sunk and also throughout the whole period of Atlantis, which was over 200,000 years.

The last portion of Atlantis was destroyed about 12,000 years ago. The "Mixtures" that had various animal parts still lived in ancient Egypt while only some lived in 10,500 B.C. Many of them were wiped out in the flood. (Noah, 22,006 years ago.)

The Earth itself was created over ten and a half million years ago, the Readings state.

There were various types of beings living in Lemuria for all those years.

> For the Projections of these (Thought Forms) had
> come from those influences that were termed, Lemure,
> or Lemurian, or the land of Mu.
> (877-10)

94

...that land now known as Mu, or the vanished land
of the Pacific.
(630-2)

Parts of Lemuria that still remain today are in Arizona, Nevada, New
Mexico and Utah and also parts of South America, as in Peru.

One person was told of a cave drawing that he or she did in Arizona
ten million years ago. He or she drew pictures still existing today.
God was called ZU_UUUUU in that period of Lemuria.

> The One God, as called in this period. In that period
> He was called Zu-u-u-u-u; in the next Ohm–Oh-u-m;
> in the next (now known as Egypt) with Ra-Ta, He was
> called God – G-o-r-r-d !
> (436-2)

("The Pacific coast of South America represented the extreme
western portion of Lemuria", as per "Earth Changes Update".)

Many Lemurians escaped before the major destruction to settle
in portions of western America which must have been part of the
original continent if someone painted in a cave there ten million
years ago.
The Lemurians who migrated to the western U.S.A., as it was
sinking, brought with them the teaching of the "Law of One."

There was a deeply spiritual group that was of the Law of One.
These souls had not forgotten their spiritual Source and were
projecting their Astral or spiritual bodies not mixed with animal
flesh. Then there were other souls who were mixed in with animals.
Two opposite groups were developing at the same time. One group
sought to manifest the Oneness of God and one group sought self
indulgences, self glorification and selfishness.

We can be our own portion of the creative forces but NEVER the Whole. We can be One with God yet separate in attaining our own identity as our individual portion of the Whole, is the Law.

> ...at an At-Onement with same, a portion of same, but NEVER the Whole.
> (256-2)

After Lemuria (which was in the South Pacific) vanished, the "Mixtures" still continued on to live and function in Atlantis. There were souls trapped in these "Mixtures."

> ...Lemuria began its disappearance - even before Atlantis...
> (364-4)

Poseidia was one of the first and the last and highest flourishing centers of Atlantis.

> ...at that particular period (Poseidian) - or the highest that had been save that which had been part of the Lemurian age.
> (877-26)

Evidently Lemuria was even more advanced in development in the use of the elemental forces of nature.
Atlantis was highest in scientific achievements.

Mu was a sage and ruler and Law giver of groups of people known as colonies who gathered together for a common purpose.

> The land under those influences of Mu became as what would be termed in the present as among or the highest state of advancement in MATERIAL accomplishments for the benefit or conveniences for man's indwelling, or the less combative influence of

the ELEMENTAL or of that man knows as nature-in the raw.
(877-10)

Colonies were like collective family groups or a group soul.

For those who were of the ruling forces were able by choice to create or bring about, or make the channel for the entrance or the PROJECTION of an entity or soul, as the period of necessity arose.
Then such were not as households or as families, like we have today, but rather as groups.
(877-26)

The Mu colonies were able to harness nature to use for their benefit.
The Lemurians and Atlanteans knew the secret of overcoming gravity.
They could levitate large stone objects and control the weather as they were united in a collective soul group effort giving them more Power than an individual alone would have.
They had procreation that was a form of Projection that was spiritual and not sexual.
They were the first to bring in monogamy and were in the process of disentangling themselves of animal associations.
They were becoming the first separate entities rather than part of a collective group.
They were builders with timber and made clothing from flax, leather, ramie, silk, linen.
The Mu colonies were workers in metals: Gold, silver, lead, radium.
Mu was known as the Lawgiver, Prophet, sage, and the father of Muzuen, an entity later having a Cayce Reading.
It vaguely refers to Mu as being the SOUL of that one who became the Savior (Jesus Christ) in its final Earthly experience.

> This then we find as the period when there was the
> CHOICE of that SOUL that became in its final
> earthly experience the SAVIOR, the SON in the Earth
> indwellings, or of those as man sees or comprehends
> as the children of men.
> (877-10)

The Golden City was a domain that covered over a hundred
thousand miles. The Temple of Gold was in the Gobi land but must
have been part of Lemuria then as well.

Muzuen, the son of Mu, became the Prince and builder of the City
of Gold in the Gobi or Mongolian land which Cayce predicts will
be found one day again. He was at first called Zu-zezn.

> A description of the entity, and of the household and
> of the ruling forces, comes.
> Stature, what would now be five feet eleven inches.
> Blue of eye. Hair dark gold. Six-fingered; five-toed.
> (Muzuen, the Prince, son of Mu).
> ...the fine works in laces, fabrics, spun gold, silver,
> carved ivory and the like...
> (877-10)

> As to the manner of locomotions in the experience,
> the entity injected much of that which – when there is
> the discovery of the Temple of Gold – will be found;
> lifts or elevators, the one-line electrical car, the very
> fast aerial locomotion – there were a portion of those
> experiences with which the entity had much to do.
> (877-11)

In the City of Gold they developed art and music and had a
communal lifestyle in which there was one common storehouse and
all shared the material goods.

All people worked from twelve years of age up unless sick, lame, blind, or pregnant. The very OLD were MERCIFULLY put away.
They made the first gold coin which was a square with a hole in the center. A piece of gold was for a day's labor for all.
These gold coins were often worn around the neck on a cord or around the waist.
All people were treated equally regardless of sex or position.
Their religious gathering was called a Forum and was similar to the Quakers as any could speak as inspired by the Spirit from within.
Only the Prince and royal household had the last word but they NEVER acted as Lords or DICTATORS over the people but as interpreters of the Law between man and man and man and God.
There was equality among the sexes and only monogamy, never EVER was polygamy practiced.
Because all peoples were considered equal within the Muzuen group, they had fewer social classes than the Atlantean and Indian groups.
The people of the City of Gold were the FIRST to trade goods with India, Egypt, Caucasia, Pyrenees and Atlantis.
(Were these groups part of the Five Races projected by Amilius? Or before?)

Disturbances came about in the second generation AFTER Muzuen.

> In the exchange between those of other lands when these associations were established, there were the spices from India, linens and cut stones from Egypt. These were especially for the women.
> …with the mixing of those from India and especially from Caucasia – made for the disturbances in the second generation after Muzuen.
> (877-12)

Ra Ta of ancient Egypt is mentioned in the Muzuen Reading which means that the period might be AFTER Adam entered the Earth, not pre-Adamic as thought. Or it could be describing the Egyptian area that Ra Ta proclaimed later.

> The entity in its associations, by the heralding of this union of purpose from the varied centers as proclaimed by Ra, or Ra-Ta, journeyed forth into the lands of those various groups.
> (877-10)

The same soul who was Muzeun is born into Poseidia in Atlantis in his next incarnation in which the Five Races are mentioned which is definitely during the Adamic period.

When the final disturbances came In Lemuria, many traveled to western America and established the Law of One there.

> Before that the entity was in that now known as the American land, in those places about what is now a portion of Arizona, New Mexico, Colorado.
> There the entity was among those who were the outcome of those who had come from the land of Mu or Lemuria.
> There the entity began the dwellings as of a separate people into groups when they had been bound together by the necessities then.
> The entity as a ruler then, in the name Tutotu, made for the dividing or grouping of groups for some SPECIFIC activity; yet as DEFENSE all came together as ONE.
> (962-1)

The above Reading gives a glimpse of what a group consciousness was like.

It seems they were forming into their own individuality but still returned as one "group Mind" in emergencies.

Material Life on Earth was not intended to be eternal and the flesh and blood bodies of the animals would eventually die.

Therefore, the trapped souls would experience death along with the animals they had inhabited.

After death, the souls could still not return to their higher state of Heavenly consciousness as they had forgotten their identity with God. The only way to return to the familiar fallen level they found themselves in was to incarnate as another Earth being.

Even when they experienced higher realms of consciousness in the planetary system, they always came back to Earth.

They had become Earthbound.

I wrote a short story about what it might have been like for an Angel or a soul to fall into being an animal during this early period.

Here is an excerpt:

> "...did Lucifer decide to isolate this planet from the rest of the creation and claim it for his own? What were all these celestial beings down here doing? Why was I here? Oh, now I remember, I got caught up in that rebellion in Heaven. It sounded right at the time. The young Son had no experience. Why should we worship Him, since He had no memories in His newness? We, who were there before Him were the real stars of Heaven...How could we give Him equal status with the Almighty God? He had not formed into that reality as yet. He rose up with His Angels to prove Himself and won. I was not sure who was right and yet I was cast out by association. Was that fair?
>
> How could this have happened to me?
>
> Now we were just fallen stars. Homeless.
>
> I seemed to have forgotten myself or lost my identity somehow.
>
> All my thoughts were slowed down now, time lagged, space contained, shut in and restricted. This was painful. Movements were difficult. My vision was blurred. I woke up in an animated cartoon.
>
> Nothing was real anymore, not even me.

I saw a small herd of horses and was especially attracted to one white mare as she galloped and snorted and ran across the plains, with her long mane and tail flowing in the wind, kicking up a dust cloud as she went.

How beautiful she was and yet unaware of her outer self. She couldn't take any pride in herself as she couldn't see herself. She was just being the best she was created to be instinctually.

I used to be like that too, just being the best of what I was made to be and it was sheer happiness and joy. Our "holier than thou" pride made us refuse to admit our mistakes.

The other beings tempted me to try to experience the mare as they were doing with the other horses. "Look at me, Look at me!"

I watched and it was fascinating to see how they could enter the animal and then leave it again. It looked so easy. This might be a fun diversion. I missed my lost self.

I remembered being in the atmosphere of God. I loved singing praises to God and being a part of all the Heavenly glory.

I was tempted to jump in and see what it felt like to be that horse, to be her, just for a moment...

My thought became my choice almost instantly. What you think happens fast down here, too fast sometimes, other times it takes so long that you forgot you imaged or desired it.

I dived into her, head first, my head into her head. It was like jumping into water with a splash then a thud. I became submerged within her. I became that horse. It was a big shock to the consciousness, like hitting the rocky side of a cliff. SLAM!

Hot fiery snorts came out of my nostrils and my tongue was thick and coarse, a harsh braying came out of the mouth instead of the sound I knew as my own voice. "Whoa!" I called, "Slow down." The horse didn't seem to respond to me.

I was horrified. The heaviness, the hot flashes, the pounding heart, the muscle pain with stretched movements, the embarrassment I experienced at the elimination of wastes through the animal body. This was NOT fun!

I was an Angel of the Most High God, separated not only from the rest of myself but from my God and my own form having lost a part of my reality and identity...I had gone down, down, down, down into hooves instead of hands, braying instead of singing with the Angels.

Now instead of being a part of creating with God, I was the result of my own creation, stuck in animation, awake in unreality.

Third dimensional matter is not real.

This type of matter can only be sustained temporarily by Spirit.

It dies, decays, evaporates, rots and dissolves. I had to keep recreating new forms to inhabit as they wore out. I did not want to be an animal. But what else can I be down here? A tree?

I was not an animal yet here I was stuck inside this horse. I felt trapped. I did not want to be even less of myself than I already was. Was I going to lose all of me in the horse?

I could not seem to dislodge myself. Why did I listen to them?

This was a brutality to the Mind, which was frightening.

In a panic, I ran with the horse as fast as I could trying to get away from this realization.

My soul rose up and cried with all my being, I yelled for Help... "Save me O God...'"

Remember that we were created as perfect beings who were made in His image. We are not the distorted ego images that we have become which separates us from our real spiritual self.

We are meant to be companions of God through Christ.

Joan Clarke

It is our destiny to be conformed to that image of perfection again.
Whatever it takes, He is going to help us get back into our true state
of consciousness as long as we are willing.
His Love will draw us, like a magnet.

> Because we were made for the purpose of being
> companions with Him, a little lower than the Angels
> who behold His face ever, yet (we are) as heirs, as joint
> heirs with Him who IS the Savior, the Way…
> (1567-2)

> The Creator intended man to be a companion with
> Him.
> Whether in Heaven or in the Earth, or in whatever
> consciousness, a companion with the Creator.
> How many (Lifetimes) will it require for thee to be able
> to be a companion with the creative forces wherever
> you are?
> (416-18)

How many Lifetimes it requires us to return to God in a state that
is companionable is up to our own individual choices.
Our energy frequencies need to be high enough to blend in with
those of our Creator for all negative qualities will be burned out and
we will be pure enough to enter in.

Let us continually choose Light, Love, and the consciousness of
Christ in our daily lives.

CHAPTER V

THE AMILIUS ERA IN ATLANTIS (PRE-ADAMIC)

...the First Begotten of the Father that came as Amilius in the Atlantean land...
(364-8)

...these (sons of God) were all together in (Spirit with) Amilius.
(288-29)

In the beginning when the First of the Elements were given, and the forces set in motion that brought about the sphere... called the Earth plane...
This entity (Edgar Cayce) came into being with this MULTITUDE (of souls).
(294-8)

That from which, through which, in which may be found all things, out of which all things come. Thus the FIRST of everything that may be visible in Earth,

in Heaven, in space, IS of that LIGHT - IS that
LIGHT!
(2533-8)

Amilius, was the name the Only Begotten Son was called, as He
entered the Earth plane and its planetary system with a multitude
of souls still in Oneness with the First Cause.

Why did the Only Begotten Son manifest as or into a soul?
Since becoming an individual soul was the pattern for all the
companions, He was first to demonstrate the Way.

The Amilius group's purpose was to reawaken the sons of God who
had lost their identification with their spiritual reality due to their
entanglement in material encasements and their influences.

Amilius was the First Adam in Spirit Body before the flesh and blood
form was created, thus the beginning of mankind in the Earth.

It was a rescue mission.

The multitude of souls that entered into the environments of the
Earth plane with Amilius were as a group of souls still inter-connected
within the Christ.

Souls existed in Amilius as a sort of collective consciousness or
group soul. Like many wheels (souls) within a wheel (Christ) who
was within a wheel (God, the First Cause.)

These (sons of God) were all together in Amilius.
(288-29)

Christ and His younger brothers and sisters as a "group soul"
incarnated into the soul expression of one named Amilius and AY
or Ai which was the other half or female aspect of the Amilius soul.
The male and female traits are of the Mind and Spirit in one united

soul entity. The Yin Yang symbol is a perfect description of the androgynous mystery of the Twin Soul self combined in a Whole entity.

This is the First Manifestation of the Only Begotten Son as a soul that we have a record of in the Readings.

Many souls were still forming and had not become fully individualized as yet.

> Then came into the Earth materiality, through the Spirit pushing itself into matter. Spirit was INDIVIDUALIZED...
> (3508-1)

> Then, as the sons of God came together and saw in the Earth the unspeakable conditions becoming more and more for self–indulgence, self-glorification, the ability to procreate through the very forces of their activity, we find that our Lord, our Brother, CHOSE to measure up, to earn, to ATTAIN that companionship for man with the Father through the overcoming of SELF in the physical plane.
> (262-115)

Amilius and His group of souls sought to "make manifest Heaven and Heaven's forces" in the Earth plane to provide a Way for those in error to return to God. The souls with Amilius were like many small sparks of Light (souls/Minds) within the Christ Consciousness Light.

> ...that entity, that part of the Whole, would through these creatures of the High Heavenly make manifest Heaven and Heaven's forces through those elements.
> (341-8)

A divine plan was envisioned to give the lost souls an opportunity to awaken and to inspire the desire to return to God.

107

In order to establish a standard of perfection by which souls entrapped in their distorted mental-ego-monster encasements, could measure themselves, the Christ offered Himself in the soul of Amilius to be the divine image and pattern that they needed.

The highest point in spiritual development in the Earth was reached in Atlantis when Amilius ruled.

This was referred to as the "First Eden" of the world and it was more of a fourth dimensional spiritual manifestation than a third dimensional physical one, yet a BLENDING of BOTH dimensions.

When a soul first entered into the Earth plane, it was NOT in a physical form but in a soul Body as a spiritual entity.

Matter exists throughout the universe as it is a portion of God, the First Cause. Spiritual matter is of a different frequency or vibration than that of physical matter. Souls had bodies as vehicles of expression before the First Flesh and Blood Body (Adamic form) was made by God.

> For thy Body is indeed the pattern of the Heavenly Body...
> (2533-8)

> The Body is a pattern, it is an ensample of all the forces of the universe itself.
> (2153-6)

Amilius, Son of the Most High was the Christ and Only Begotten Son. Amilius and His soul group were in perfect accord with God and the Laws already set in motion.

> ...as the First Begotten of the Father that came as Amilius in the Atlantean land...
> (364-8)

> ...the highest point (in Atlantis) was when Amilius
> ruled with those understandings, as the One that
> understood the variations...
> (364-4)

The variations are referring to the "Mixtures" which were souls
who were infused with animals that were trapped in Earth's matter.
Amilius understood their identification with the material.
The lost souls had desires, which were now fed by the animal
instincts for procreation and continuation of the species.
The animals were of flesh and blood and contained the natural or
normal instincts of self-preservation and the satisfying of appetites.
This was normal for the animal Kingdom but not normal for soul
entities that were intended to be companionable to God. The
animal traits and instincts brought about confusion that created
habit patterns and appetites STILL existing in man today.

> Before that we find that the entity was in the beginning,
> when the sons of God came together to announce to
> matter a Way being opened for the souls of men, the
> souls of God's creation, to come again to the awareness
> of their ERROR.
> This entity, as indicated from those experiences, was
> among those announcing same.
> (2156-2)

In the animal Kingdom male and female qualities were separated
into different body forms for procreation.

The soul entities were androgynous or a perfect balance of male and
female in One soul. This is the image in which souls are created to be.

Souls are a combination of male and female or positive and negative
vibrational QUALITIES in one entity. They are non-sexual beings
as sex is of flesh which is of the animal Kingdom and does not exist
in the Spirit.

The Creator as the Parent or Father/Mother God is the perfect male and female polarity in one person. This is the pattern. Christ is the pattern from which souls were formed in Spirit.

Many of the souls that were trapped in matter had divided their soul forces in an effort to experience animal sexuality. This was a division of the soul-self, which was not in the will of God.

To experience the male and female essence of animals, souls divided themselves, separating their Wholeness into two selves.

It is indicated that some souls may have fragmented their male-female self even farther after it was divided. (Cayce refers to this as multiplicity.)

Individual soul essence was scattered into bits and pieces of the self or selves. This was a shattering of the soul Oneness.

> In the beginning, as was outlined, there was presented that that became as the sons of God, in that male and female were as One...
> (364-7)

> - as He gave - is neither male nor female, they are then both - or One.
> (5749-7)

> ...in the land known as the Atlantean...when there were the separations of the bodies as male and female...
> (2121-2)

> ...when there were the divisions of sexes... among the first offspring of such divisions...
> (2753-2)

I visualize the Lemuria and early Atlantis period of creation in the Earth as multi-dimensional.

They were higher dimensional mental-spiritual beings with "Thought Form" bodies co-existing with third dimensional matter that was not as hardened as our matter of today.

It was more of a gelatinous material that was formable or able to be changed and remolded at will. Matter is vibrational and can be changed or formed and reformed.
Some of the bodies in Atlantis could form various limbs as needed such as extra hands or eyes.
This was a merger of Life forms combining third, fourth and fifth dimensional energies. The result was various types of hybrid forms.
There was a shifting of forms involved during this time.
Souls moved in and out of form, shifting in consciousness.
Many were like Changlings who appeared and reappeared in different Body forms.
The Readings do not make a clear distinction between the Root Races or Body forms during this long period.
We can assume that there were many different types of Body forms at one time.

Amilius established Laws and created a balance in the Earth.
It was He that first established the various seasons of the year.
Amilius is responsible for the setting of TIME which is still functioning as He set it.
Amilius built the first altars upon which sacrifices were offered to God from the fruits of the field and forests as a form of tribute.
Amilius taught the Love of the Law of the One God, the One Spirit.

> ...altars were set up to tie up the meanings of "The Lord thy God is One." The building up of this thought makes no bonds, no slaves among any peoples.
> (3581-1)

> ...Law of One – as one wife, one home, one state, one religion, One God, one purpose...
> (2437-1)

The sons of God who had entered the Earth to aid Amilius were able to draw from the living elements surrounding them until they rapidly developed a material-physical form or Body in which to communicate with the lost sons and daughters trapped in flesh matter.

It is possible that those lost souls in the "Mixtures" who were now in the third dimension and mixed with animal flesh and blood were not able to see the higher, lighter, vibratory bodies of Amilius and the souls with Him in the Oneness.

Thus, there was the need for the celestial bodies to project themselves into "Thought Forms" and to become semi-solidified with living elements of the third dimension of matter to become visible vehicles of expression to be able to communicate.

They did not become part of the animal Kingdom.

However, even though they became material bodies, they were not as yet all of flesh and blood. Adam was to be the First Flesh and Blood Man created by God later.

> In the period then - some hundred, some ninety-eight thousand years before the entry of Ram into India - there lived in this land of Atlantis one Amilius, who had first noted...the separations of the beings as inhabited that portion of the Earth's sphere...into male and female as separate entities, or individuals.
> (364-3)

Atlantis was said to be between the Gulf of Mexico on the one hand and the Mediterranean on the other. Evidence of this lost civilization is said to be found in the Pyrenees and Morocco on one hand and British Honduras, Yucatan and America upon the other. Evidence in the British West Indies or the Bahamas may be seen in the present time; however, geological surveys in Bimini and in the Gulf Stream are yet to be determined.

The Amilius bodies were like the form of our bodies today but much lighter and more flexible. Even though they were Thought Forms, they had bodies.

Some of these bodies were able to change color, like a chameleon, who can match whatever color its Body rests upon.

They could form extra limbs at will, and many had an extra single eye in the center of the forehead which could be moved to any other part of the Body as needed to see.

> As these took form, by the gratifying of their own desire for that as builded or added to the material conditions, they became hardened or set – much in the form of the existent human Body of the day, with that of color as partook of its surroundings much in the manner as the chameleon in the present.
>
> (364-3)

These forms that the Amilius group inhabited may have been the "Third Root Race."

The Amilius group was not mixed in with the animals or the animal people they were trying to help.

They kept their bodies pure and separate from those of the "Mixtures."

A Reading for an entity that may have been part of the Amilius group whose main purpose in Life was to subdue the animal influences in both man and beast said that the animal Kingdoms at the present time dread his presence as he still had the ability to subdue them with Love.

> ...in the land of Alta (Atlantis), when the country was in the first developing, and the entity's main force and development was in that of SUBDUING the animal LIFE in both man and beast, and in this we find that ALL animal Life DREADS this present entity, though with Love this entity may subdue.
>
> (304-5)

Here is another Reading for one of the entities that was most likely NOT one of the Amiliius group but this Reading gives us a hint as to what a being at that time was like.

This was a soul incarnation as the person is called an "entity." The person was a "Thought Form" with a physical being having both male and female reproductive sexual centers.

> Before that the entity was in the Atlantean land and in those periods BEFORE Adam was in the Earth. The entity was among those who were then "Thought Projections," and the PHYSICAL being had the union of sex in the One Body, and yet a real musician on pipes and reed instruments.
> (5056-1)

This entity was a "Thought Projection" and had not separated the soul forces into male and female but had the union of both sexes in one Body (Note the words "physical being" indicating flesh.)

Are the legendary hermaphroditic beings some of the "Mixtures?" The Reading stated that he tried to be both sexes at once and was not successful at either (that past Lifetime was an influencing factor causing his homosexual tendencies in the present Life.)

> Before that the entity was in the Atlantean land when there were those periods of activity in which there was the changing of individuals from the DOUBLE SEX, or the ability of the progeneration of activities from self.
> (2390-1)

Even though they were part Thought Forms, they played musical instruments. Reed and pipe instruments are very real and of physical matter.

These Thought Form entities were not like ghosts, who cannot eat or drink or paint pictures or participate in sexual activities on a physical level. They were "Thought Forms" with physical Body attributes as well.

114

Many of these Thought Form bodies ("Mixtures") were part animal, yet others, especially those of the Amilius group, were very similar to those we inhabit today.

Mind control was being used by the sons of Belial which was the other group in control besides the Law of One.

> In the one before this we find in that land known as the Atlantean, and in that period when there were the beginning of the peoples harkening to those influences wherein one controlled another by the mental being. The entity rebelled against the mis-application, the mis-use of those forces...
> (428-4)

The Earth is over ten million years old.

Lemuria lasted many centuries BEFORE Atlantis and a portion of it was still left and functioning during the last period of Atlantis.

The Readings state that parts of western America were settled by Lemurians. A person was said to have done a cave painting there millions of years ago and it is still there.

The civilization of Atlantis lasted over two hundred thousand years.

Amilius was active in Atlantis for its whole duration, whether in the Spirit or material world.

Amilius set time, therefore He was here since before the beginning. Today's time is still functioning as it was set by Amilius. Since Amilius is the Christ soul, He has been involved in ALL that has been created.

Amilius wanted to reawaken the souls who had drifted away from their relationship and awareness of the Creator.

His mission was to bring them back home or back into God Consciousness.

It is thought that some of these lost souls were in actuality fallen Angels who left with Lucifer when there was the rebellion in Heaven. Some of them must have regretted their choice and longed to be One with the Creator again.

Other fallen Angels were on a mission to pervert, deceive, distort, and trap the souls of God.

The Readings indicate that the Forces of Darkness, Lucifer or Satan, had persuaded the companions to PUSH themselves into matter for self- indulgence. It was the same SPIRIT that influenced Adam and Eve to disobey God in the Garden of Eden at a later period.

> In the day ye eat or use the knowledge for thine own aggrandizement, ye shall die.
> But HE that hath PERSUADED the Spirit, the souls that God had brought into being, to PUSH into matter to gratify desire for self-expression, self-indulgence, self-satisfaction, said, "Ye shall not surely die"...
> (3976-29)

Some of those called fallen Angels were actually sons of God.

It is difficult to differentiate between celestial beings as sons or Angels during this period of existence.

It is possible that some of the Fallen Angels got trapped in the material world, too.

Just keep the concept in Mind that when the word Angel or celestial being is used that it could mean a son or daughter of God instead of an Angel.

This does not mean there is not a difference between the two types of beings.

We are beings of Light with free will to form into individual souls with the potential of becoming worthy to be companions of God again.

The word "man" is used to describe spiritual man, mental man, and flesh man. (Mental/spiritual man as "Thought Form" Projections with Amilius, then the "Thought Form" beings that were mixed with animals and nature, and then later the flesh man with the Adamic group.)

When the Readings refer to man, we need to know to which creation it refers as sometimes it means the spiritual/mental man in Amilius before Adam was created by God. Adam's Body was the First Flesh and Blood Form deemed suitable for soul inhabitation and created by God.

The Readings refer to Amilius as Adam at different times and it is difficult to discern if it meant that Amilius was the higher self of Adam when Adam was in the Earth. Or if it meant Amilius was this higher self in an earlier time frame before the Body of Adam was made. Sometimes reference is made to Amilius' Life experiences in Atlantis before Adam was created. Sometimes when Adam is in the Earth, He is called Amilius who is the higher self of Adam.

The First Spiritual Creation is of "man" as a soul, (all souls) who were born in and through the Christ or Only Begotten Son. These free willed celestial Spirit beings have a soul to be made through individualized choices and experiences in Heavenly realms.
This "man" is the spark of Light that came forth from Christ with all the other souls in the beginning (us).

The next creation is in Mind or the mental levels of consciousness with the soul Projections of the Christ as a First Soul Incarnation in Amilius who entered into the Earth plane. Amilius and the "Thought Form" souls with Him came to show the lost celestial beings (and Angels?) the Way to return to God. This "man" is referring to those souls who entered into the Earth as "Thought Forms" with Amilius to rescue the trapped souls.

> What has been given as the most meaning of all that written? "HE has not willed that ANY soul should perish"…
> (262-56)

I do not believe that the Amilius "Thought Forms" were mixed in with the animal Kingdoms because they had come to set those souls trapped in the beasts free from animal matter. The Amilius group had bodies more like their Astral bodies. They appeared in their celestial form which is similar to our bodies of today.

The Third Creation is of "man" in flesh as Adam or the First Mortal Man also as a group soul incarnation in five places at once but only called Adam in one. This is God's creation of man as a group in flesh and blood. This is referred to as the "Root Race."
This can be very confusing and hard to keep in the order of time frame because we have the illegal entry of fallen, rebellious souls and their distorted creations going on at the same time. (The "Mixtures" and the "Things".)
Then there are the fallen Angels in the Spirit and in the physical to deal with as well.
It is not difficult to imagine that these fallen Angels had the Power to materialize into various forms and to confuse souls in the Earth.

Amilius is the soul name of the Only Begotten Son, who is Christ and is the spiritual identity and super conscious self that later became Adam and eventually Jesus.
Amilius ruled and established the seasons of the year and other methods to help draw back the lost souls from their rebellion.
Atlantis was a peaceful place when Amilius ruled.
There was a continual influx of souls entering from other worlds or Heavenly realms of consciousness to reinforce the mission.
The following Reading demonstrates the constructive use of free will in Spirit and soul forces of entities functioning in accord with divine Law while the Earth was being created.

> In the one (Lifetime) before this, we find when the waters were divided, and the Earth's sphere was changed, this Body in the Spirit and soul forces was the Guide of the forces that chose the better Way.
> (2481-1)

It is stated that the war-like influence that was in other portions (planets?) of the universe did not exist in Atlantis.

(The other war-like portions of the universe could mean the combative influences in Spirit between the fallen Angels and the Angels and souls of Light or it could have to do with planetary influences of the war-like planets, such as Mars.)

Atlantis was a peaceful place without competition or capitalism. This is because souls were so inter-connected and easily identified with the others in the group.

The groups were like family clusters and were like those that began in Lemuria. Lemuria was before Atlantis but a portion of it existed throughout most of the Atlantean period.

The rights and needs of one was the need of all. Spiritual Oneness was maintained and they called themselves, "Children of the Law of One."

To harm another would be like harming one's own self.

They were each as cells (souls) in One Body, Mind, and spiritual consciousness.

The groups or family clusters were in the process of forming into more individualized personal beings as they separated themselves from the groups.

> ...in that state of evolution of developing their mental abilities for single or separate activity.
>
> (2464-2)

The souls that were still functioning as a group soul in Amilius were all in contact with God as companions. They had not fallen into matter. (AS YET!) They were using matter to demonstrate the Christ Consciousness and the Law of One.

Fast developments in the physical were obtained by recognizing the Spirit in the material elements about them to be a part of themselves.

The supply of the necessary food to sustain them as well as that of apparel was all easily supplied from the natural elements about them. In the beginning they did not require food but were sustained from the creative energy force from within. As they became more hardened in material substances, they ate food that was vegetarian to remain clean in Body. Some of the fallen ones were eating flesh even though permission to eat it was forbidden.

> ...and these then were of those ABOUT them that were given as meat, or used as same-that partook of the herbs. These were those same herbs that the seed were to have been for food for the man in self, and only those that partook of same may be called even CLEAN - in the present day.
> (364-11)

Since the whole period of Atlantis lasted so many years (200,000), we do not know how long Amilius and his group of souls ruled as the Children of the Law of One in Harmony with God. However, the Readings mention that in the LAST portion of the development of the Amilius group, they began to pollute themselves with the Mixtures or sons of Belial.
We do know that the Law of One continued on into ancient Egypt during the time of Ra Ta which was at the time of the last destruction of Atlantis around 10,500 B.C. or 12,500 years ago.
This was the period of Ra Ta when many Atlanteans left before it sank and migrated to Egypt.

The Readings stated that in the highest form of Atlantis, the natural trend was the use of occult and mystical science which was as natural to them as it is today for us to eat.

> ...as to what is meant by occult or mystic science; for the NATURAL trend - or the NATURAL condition of individuals, or entities - was the USE of these; as it is natural to eat!
> (364-9)

They were very psychic and in tune with higher realities of Spirit.

> ...the Alanteans were a thought people, those of an intuitive influence.
> (255-12)

> The entity, then, was the teacher in the psychological thought and study, especially as that of the transmission of thought through ether.
> (187-1)

This time of Amilius was called the aerial age or the electrical age. They could levitate large weights and had airships which were used for transportation that could also travel under the water as well as in the air. They could also travel psychically or in soul flight to other realms of the universe.

> ...supplying then the modes and manners of transposition of those materials about same that did not pertain to themselves bodily; for of themselves was transposed, rather by that ability lying within each to be transposed in thought as in Body.
> (364-4)

> ...that land known as the Atlantis, when the peoples were in the stage of civilization...with the ability to apply so many of the Laws of the universal forces.
> (2720-1)

> For the manners of transportation, the manners of communication through the airships of that period were such as Ezekiel described of a much later date.
> (1859-1)

> In these things, then, did Amilius see the beginning of, and the abilities of, those of His own age, era, or period, not only able to build that as able to transpose or build up the elements about them but to transpose them bodily

from one portion of the universe to the other, through the uses of not only, those RECENTLY re-discovered gases, and those of the electrical and aeriatic formations - in the breaking up of the atomic forces to produce impelling force to those means and modes of transposition or of travel, or of lifting large weights, or of changing the faces or forces of nature itself, but with these transpositions, with these changes that came in as personalities, we find these as the sons of the creative force as manifest in their experience looking upon those changed forms, or the daughters of men, and there crept in those pollutions, of polluting themselves with those MIXTURES that brought contempt, hatred, bloodshed, and those that build for DESIRES of self WITHOUT respects of others' freedom, others' wishes – and there began, then, in the latter portion of this period of development, that that brought about those of dissenting and divisions among the peoples in the lands.

With the attempts of those still in Power, through those lineages of the PURE, that had kept themselves intact as of the abilities of forces as were manifest IN their activities, these (souls) BUILDED rather those things that ATTEMPTED to draw BACK those peoples...
(Pure souls mating with the polluted Mixtures.)
(364-4)

As the soul personalities began to change in the development of their individuality of the Christ-like souls, they looked upon the daughters of men and found them fair. (The daughters of men are the fallen souls who had mixed with animals or their offspring that Amilius had come to save and show the way back home again.)

Many of the mixed forms had become quite beautiful. The pure souls uniting with the polluted souls brought contempt, hatred, bloodshed and those desires of self indulgences without respect of another's freedom or wishes.

Someone asked the Source of the Readings if the Thought Forms were inhabited by souls or were they of the animal Kingdom.

> That as created by that created, of the animal Kingdom. That created by the Creator, with the soul.
> (364-7)

> And the animal seeks only gratifying of self, the preservation of Life, the satisfying of appetites.
> (2072-8)

> ...add fearing to the sense of animal senses.
> (900-47)

> Q: Explain the difference between experience as in an animal and experience as in man, as related to Mind.

> A: In animal is that as appertains to the consciousness of the animal Mind, with Spirit.
> As in man, that is of consciousness co-related with man's development, or the higher elements of Mind and of matter. Hence man developed, becomes Lord and Master over animal Kingdom. Man degraded becomes the companion, the equal with the beast, or the beastly man.
> Then we would find this illustrated as in this:
> Experience to man gives the understanding through the subconscious obtaining the remembrance. The animal only the animal forces, as would be found in this:
> Fire to man is ever dread, to an animal only by sense of smell does it know the difference. The experience does not lead it away.
> (900-31)

Amilius developed the concept of the One God and those who continued to serve God were called the Children of the Law of One.

The "Mixtures" were referred to as the sons of Belial and they had no standard except that of selfish interests. Belial is associated with Satan, called Beelzebub or of being influenced by the Dark Forces. Both of the groups were in Lemuria as well as in Atlantis.

There were also the "Things" which were laborers produced by the Belial group. These "Things" were misused and abused.

The Children of the Law of One also used these "Things" as laborers and we do not know if they were different or the same ones used by the sons of Belial. We do know that these beings were a concern of the souls serving God.

The "Things" were said to be usually without souls and to be extensions of their makers or producers (group) and part animal. These "Things" were a special type of Mixture who were exploited. These beings were probably cloned creatures, but as all animals do, had feelings but they were treated as just machines. Some of them were the offspring of the sons of Belial (and later the sons of God) mating with the "Mixtures."

They were treated even worse than we treat our animals of today. Many of our chickens, who are farmed to lay eggs are not allowed to have a natural Life. We still do not treat our animals as we should but as machines.

Some of the "Things" were sexually abused by their producers and offspring resulted, creating more half human and half animal bodies with even greater problems.

There were disincarnate souls that began to search for bodies to express in the Earth and some of them entered the "Things" which caused more problems with which to deal. Souls got trapped in the "Things" as well as in the "Mixtures."

The Amilius group tried to help these souls by uplifting and regenerating them as best as they could and also to provide protection.

Many of these creatures were not mentally able to care for themselves. They were similar to our mentally slow people who can be quite charming but need our Love and protection from those who might take advantage of their gentle, innocent natures. Evidently some of the "Things" could talk and think as the Children of the Law of One wanted them to have "freedom of speech" and "thought" and saw the possibility of growth for them.

> ...in the Atlantean land (BEFORE Adam) the entity was the timekeeper for those who were called "Things", or workers of the peoples and the entity felt the wanting to reform, to change things, so that every individual soul had the right to freedom of speech, freedom of thought, freedom of activity...found the desire to improve, to make better those environs for the workers...felt the need of God's hand in what evil, or Satan, had brought in the Earth.
>
> (5249-1)

> The entity acted in the capacity as the Prince to the ruling forces in the land, and ever stood for those tenants of Truth, for the UPBUILDING, for the regeneration of those peoples that were PARTLY as "Things" – or those not capable in Mind to care for their own activities.
>
> (3507-1)

In spite of the efforts of Amilius and his group of pure souls to bring the lost souls back home again, they also fell into the material temptations.
Many of the Amilius group began to choose friendships and also mates from the sons and daughters of Belial.
The sons of Belial enticed secrets from the Children of the Law of One so they could use the hidden methods of spiritual energy for selfish purposes, like indulging appetites and for the ease of material benefits. The Amilius souls that got involved with the Belial group lost sight of their spiritual ideals and purposes.

Joan Clarke

Third dimensional matter in flesh was addictive and when partaken of, it overpowered the will of the soul.

An entity was said to be in that household of the Children of the Law of One just BEFORE the second DIVISION of the land of Atlantis. This entity chose companionship with a son of Belial which brought confusion and destruction as spiritual things were used for appetites and material benefits.

> ...the entity was in Atlantis, just before the periods of the division, or the second division of the land, during those activities when Amilius was in the position of carrying forward IDEALS.
> The entity was of that household and thus of the Children of the Law of One; yet chose companionship among the sons of Belial causing consternation among those of Amilius' activities, and brought confusion and eventual destruction in the USE of spiritual things for material benefits and appetites.
> (3298-1)

A Reading for another entity said...

> ...the entity was in Atlantis when there was the second period of disturbance - which would be some 22,500 before the periods of the Egyptian activity; or it was some 28,000 before Christ.
> (470-22)

The sons of Belial sought to alter the spiritual method of propagation of the Children of the Law of One.

> The entity was among the Children of the Law of One, and yet cohorted with the sons of Belial in the usage of their efforts to use those tenets attained by the entity for the propagation in an UNSEEMLY manner.
> (3307-1)

The following Reading mentions changing the sex from the One androgynous Body to the male and female split into two separate forms. The Adamic race which was the First Flesh and Blood Form began as androgynous as that is the pattern of the complete soul. But we know that Eve was taken out of Adam so the androgynous state was not permanent.

> ...in that land known as the Atlantean, during that period when there were the separations of the bodies as male and female...
> (2121-2)

> The entity was in the Atlantean land, in those periods when there was the changing within the Body forces of the sex of individuals.
> (3307-1)

There was much turmoil between the Law of One and the sons of Belial. Those who worshipped Belial sought the satisfying of physical desires and sought ease and pleasure at the expense of hurting others, if necessary, as they had NO standard of morality except self, self indulgences, and self aggrandize-ment.
They took what they wanted without thought of how their actions might cause harm. They were too self-involved and narcissistic to consider others.
The difference between the two groups was that the Children of Light sought to use energy to spiritualize matter, lifting it up for spiritual purposes. It was most important to maintain a flowing contact and communion with God to be in His will.
The Children of Belial sought to use spiritual energy for material gain in greed, in lust, and for all the selfish purposes imaginable.

The Children of the Law of One sought to manifest Love and kindness to all and to use spiritual forces for constructive purposes. They wanted to help the fallen ones to cleanse their bodies of the animal pollutions and reawaken their souls to Christ awareness.

>...the Way of the Law of One-or that manifested in
>the present as the Christ Consciousness...
>(884-1)

Who knows how many souls were rescued.
This was a period of over two hundred thousand years.
People lived to be hundreds of years old then.

>The Life existence of the entity, as compared to the
>present, would be years instead of weeks; or, in that
>experience, to live five to six to seven hundred years
>was no more that it is to live to the age of fifty, sixty or
>seventy years in the present.
>(1968-2)

>For the entity lived to be a thousand years old, in years
>as termed today, and saw great changes come about,
>not only in the Earth but in those Ways in which
>preparations were made for the advent of the souls
>of men to be brought to their relationships with the
>creative forces or God.
>(3579-1)

There was a continual influx of souls entering the Earth from other
planetary dimensions and surely some of them were the rescued
ones who returned to help the other souls as well.

One of the main disputes between the Children of the Law of One
and the sons of Belial was over the "Terrible Crystal," which was
also called the Firestone and the Tuaoi Stone.
This was a huge white stone shaped as a six-sided figure.
This Crystal was used as a form of communication that the Children
of Light had with the "Saint realm" or the "divine."

They gathered together and chanted themselves into a higher realm of consciousness in which they were able to commune as a group in Spirit.

> The temples there, the enormous prisms that were as the lights and the guiding influences in those sojourns.
> (540-1)

There were actual voices that they heard which emanated from the stone as prophetic messages to guide them which came from those influences of the divine.

This general format of the Crystal was eventually used for more everyday purposes and there were various power stations constructed. Solar energy was the main source of energy used.

The stone was set as a Crystal of large cylindrical glass with many lights coming from it on all sides, reflecting energy and colored light absorbed from the sun and other stars in the planetary system. This energy was used as power for electricity, heat and even fuel in the form of various gases for transportation vehicles as well as for photography at a distance, television and voice transmission to various destinations as set or designated.

It was like a power station. The same energy that was used for regeneration of the Body could also be used destructively as in weapons of war. The sons of Belial wanted to use the Crystal for selfish purposes that were harmful to others which was in conflict with the beneficial and uplifting motivations of the Children of the Law of One. The Belial group sought Power over others.

The Crystal was housed in a dome shaped building lined with materials that could withstand high heat but these materials are as a lost art now. They were described as to be similar to asbestos or bakerite.

>...the entity there made use of the metal known as iron, or the combinations of iron and copper - which have long since been removed from use in the present...
>(470-22)

The top of the dome could be rolled back and opened to enable the influences of the planetary system to enter the capstone.
The gases from the center of the Earth were tapped as well and utilized for various purposes.

>These were not only the rays from the sun, set by the facets of the stones as crystallized from the heat from within the elements of the Earth itself, but were as the combinations of these.
>For it was these gases, these influences that were used for what we call today the conveniences as for light, heat, motivative forces; or radial activity, electrical combinations; the motivative forces of steam, gas and the like for the conveniences.
>(877-26)

The preparation of constructing the Crystal power stations was a secret guarded by the Children of the Law of One who were called, "Initiates."

>The preparation of this stone was in the hands only of the Initiates at the time...
>(440-5)

Thus, the Children of Belial wanted this information and sought to seduce the Children of Light and thereby gain access to these secrets.

I had several interesting dreams about a Lifetime during the Atlantis period as one of the Children of the Law of One.
I dreamed that I was in a man-made airplane, fashioned like a flying snake or bird like creature without wings with several others during the time of Atlantis flying over western America.

The airplane was definitely NOT a living creature but looked like one. The front of the airplane had the shape of a creature's face with an open mouth that could have been a snake or a bird. It sort of resembled some of the early Mayan snake sculptures. I thought of the B-29 airplanes in World War II that had creature faces painted on them with an open mouth and teeth. I always wondered WHY they did that. Perhaps it was a memory from Atlantis.

There are many snake symbols in Native America, Mayan, and Egyptian symbology. People were inside of snakes or riding on their backs or peeping out of the mouth of a snake. What did it mean? The snake has the ability to strike or fly into the air which is symbolic of soul travel.

I thought it was referring to the snake as the Kundalini Life force in the human Body that can be used to project the soul Body into a type of Astral flight. The Atlanteans could TELEPORT and TRANSPOSE themselves from one place to another. They could go back in time and read records or view the past, similar to time travel.

The Atlanteans could teleport to different areas using their bodies without machines.

I thought that some of this transportation was like Astral or "soul flight."

My dream vehicle was painted, then etched with semi-precious stones. (One of the people in the airplane was a Princess from Poseidia who is my nephew's wife today.)

In the bottom of the plane there was a large screen which resembled a TV screen with dials that could be set to zoom down and magnify animals or insects on the ground very close up. There was a power station in a mountain hidden in a rural area yet to be rediscovered. (New Mexico?) We had a cone shaped object that when activated had various openings. Energy-like electricity and light shown out of it as it twirled in a circle which sent beams out for long distances as it made a humming noise.

It was less than two feet tall and had many uses.

I thought it might be a form of the Atlantis Crystal that could be carried about in travel.

In another dream, I activated this object since I had the memory key and it still worked. Often I have thought about trying to find it but now it would look like a piece of rock and barely recognizable.

The technology of the Crystal was given by the divine and will not be given to mankind again until we reach a higher spiritual level of awareness to be able to use it according to God's will.

The problem with the historians of today is that they think of us as the highest civilization of all time, so they reject any information which goes against that accepted rule.
This egotistic notion blocks us from seeing the Truth about our origins. Plus, they have the time frame wrong according to Cayce.

Until we become more humble and Christ centered and become our brother's keeper, we will not be given this secret again.
The tuning of these facets of the Crystal too high brought destructive forces in that period and broke up the land of Atlantis into isles.
This was called the second destruction in which it was broken up into five islands and eventually only three were left.
There were three major destructions in Atlantis, the last one being the final one which was only about 10,000 B.C. The second destruction was near the Noah period with the ark and flood.
We know that Noah was a descendant of Adam.
Therefore, the second destruction was AFTER Adam.

In another dream, I stood with others around the Crystal in a circle and above us there was an open circular room surrounding the capstone or top of the Crystal. We, as a group in Oneness of purpose, chanted and sang until we entered the Spirit, then we levitated up to the higher room and once there, we were able to hear the messages given. If even one of us were out of Harmony with God, we could not enter into the Holy Place. Reaching the upper room required a joint effort of all being on ONE accord, as one person alone did not have the ability or Power to rise up there.

There is the concept of the legend of Lilith, which most of the early Cayce people, as well as those of today, believe to have been a companion made by Amilius from a form of Immaculate Conception in Mind and Spirit.

It is believed that Lilith was formed out of the Spirit of Amilius using his female energies in the same way that Eve was later formed from out of the soul of Adam.

This is a controversial subject which I no longer believe to be true.

Juliet Brooke Ballard discussed this issue with me years ago, which caused me to question the validity of it.

Juliet Brooke Ballard wrote, <u>Pilgrimage Into Light</u>, a Cayce creation study. Ballard did not think Lilith was involved with Amilius at all because Lilith was one of the unclean "Thought Forms" or "Mixtures."

Eula Allen, who was one of the original Cayce group, taught in depth about the creation of Lilith as being a perfect companion made by Amilius in a form of Immaculate Conception in which the soul forces as a cosmic ray were divided. This was important, she stated, as the Immaculate Conception is the method intended as the highest way of procreation by souls when in the Earth. It is a beautiful concept which I agreed with in principle.

There have been highly spiritual individuals throughout time who have been able to produce offspring in this manner.

One was the Virgin Mary who gave birth to Jesus. The Virgin Mary was also an Immaculate Conception herself according to the Readings. Ra-Ta, an incarnation of Edgar Cayce, was said to have been an Immaculate Conception by his mother, who was from the tribe of Zu. It seems indicated that this was the form of propagation used in Lemuria and Atlantis by the Law of One.

But most of us will have to wait for the next Root Race for this to be a reality.

I believe in the concept of the Immaculate Conception that Allen taught, but I do not think that Lilith was the other portion of the Amilius Spirit.

Most of today's Cayce writers believe in this concept of Lilith as the Twin Soul of Amilius during the Atlantis "Thought Form" incarnation.

Hugh Lynn Cayce taught that Lilith was a Projection into the animal Kingdom, which was the earlier method of creating a companion during the Amilius era. Eve was drawn from the actual soul entity by God, which is a higher creation (the coming of man).

Juliet Ballard put a doubt in my mind about Lilith in the 1980s. I have not been given a definite inner answer to this "Lilith" question as yet so while not 100% positive, I tend to find myself agreeing with Ballard on this one. I think we misinterpreted the Lilith Reading and made false assumptions.

The Readings do indicate that Lilith was a type of companion but did not specify if she were a companion directly to Amilius.

It could mean that Lilith was the type of companion being used by the rebellious souls BEFORE the helpmeet and real companion was taken from within Amilius as Adam. He (Adam) manifested outwardly as a portion of His own inner self and feminine nature in Eve.

Remember there are many companions but only one Twin Soul for each entity (except for those who fragmented the soul forces into many divisions of multiplicity).

In April 1932 a question was asked:

> Q: How is the legend of Lilith connected with the period of Amilius?

> (Note that the question asks about the PERIOD of Amilius.

The period of Amilius is NOT connected to Amilius personally).

A: In the beginning, as was outlined, there was presented that that became the sons of God, in that male and female were as One, with those abilities for those changes as were able or capable of being brought about. In the changes that came from those "THINGS", as were of the Projections of the abilities of those (rebellious) entities to project, this as a being came as the companion; and when there was that turning to the within, through the sources of creation, as to make for the helpmeet of that as created by the First Cause, or of the creative forces that brought into being that as was made, THEN-from out of self – was brought that as was to be the helpmeet, NOT just (a) companion of the Body. Hence the legend of the associations of the Body (bodily associations of the rebellious souls) during that period before there was brought into being the LAST of the creations which was not of that that was NOT made, but the first of that that WAS made and a helpmeet to the Body, (of Adamic man) that there might be NO change in the relationships of the SONS of GOD WITH those relationships of the sons and daughters of men (the Thought Form Mixtures).

(364-7)

"...Lilith represents the Projections or Thought Forms created by the rebellious souls. We know that it is because of the unspeakable conditions that Amilius decided to lead the souls back the Father.

It is therefore extremely unlikely that He was participating in making such Projections.

... the point is made that Eve was created so that there might be NO CHANGE from the spiritual

relationships hitherto maintained by the sons of God
and now to be maintained by the Adamic Race.
...It is quite evident that there was no direct connection
between Amilius and a Lilith-form."

(Juliet Brooke Ballard, <u>Pilgrimage Into Light</u>,
p.16)

Lilith is mentioned in various legends as a fallen Angel or Demon. It
is stated that Lilith is the first wife of Adam. This could be referring
to Amilius as the upper Adam.

Lilith is said to have become the snake in the Garden of Eden who
tempted Eve out of jealously of being replaced by another wife.
How can a portion of One's own self be replaced? Lilith seems more
of a suitable companion for Lucifer than for Amilius.

Lilith has been given a very bad reputation in many cultures, such
as Mesopotamian mythology, Jewish traditions, Dead Sea scrolls,
Talmud, Kabbalah, the Bible, Greco-Roman myths, and Arabic
myths. Lilith is a recorded myth in the Romantic and Victorian
periods and even in the modern day Occult and Wicca groups.

One legend (the Alphabet of Ben Sira) says Lilith was Adam's first
wife who demanded equality with him. God was said to have taken
her children away because she refused to return to Adam. For
centuries Lilith was considered a threat to women in childbirth and
she was blamed for the loss of infant lives.

Lilith seems to have been a very seductive Goddess of the night who
was able to bear demonic offspring.

In an Armenian legend, Lilith is Adam's wife but made out of fire;
whereas, Adam is made out of dust. Lilith escapes from Adam with
Satan in the shape of a snake.

Lilith is symbolic of lust. Lilith could be a fallen Angel who mixed
with the animal influences. Lucifer also thought Adam beneath him
because he was made of fire and Adam of clay.

Amilius represents the Law of Love and Oneness with God who was in a Thought Form Body type in pre-Adamic Atlantis.

Amilius was non sexual in a Body that had not mixed in with the beasts. Therefore, Lilith certainly does not seem like a female Projection of the Amilius/Christ soul.

However, Lilith could have been given a false image by superstitious people.

Eve seems like a more suitable companion and help–meet than Lilith.

There is a Reading in which the question was asked, "Is there a planet anciently known as Lilith or Vulcan?"

> A: Pluto and Vulcan are one and the same.
> No Lilith. Lilith is a personalilty.
> (826-8)

The Reading does not even call Lilith an entity, just a personality which is an interesting statement tending to indicate she WAS one of the "Thought Forms" or "Mixtures."

Mesopotamian tablets from 2300 B.C. depict Lilith as a winged, bird footed, long haired female accompanied by owls.

This sculpture resembles a being who was a "Mixture" of part bird and part human female.

The Readings indicate that a help-meet is a higher form of partner than just a companion of the Body (physical).

There is a Reading in which Amilius is given a second name of Ai or Ay. Gladys Davis Turner said Edgar Cayce believed Ai or Ay might be the REAL Twin Soul of Amilius.

It was Ai or Ay, pronounced "I" but held like iiii.

> Q: Who was I? (Ai? Ay?)

> A: It's been given!

> ...with these changes coming in the experience of Amilius and I (Ai? Ay?), Adam and Eve...

influences that fire the imaginations of those that
are gifted in ANY form of depicting the high
emotions of human experience...or through desire
submit themselves - as did Amilius and I (Ay) to
those ELEMENTS, through the forces in the Life
as about them.
(364-6)

It makes sense to me that Ai or Ay is the feminine aspect of Amilius
that became Eve. If Lilith were the Twin Soul of Amilius, she would
have been mentioned instead of Ai or Ay.
The Readings state that Amilius allowed Himself to be led into the
ways of selfishness.

...or as the First Begotten of the Father that came as
Amilius in the Atlantean land and allowed Himself to
be led in ways of selfishness.
(364-8)

Evidently at a later point in time, Amilius experienced DESIRE for
relationship with the beings or the matter about Him just like the
rest of the souls did.
We do not know that He acted upon this desire. It could have just
been a thought.
It is possible that a Lilith type personality in "Thought Form" could
have been involved. However, I personally do not think Amilius
created this Lilith out of Himself. The Reading below says that
Amilius was with that Projection of self (HIMSELF) indicating it
was a Projection of his Twin Soul as Ai/Ay and that both of them
had the awareness of DESIRE for relationships with the beings or
matter ABOUT them which indicated the "Mixtures" outside of
them. This was an influence OUTSIDE of them both. The Reading
says that Amilius allowed Himself to be LED, indicating He allowed
the influence of selfishness to lead Him and His Twin Soul or the
Projection of self.

> ...we have had how One Amilius with that Projection of
> self brought into being the awareness of desires as related
> to relationships with the beings – or matter - about.
> (262-115)

No other details are given but it is good to read this whole Reading
as it contains many creation insights.

It was at this point that the Christ Spirit in Amilius realized that a
Pure Physical Race could be formed using Himself as the pattern
in the soul of Amilius. He came to help His younger brothers and
sisters who were trapped to become aware of their error.
He wanted to awaken them and help them to make choices to be
able to return home again and into companionship with God.

Third dimensional matter was so seductive that Amilius Himself got
confused and fell into the same trap as the souls He was trying to rescue.

Amilius stood up in Spirit once more determined to try again.
This time He would use a flesh and blood Body that would be
a more fit vessel for the third dimensional vibrations which were
already commingled with flesh and blood.
There would be no longer any need to mate with animals as the
trapped souls were doing because He realized that His own feminine
soul forces could be drawn out of Himself to form a being for
companionship as a help–meet.

Note that the names of Amilius and Adam are used as the same
person (this is before Adam entered in the Garden).

> ...that this Amilius-Adam, as given - first discerned
> that from Himself, not of the beasts about Him, could
> be drawn...that which made for the propagation
> OF beings IN the flesh, that made for that
> companionship... in the material worlds about same.
> (364-5)

Amilius is responsible for ALL that pertains to man in the material world. He chose to be the means for souls to attain companionship with God by overcoming of self in the material plane.

> ...(Amilius) a teacher of a peoples that separated for that definite purpose of keeping alive in the Minds, the hearts, the SOUL Minds of entities, that there may be seen their closer relationship to the divine influences of creative forces, that brought to being ALL that appertains to man's indwelling as man in the form of flesh in this material world.
> (364-5)

> ...our Lord, our brother CHOSE to measure up, to earn, to ATTAIN that companionship for man with the Father through the overcoming of SELF in the physical plane.
> (262-115)

Cayce gave a talk about this period in the Earth to his Sunday school class. He explained how the conditions that existed with souls trapped in the Thought Form "Mixtures" made the NEED for God to create a perfect man for souls to return to God.

> "These beings were male and female in One: They were images (in Spirit) of that God-Spirit which moved and brought Light into being. Consequently, they also had the ability to push out of themselves, or to divide into various manifestations. They began to do this for their own selfish gratification, or for the propagation of their own selfishness, rather than the glory of their Creator.

> Unless we can get a glimpse of such a state existing in the Earth, it will be impossible to see the necessity,

later, for God creating a perfect man, through which all souls might return to their original Source."
(Edgar Cayce's words to the Sunday school)

A Way of escape must be made for those fallen Children of God in matter to return to their higher state of consciousness.
They had chosen selfishness. They needed to make choices that would lead them back to God and into their true natures of Goodness. Celestial beings were trapped in grotesque animal bodies that they had created. Those forms were the result of their activity in Body, Mind and Spirit which invaded the animal.

> The Spirit chose to put on, to become a part of that which was a command not to be done!
> Then those so entering MUST continue through the Earth until the Body-Mind is made perfect for the soul, or the Body-celestial again.
> (262-99)

> As man applies the Laws of which he becomes conscious of, the development of man brings forth those results merited by that knowledge.
> (900-70)

As the soul manifests the Truth which is the will of God in his experience, he GROWS toward his purposes and develops into the knowledge of Good.

> The destiny of the soul—as of all creation-is to be One with Him; continually growing, growing, for that association.
> (262-88)

To be One with Him means we as souls are of the Christ Spirit. We are as individual consciousnesses in the Cosmic Christ Consciousness.

...as it is indeed in Him that we live and move and have our being.

Hence the purpose is to GROW in Grace, in knowledge in understanding, for the indwelling in that Presence.

(1861-4)

If the soul chooses selfishness, self–indulgence and self-glory, then he manifests that which is evil.

The soul of each individual is a portion then of the Whole, with the birthright of creative forces to become a co-creator with the Father, a co-laborer with Him. As that birthright is then manifested, GROWTH ensues. If it is made selfish, retardments must be the result.

(1549-1)

...the coming into the Earth has been and is for the evolution or the evolving of the soul unto its awareness...

(5749-5)

...as man's concept became to that point wherein man walked not after the Ways of the Spirit but after the desires of the flesh, SIN entered – that is, away from the Face of the Maker.

(900-227)

For in flesh must the entity manifest, and make the will One with the God, or creative force in the universe...

(900-25)

Life in its manifestation is vibration. Electricity is vibration. But vibration that is creative is one thing. Vibration that is destructive is another.

Yet they may be from the same Source.

(1861-16)

...that vibration that is creative is of that same energy
as Life itself.
(2828-4)

We need to keep in Mind that the spiritual world is the REAL level
of our functioning.
We are Children of the One God and are spiritual beings composed
of Mind, and Body as well as soul, with the continuity of Life from
before the beginning to beyond the end of the world.
The third dimension is a PROJECTION of that which is being
built in the higher levels of Mind and Spirit. The physical is the
RESULT of mental and spiritual energy moving into manifestation.
This is like a slowed down motion picture of what has occurred in
Mind and Spirit. Our mental-spiritual choices are reflected in our
material-Earthly Life.

Robert Krajenke,* a Cayce author, (who was also in the Eula Allen
creation class I attended many years ago) stated in his E-Bible
lesson:
"Spirit animates, Mind interprets, the physical demonstrates.
It is all One."
(*Robert Krajenke wrote the Edgar Cayce Story of the Old Testament,
Spiritual Power Points, and Spiritual Power, Healing Hands).

The highest form of vibration gives creative forces, rather than the
lowest which destroys.

Just as Mind or matter has its part in man's existence,
so does vibration...
(900-448)

That the Body is built up by the radiation of vibratory
forces...
(283-1)

> ...everything in motion, everything that has taken on materiality as to become expressive in any Kingdom in the material world, is BY the VIBRATIONS that are the motions - or those positive and negative influences that make for that differentiation that man has called matter in its various stages of evolution into material things. For it enters and it passes through. For - as is the better understood, and as will be proclaimed, all vibration must eventually, as it materializes into matter, pass through a stage of evolution and out.
> For it rises in its emanations and descends also.
> Hence the cycle, or circle, or arc, that is as a description of all influence in the experience of man. And very few do they come at angles!
> (699-1)

When in the Earth consciousness, we have to deal with the Laws and elements connected with that functioning.
There is the triune self, that is, the Spirit is the Life, the Mind is the builder, and the physical is the RESULT.

We must also deal with the concepts of reincarnation and Karma and Grace.
The third dimension is time and space and patience.
We can best understand God by the concept of the Holy Trinity of Father, Son, and Holy Spirit because we are Body, Mind, and Spirit.

> Thou art Body, Mind and soul...in a three-dimensional consciousness. Hence ye find the Godhead, to a consciousness of an individual in the Earth plane, is three-dimensions: Father, Son, and Holy Spirit.
> Each are individual, and yet they are One. So with the Body-consciousness: the Body, the Mind, and

the soul. Each have their attributes, each have their limitations, save the soul. Nothing may separate the soul from its Source save the will of self.

(5089-3)

The period of Atlantis was long as we count time, lasting over two hundred thousand years (200,000).

Only the early periods of Lemuria and Atlantis were more of a Thought Form world. Atlantis was very physical and had human type bodies for about the last 100,000 years.

Atlantis is one of the locations where the Five Races were projected by Amilius in Adam as the First Flesh and Blood Forms of Man created by God.

Therefore, Atlantis was not as yet destroyed when there was the Garden of Eden and Amilius awoke as the First Flesh and Blood Man in Adam created by God.

> Before that the entity was in the Atlantean land, when there were those activities when One individual first saw those changes that eventually made for that opening for the needs of, or the preparation for, the Universal Consciousness to bring into the experience what is known to man as the First Created Man.
>
> This entity was the companion of that beginning of activity in the Atlantean land.
>
> Thus, not as the mother of creation of those activities, but as an advisor to those who would change in their form of activities; or the attempts as later expressed in the entity of being rid of the appendages of materiality.
>
> (2454-3)

...the time came for the dwelling of man in physical forces, the sons of God came together.

As is given, in the beginning was the Word, and the Word WAS God.

The same was in the beginning.
ALL THOSE FORCES THAT, CO-RELATED,
MAKE THE UNIVERSAL FORCES IN THE
SPHERES ABOUT THE EARTH WERE
BROUGHT TOGETHER, AS IN ONE.
(137-12)

What greater manifestations could there be in the inner soul of anyone in a material plane than bespeak those things of the Son of the Father in such a Way and manner that those that hear may know that thou hast indwelling in thine inmost soul the knowledge of the Father, in the Son, and the LOVE of the Father to the "sons of men!"
(262-58)

CHAPTER VI

CREATION OF ADAM

> I Am Alpha and Omega,
> the beginning and the end,
> the first and the last.
> > Revelation 22:13

> In the beginning God created the Heaven
> and the Earth.
> > Genesis 1:1

In the beginning GOD...
The first premise is that God IS and IS the SOURCE of all
that is created.
God is the Father, the Son, and the Holy Spirit in Oneness.
God created...
The Heaven and the Earth.
Heaven and Earth are two separate states of consciousness,
two spheres of awareness that are divided.
All manifested things in the Earth have a beginning in the Spirit or
in the higher realms (Heaven).
Everything we see and experience in the Earth has an UNSEEN
beginning in a higher realm.

We carry these two spheres of reality within ourselves;
our spiritual reality and our manifested reality.

This is a dialogue between God the Father and God the Son
discussing the creation of the First Flesh and Blood Man.

> And God said, "Let us make man in OUR image,
> after OUR likeness; and let them have dominion over
> the fish of the sea, and over the fowl of the air, and
> over the cattle, and over all the Earth, and over every
> creeping thing that creepeth upon the Earth."
> So God created man in His own image, in the image
> of God created He him; male and female created He
> them.
> And God blessed them, and God said unto them, "Be
> fruitful and multiply, and replenish the Earth, and
> subdue it: And have dominion over the fish of the
> sea and over the fowl of the air, and over every living
> thing that moveth upon the Earth."
> Genesis 1:26-28

Bible scholars tell us that when the Bible says:
"In the beginning, God created the Heavens and the Earth,"
that the Hebrew word, "Elohim" is used for God which is the
plural noun for deity. To Christian Bible students, this is indicating
the Holy Trinity as the Godhead within itself (the singular word
for Elohim is not enough to set forth all that is intended in the
meaning.)
This also indicates that all the created souls were there within the
collective Christ Consciousness in the beginning as well.
God is a collective-being composed of God the Father, God the
Son, and God the Holy Spirit.

All the sons of God were there in Spirit and were present at the
creation of Earth and at the creation of the First Man in Adam.

The First Man in Adam was an individual but also was a GROUP, just like before when with Amilius in the Spirit, they entered as a GROUP consciousness of souls all of One accord with Christ and each other.

Therefore, when we think of Adam we need to remember that besides a specific soul, Adam is also a group of souls.

Adam represents the First Flesh and Blood Form created by God to be deemed worthy for souls to enter in as mankind.

> These were all together in Amilius.
> They were material bodies as came in Adam.
> (288-29)

> For in Him we live, and move, and have our being; as certain also of your own poets have said, for we are also His offspring.
> Acts 17:28

The male and female or androgynous soul entity ("them") was in Amilius before the soul forces were divided in Adam to form Eve.

This is the spiritual creation which, being before the Body of Adam, was created from the dust of the Earth.

The spiritual creation of the soul came BEFORE the PHYSICAL manifestation. The soul is comprised of Spirit, Mind, and will, and when entering the material plane, we have the conscious Mind.

> As the Earth plane became in that state wherein man may find residence, the Spirit forces as are developing through the spiritual forces to make One with the Father, GIVEN the SOUL of man to make manifest in the flesh.
> (900-70)

The pattern of creation in the Earth had been distorted beyond recognition of its Creator. Souls were trapped in their ego distorted images in the plant, mineral, and animal Kingdoms.

The influences of the flesh and third dimensional matter were stronger than the reality of the Spirit. They had forgotten God.

The Christ Spirit knew the sad darkness of the soul entrapment those many selves that were a part of Him had fallen into, causing them to lose their identity and companionship with God.

Christ took it upon Himself to draw a new pattern from within Himself to lead His children, His younger brothers and sisters, out of the darkness and into the Light again. Souls could go through Him as the Way to return to the Father.

The new physical form would contain within it everything Good and creative that was already outside of it. It would not contain any evil or negative influences. It would be a clean vessel.

> The Body is a pattern, it is an example of all the forces
> of the universe itself.
> (2153-6)

The Light Body and soul of Amilius was projected into the flesh Body of Adam and Adam became a living soul.
Amilius is the upper Adam or archetypal man who preceded the Earthly Adam and the material creation.
The Only Begotten Son, the Christ, as the soul of Amilius, entered the Earth as the First Flesh and Blood Man in Adam.
Christ, the Word, the Light of God, was manifested in and through an incarnate person as a soul (Amilius) in Adam.
Amilius is the super consciousness or higher self of Adam.
Amilius is the personification or soul self of the Only Begotten Son or the Logos.

The forming of the physical Body of Adam out of the dust of the Earth was a second or separate creation as "They" were already created in Spirit first.

The "dust Body" is a symbol of the atom or cellular beginning of the physical Body. All the vibrational elements in the Earth were used to form the first Body of man. Dust is the smallest particle of matter visible to us.

> And the Lord God formed man of the dust of the ground, and breathed into his nostrils the breath of Life; and man became a living soul.
> Genesis 2:7

> ...all the elements that are WITHOUT man may be found in the LIVING human Body.
> (557-3)

> For He, the Maker, the Creator, came into a Body, flesh and blood, that it might be shown man - as to what is the ideal manner to meet every experience.
> (1440-2)

The atom (Adam) is symbolic of the energy of Light as "in the beginning LIGHT." This Light within is the individual ability of a soul to manifest its own concept of that Light in a material Body and Life expression.

Since the Body is formed of all the elements and is a pattern of all the forces in the universe, I like to think that the real Body is composed symbolically of STAR DUST and is part of the Whole universe.

This is the physical creation of breathing the living – Life - breath into the flesh Body of Adam, which came after the soul creation of THEM in Spirit (in the Bible/Cayce accounts.) Adam then has the "breath of Life" which is Life and conscious awareness begins.

> For, BREATH is the basis of the living organism's activity...for breath is Power in itself...
> (2475-1)

The Word is the Christ Consciousness or the Christ Spirit that was in Amilius, Adam, and later Jesus.

> For when God said, "Let there be Light," there came Light into that which He had created, that was without form and was void and it became the Word, and the Word dwelt among men and men perceived it not.
> (3976-29)

> Then, though He were the first of man, the first of the sons of God in Spirit, in flesh, it became necessary that He fulfill all those associations, those connections that were to wipe away in the experience of man that which separates him from his Maker.
> (5749-6)

> He, that Christ-Consciousness, is that first spoken of in the beginning when God said, "Let there be Light" and there was Light. And that is the Light manifested in the Christ.
> First it became physically conscious in Adam.
> (2879-1)

Water was the element that God used to bring forth His creations. From the spiritual cosmic sea, water became manifested in the Earth as well as the Heavens.
Three fourths of the Earth, three fourths of the universe(s), and also three fourths of the human Body consist of water.
Water is the Mother and the Life of all material experiences.
Water is necessary for sustaining Life in the material plane.
Water has a spiritual nature and is a symbol of the Spirit.

> For as the Spirit is the beginning, water combined of elements is the Mother of Creation.
> (2533-8)

Hence WATER – the most flexible, the most solid; the most destructive yet the most necessary; three-fourths of the Universe; three-fourths of the human Body; three-fourths of all that is- contained in water. Hence all expression as manifested in a three dimensional world arises from same. For, it is three-fourths of the Whole.
(1554-6)

For, as indicated, from the basic principle; first: "H20", two elements not of material gases, but of air, of the divine itself, combined to form what ye call water.
(5148-2)

...there is solid matter, there is liquid, there is vapor. All are One in their various stages of consciousness or of activity, for what? Man – GODLY MAN!
(5757-1)

Edgar Cayce was told that water was to be a saving force in his Life because he first manifested in the Earth when the waters were on the Earth and ABOVE the Earth.

...for this entity we find was first manifest in the Earth plane through the waters as was on the Earth, and above the Earth.
(294-8)

He needed to be near large bodies of water for this reason, which is why Virginia Beach was chosen as the place for him to live.

The soul of Amilius fell into selfishness in the Atlantean land.
Now He must rise up and try again to complete the mission that He started.

A new type of vessel or Body was needed to function in the material world.

The new physical form would contain within it psychic or spiritual centers (Kundalini/Chakras of the endocrine glandular system) which the soul could activate in the Body to remain in contact with God and keep its spiritual reality.

The sons of God with Amilius were all involved in the First Creation of Man. Many of the souls were part of announcing this coming creation.

> In the Atlantean land when one individual (Amilius) first saw those changes that eventually made for that opening for the needs of, or the preparation for, the Universal Consciousness to bring into the experience what is known to man as the First Created Man.
> (2454-3)

> ...in the beginning when the sons of God came together to announce to matter a Way being opened for...the souls of God's creation, to come again to the awareness of their error.
> (2156-2)

> ...and the sons of God came together, and the sounding of the coming of man was given.
> (234-1)

The soul of Amilius was the first to enter as man in a flesh and blood Body created by God and called Adam.

> Ye were with Him in the beginning. Ye were both then, as the WIND...upon the waters, that announced the glory of the coming of man! Hence ye were both as spiritual imports and purposes when Adam first walked in the Garden.
> (1857-2)

The First Man was created through the Mind of God.
Man was made up of all the elements in the Earth combined with
the Mind, soul, and Spirit.

> For within the human Body – living, not dead-
> LIVING human forces – we find every element,
> every gas, every mineral, every influence that is
> outside of the organism itself. For indeed it is One
> with the Whole.
> (470-22)

> All those essential forces as are manifest in the
> universe is manifest in the living man, and above that
> the soul of man. The chemical or animated forces as
> are seen in all animal, vegetable, mineral forces, with
> their combinations, are found in the combinations
> of man...
> (900-70)

The Spirit of God is aware through ACTIVITY.
To me, this means that God is aware of Life through us.
I was shown this many years ago that God experiences the essence
of our lives through us. Not that God or Christ enters into our
selfish acts but when we are noble and give of ourselves and our true
nature that is part of Him in Love and kindness, He is aware of us
in a personal Way. He shares our consciousness with us as we express
His nature in Love.

The soul was first a celestial Body and Mind in Spirit before it
became an Earthly Body.

> The Spirit of God is aware through activity, and we see
> it in those things celestial, terrestrial, of the air, of all
> forms. And ALL of these are merely manifestations!
> The knowledge, the understanding, the
> comprehending, then necessitated the entering in

> because it partook of that which was in manifestation;
> and thus the PERFECT Body, the celestial Body
> became an Earthly Body and thus put on flesh.
> (262-99)

Celestial souls who were in their perfect Body had to take on flesh because they partook of that which was in manifestation and this was forbidden.

Now they had to become consciously aware of their error and to be purged to become fit companions of God again.

> First, the entering of EVERY soul is that it, the soul,
> may become more and more aware or CONSCIOUS
> of the divine within, that the SOUL-BODY may be
> purged that it may be a fit companion for the GLORY
> of the creative forces in its activity...
> (518-2)

This means the souls had to become a part of the third dimension with its plant, animal, and mineral Kingdoms.

The development of Earth matter was interrupted by the fallen celestial beings who influenced the growth and altered the manifestation process which had not been completed or had not reached its fruition as intended.

All these alterations in matter needed to be corrected as much as possible. Souls lost in animal beings needed to be set free.

> But when an entity, a soul, uses a period of manifestation
> – in whatever realm of consciousness – to its OWN
> INDULGENCES, then there is need for the lesson,
> or for the soul understanding or interpreting, or to
> become aware of the error of its Way.
> (815-7)

Matter can only be changed by Mind and Spirit as it is a result of a higher activity.

> For, of the dust of the Earth was the Body-physical created. But the WORD, the MIND, is the controlling factor of its shape...
> (263-13)

Matter of itself does NOT evolve, it repeats itself.

> ...there is the evolution of the soul, evolution of the Mind, but NOT evolution of matter – save THROUGH Mind, and that which builds same.
> (262-56)

The plant Life has one purpose, the animal Life has two purposes, and man has three purposes. Spiritual man has four purposes.
All the various Kingdoms are developing and moving toward the spiritual Source from which they came, including man.

> Now, that will, then, is heredity. That environment is the evolution. There you have reincarnation, there you have evolution, there you have the mineral Kingdom, the plant Kingdom, the animal Kingdom, each developing towards its own Source, yet all belonging and becoming One in that force as it develops itself to become One with the creative energy, and One with the God.
> The one then surviving in the Earth through mineral, through plant Kingdom, through the vegetable Kingdom, through the animal Kingdom, each as the geological survey shows, held its sway in the Earth, pass from one into the other; yet man given that to be Lord over all, and the ONLY survivor of that creation.
> (900-340)

> Know that man… was given dominion over all, and
> in the understanding of same may use all of the Laws
> as pertaining to same for his benefit.
> (1895-1)

The Only Begotten Son, who was the soul of Amilius, entered the flesh and blood Body of Adam and became the First Man Created by God. (I am repeating this concept to make sure it is grasped.) Amilius entered His OWN creation as Adam which was a fleshly Projection of Himself.

The Adamic Body contained the seven spiritual centers that the animal Mixtures and fallen celestial beings did NOT have in their make-up. There are actually twelve psychic centers but only seven are now functioning.
Adam may have had all twelve centers functioning because He was in direct communication with the Father-Mother God.

This endocrine glandular system was for the purpose of connecting the physical Body with the soul Body of the entity to be able to communicate with God. These glands are like psychic electrical outlets which can be activated by Mind and Spirit enabling communion with the Creator. The Silver Cord makes the connection with the glandular system when the soul enters the Body at birth.

Amilius as Adam entered with many of those souls that were still a part of Him who were becoming His individual selves.

> …the Son of Man entered the Earth as the First Man.
> Hence the Son of Man, the Son of God, the Son of
> the First Cause, making manifest in a material Body.
> This was not the First Spiritual Influence, spiritual
> Body, spiritual manifestation in the Earth, but the
> FIRST Man – FLESH and BLOOD; the First Carnal
> House…
> (5749-3)

Adam was a special creation and not related to the evolutionary process that was going on with the rest of creation.
The Adamic Body did not have the animal parts or influences of the "Mixtures."

> ...Let us make man in our image, after our likeness...
> Genesis 1:26

> ...and this was the entity Adam.
> And this was the Spirit of Light.
> (5023-2)

The overcoming of self in the material plane would involve many Lifetime experiences. Amilius, in Adam, knew that the androgynous nature of the soul forces were already divided into male and female by the rebellious souls in the Earth.

Their purpose was rebellion in Mind and flesh that involved sexual indulgences. This, in turn, resulted in animal appendages in the Body, animal desires, and instincts which over powered the spiritual nature of the soul.
Consequently, this behavior created appetites and habits still within man today that must be controlled.

Amilius knew that with the same division of the soul forces in Spirit, companionship could be drawn from within Himself as a spiritual, mental, and physical helper. This feminine aspect of His own soul could be put into another flesh and blood Body which would create a balance. His own Twin Soul, the other portion of His own soul self, would be a mental companion and a human counterpart to help meet all experiences.
This would be the "new pattern" of souls in the Earth, divided into male and female bodies without animal involvement.

> "Amilius, the Son of God, had drawn from Himself a
> Garden, the Body; the Tree of Life was in the midst

of the Garden also. This Tree of Life is called by many
names: Kundalini, Spirit Fire, soul force; and in the
Edgar Cayce Readings, it is as the Christ Spirit."
Eula Allen

Out of the soul of Amilius, now known as Adam or man, Eve
was drawn. Eve was the other portion of the androgynous soul of
Amilius. (Ai or Ay) Eve is Adam's other "self."
Adam and Eve were the Twin Soul aspect of Amilius and Ai/Ay in
the Spirit and became companion souls in the physical realm.

Eve was given "intuition" besides the other abilities of Adam.
This is the "sixth sense" and it is also related to the dream level.

How received woman her awareness? Through the
sleep of man! Hence INTUITION is an attribute of
that made aware (woman)…
(5754-2)

Eve was also a "helpmeet" or able to help Adam meet any circumstance
in Life as a companion.

…when there was that turning to the within…then
– from out of self – was brought that as was to be the
helpmeet, NOT just the companion of the Body.
(364-7)

The rib refers to the feminine side of the soul forces which was
removed (divided) in Spirit and put into the female Body of Eve.

And the rib, which the Lord God had taken from man,
made He a woman and brought her unto the man.
Genesis 2:22

Q: Is it the destiny of woman's Body to return to the rib of man, out of which it was created?

A: With this ye touch upon delicate subjects, upon which MUCH might be said respecting the necessity of that UNION of influences or forces that are DIVIDED in the Earth in sex, in which all must become what? As He gave in answer to "Whose wife will she be?" In the Heavenly Kingdom ye are neither married nor given in marriage; neither is there any such thing as SEX; ye become as ONE – in the UNION of which ye have been the PORTION from the beginning!

(262-86)

The divisions of male and female in the soul forces by those in rebellion took many years as it was a long process to manifest. The male and female represent two poles as negative and positive energy necessary for polarization.

The Projection of Eve from the soul of Adam was immediate as it came from God through Christ.

...those that were the First of God's Projection – not man's but God's Projection – into the Earth; Adam and Eve.

(262-115)

Adam and Eve were a part of all of creation in the Earth as stated but their soul makeup did not include carnal or animal desires. They were nonsexual beings. They were not the heavy animal bodies we have of today but much lighter and more ethereal.

They had the spiritual centers (Kundalini/soul force) in their bodies' glandular systems to aid them in communion with the creative energy or God within.

Procreation was intended to be on a higher level than that of the animal Kingdom.

A spiritual form of conception instead of sexual was the pattern intended for Adam and Eve.
Adam did not come from an animal Body, he came from the Mind of God without the expression of any sexual act required.
The Readings tell us that Adam, like Amilius did earlier, entered as a group, not as an individual. This is a "collective consciousness" or group soul containing those souls still in Oneness with God.
Adam refers to a Whole race or group of souls besides being an individual expression (one of the Five Races).

The Projection of the First Man in the material flesh bodies took place in five places in the Earth at the same time.
Only called Adam in one historical account, the Biblical account took place in the Garden of Eden.

> These (sons of God) were all together in (Spirit) in Amilius. They were material bodies as came in Adam.
> (288-29)

> Man, in Adam (as a group; not as an individual), entered into the world (for He entered in five places at once, ...called Adam in one...)
> (900-227)

> In the beginning, the Perfect Man was given all the attributes of the Father, and placed in an ideal environment for physical manifestation.
> (262-129 Report)

The multitude of souls were all in a Oneness with Christ and each other. They were as voices of hope in the wind announcing the entrance of the companions of God all interconnected in the Oneness of Love.

What does it mean that Edgar Cayce came into being at the creation of man? It must mean he came into conscious awareness as an individual. It could imply that up until this point he was part of the group Amilius soul, not as yet personified or individualized.

> ...in the beginning, when the first of the elements were given, and the forces set in motion that brought about the sphere...called the Earth plane, and when the Morning Stars sang together, and the whispering winds brought the news of the coming of man's indwelling, of the Spirit of the Creator, man became the living soul. This entity (Edgar Cayce) came into being with this multitude.
>
> (294-8)

God blessed the male and female created in His image in Spirit and gave "Them" as in ONE Whole entity dominion over all the Earth and its contents. God meant for "Them" to have dominion over themselves as well as the environment around them (self discipline, self control, thought control, emotional and physical Body control).

"Be thou fruitful, multiply, and replenish the Earth and subdue it," He told "Them" as Adam. This was before Eve was taken out of Adam's Body of consciousness. Therefore, this was still in Spirit before Eve is manifested into a separate flesh and blood Body.

> Spirit was individualized, and then became what we recognize in one another as individual entities.
> Spirit that uses matter, that uses every influence in the Earth's environ for the glory of the creative forces, partakes of and is a part of the Universal Consciousness.
>
> (3508-1)

> For His promises throughout the ages have been, "subdue the Earth", subdue the Earth that is within thine own self.
> (689-1)

There may have been souls entering into monkeys as they were entering all types of animals and we know some of them got trapped. A monkey being could have evolved into the Neanderthal, subhuman, or beastly man but probably due to the soul involvement in that animal.

> Man DID NOT descend from the monkey...
> (3744-5)

God created the flesh and blood Form for Adam and Eve. They were to have Dominion over ALL the animals as well as the other creations on the Earth.

> Know that man - as has been expressed - was given Dominion over all, and in the understanding of same may use all of the Laws as pertaining to same for his benefit.
> (1895-1)

All the Kingdoms passed before Adam so that he would identify and name each of them.
The names would represent the traits and personality influences contained in each animal. Many of these were negative formations created by the fallen souls.
Naming the names is an important concept on many levels of consciousness. It means to correctly identify.

"All passed before Adam" means ALL of Life and not restricted to just the animal Kingdoms.

> ...all passed before Adam, and all were named that were named.
> (254-35)

...and whatsoever Adam CALLED every living creature, that was the name thereof.

Genesis 2:19

The various animals had negative traits which were injected into them by the souls entering them and the appetites of the animal were injected or absorbed by the soul.

Many of these same influences would need to be used as lessons by man since he has experienced the carnal nature of the animal Kingdom.

> ...each animal, each bird, each fowl, has been so named for some peculiarity of that individual beast, bird or fowl, and in this manner represents some particular phase of man's development in the Earth's plane, or that consciousness of some particular element or personality that is manifested in man.
>
> (294-87)

> ...Adam named those that were brought before Him in creation. Their NAME indicates to the carnal Mind their relationships in the sex condition or question.
>
> This has been the problem throughout man's experience or sojourn in the Earth; since taking bodily form, with the attributes of the animal in which he had PROJECTED himself as a portion of, that he might through the self gain that activity which was visualized to him in those relationships in the Earth.
>
> (5747-3)

The Cayce Readings tell us that when we dream of animals that these animals are traits, instincts, appetites, and habit forming patterns in ourselves which we need to recognize and deal with constructively.

We need to be able to tame the wild beasts within us as we have many of their characteristics within ourselves to control.

Hence the animal related terms:
Pets, pet peeve, as docile as a horse, a Trojan horse, a horse of a different color, horse's ass, horse feathers, one-horse-town, horse–sense, high horse, work horse, bucking horse, race horse, four horses, seven horses, (Chakras) horse sense, horsing around, horse shoe, you can lead a horse to water but you can't make him drink, hold your horses, feeling your oats, stubborn as a mule, jack-ass (horse related actions; balking, rearing, trotting, leading, trots, bridled, fenced in, bucking) as catty as a cat, a Cheshire cat grin, a black cat, strange cat, let the cat out of the bag, cat O nine tails, cat eyes, playful as a kitten, raining cats and dogs, hellcat, cat fight, cool cat, alley cat, copycat, fat cat, cat has nine lives, pussy cat, cat nap, having kittens, Tom cat, pussy-whipped, wild-cat, pussy footing, cat claws, cat walk, cat's got your tongue, something the cat dragged in, curiosity killed the cat, like a cat toying with a mouse, scaredy cat, putting on the dog, a dog is man's best friend, top dog, barking dog, pack of wild dogs, show dog, burying a bone, wagging tail, biting the hand that feeds you, the underdog, dog on a leash, like a dog doing tricks, in the dog house, life of a dog, doggone it, dogged out, dog days, give the poor doggie a bone, silly puppy, whipped puppy, a mutt, a wolf, wolf in sheep's clothing, running with the pack, foxy, sly fox, a lazy cow, fat cow, fattened calf, herd of cattle, bull, raging bull, bear hug, Teddy bear, busy as a beaver, deer, deer trophy, Bambi, buck, thirsty as a camel, a chameleon, getting your goat, billy goat, a gopher, innocent as a lamb, like a lamb for the slaughter, sacrificial lamb, sheepish, fleeced, the memory of an elephant, to tame a lion, a lioness, tiger by the tail, like a tiger ready to pounce, monkey see-monkey do; as sneaky as a snake, snake pit, like a snake ready to strike, wise as a serpent, a snake in the grass, winged serpent, coiled serpent, eat my dust, as hungry as a pig, hoggish, a pig in a poke, piggish, porker, chauvinist pig, pig headed, pig sty, you can't make a silk purse out of a sow's ear, swine, squeal, boar, kangaroo court, poor as a church mouse, sneaky as a rat, rat-fink, pack rat, ratting on a friend, a skunk, a weasel, a laughing hyena, slow as a turtle, birds of a feather flock together, ostrich with its head in the sand, a stool pigeon, soar like an eagle, winged eagle, golden eagle, fly like the

eagle, crane your neck, sitting duck, ugly duckling, like water off a duck's back, a parrot, wise as an owl, I heard the owl call my name, proud as a peacock, brought by the stork, a loon, crazy as a loon, loony tunes, bird in a cage, bird chatter, batty, blind as a bat, bats in the belfry, high perch, blue bird of happiness, a jack-daw, eat crow, a bird on the wing, bird on a wire, Phoenix rising, fluffed up, as peaceful as a dove, strange bird, fine feathered friend, a hen house, old hens, pecking hen, cocky, cock crows, a chicken, yellow as a chicken, to roost, silly goose, goosed, goose that laid the golden egg, preening, sings like a canary, a buzzard, vulture, cold turkey, love birds, cooing, mocking bird, the higher they fly the harder they fall, pecking, picking bones, lucky rabbit's foot, fishy, cold fish, hooked, fish bait. Slippery as an eel, clam up, crabby, slimy, spouting off, busy as a bee, buzz off, buzzing, buzzed, buzzing around, creep, creepy, said the spider to the fly, Lord of the flies, something that crawled out from under a rock, bugs, bugging me, a toad, a worm, eat worms, opening a can of worms, moth holes, moth to the flame, swarm, hive of bees, Queen Bee, nest of hornets, sting of a hornet, ticked off, don't let the bed bugs bite, swatting flies, flea bag, a louse, nit picker, caught in a web, web of deception, a black widow, etc.

The thorns on the roses, the stinging nettle, poison ivy, as well as various allergic reactions are the evil influences in the plant Kingdom.

The mineral Kingdoms were each gathered as separate mines before they were blasted apart and scattered all over the Earth by the rebellious souls. The minerals were as psychic centers before they were scattered which diminished their Power and influences.

In the animal Kingdom we find that the viciousness and cannibalistic nature of some animals was wrongly instilled by negativity.

Due to the close association between man and animal, both have influenced each other.

God's perfect and Heavenly state of consciousness and creation will one day be realized and, as in Isaiah, "the lion will lie down with the lamb," for hate and all negativity will be gone. It will be just as wrong to kill an animal as it is now to kill a man.

The Projection of man occurred in five places at once.

The land surfaces and atmosphere were far different than they are today as the poles have shifted since that time.

There have been many geographic changes in the continents and also in the climates of the various localities.

These Earth changes resulted in the races incarnating in different areas than they did at first for the development needed.

Adam was assisted by other sons of God in the entry into the new flesh and blood Body type(s).

The five different places would represent the areas of Five Races which became the major Five Nations in the Earth (yellow, white, red, black and brown).

> ...in what is known as Gobi, India, in Carpathia, or in that known as the Andes, and that known as in the western plain of what is now called America - the five places.
>
> (364-9)

It is stated that the physical beginning of Adam in the Garden of Eden was in the Caucasian or Carpathian.

> In the first, or that known as the beginning or in the Caucasian and Carpathian, or the Garden of Eden, in that land which lies now much in the desert, yet much in the mountain and much in the rolling lands there. The extreme northern portions were then the southern portions, or the polar regions were then turned to where they occupied more of the tropical and semi-tropical regions; hence it would be hard to discern or disseminate the change.
>
> The Nile entered into the Atlantic ocean. What is now the Sahara was an inhabited land and very fertile. What is now the central portion, or the Mississippi basin, was then all in the ocean; only the plateau was

existent, or the regions that are now portions of Nevada, Utah and Arizona formed the greater part of what we know as the United States. That along the Atlantic board formed the outer portion then, or the lowlands of Atlantis. The Andean, or the Pacific coast of South America, occupied the extreme western portion of Lemuria. The Urals and the northern regions of same were turned into a tropical land. The desert in the Mongolian land was then the fertile portion.
(364-13)

Q: Are the following the correct places? Atlantean, the red?

A: Atlantean and America, the red race.

Q: Upper Africa for the black?

A: Or what would be known now as the more WESTERN portion of upper Egypt for the black. You see, with the changes - when there came the uprisings in the Atlantean land, and the sojourning southward – with the turning of the axis, the white, and yellow races came more into that portion of Egypt, India, Persia, and Arabia.

Q: There was no original Projection in upper India?

A: This was a portion rather of the white and the yellow as represented. Let these represent the attributes of the physical, or the senses and what forms they take, rather than calling them white, black, yellow, red and green, etc. What do they signify in the SENSING? Sight, vision – white. Feeling – red.
Black – gratifying of appetites in the senses.
Yellow – mingling in the hearing.

> What is the Law of the peoples that these represent?
> Their basic thoughts run to those elements!
> (364-13)

The Five Races represent the five senses, nations, reasons and developments.

What was the time frame for the creation of the First Flesh and Blood Races created by God?

Cayce writers quote the mainstream time-line views that are given today and try to incorporate them into the Readings, stating that the Earth is four billion years old but these dates are NOT in the Readings.
The creation of Adam was not given a date. The Earth beginning is stated to be ten and a half million years old.

> The period in the world's existence from the present time being 10,500,000 years, and the changes that have come in the Earth's plane many have risen in the lands.
> (5748-2)

> When the Earth brought forth the seed in her season, and man came in the Earth plane...man appeared in five places at once-the five senses, the five reasons, the five spheres, the five developments, the five nations.
> (5748-1)

> As to the appearances or sojourns in the Earth - these are expressed or manifested, in the material Body through the senses.
> (2620-2)

These are traits, concepts, and influences with which one needs to work to subdue tendencies existing, and to understand when in that particular racial environment.

The Readings did not want the races to be called by the different skin colors but by which of the five senses that race represented. The races are not about the pigmentation of skin color; they are related to the five senses. The skin color has to do with environmental conditions.

The WHITE race represents the sense of vision and sight.
Location: Was in the Carpathian region at first (Caucasian).
The location was enlarged after the pole shift to include Egypt, India, Persia and Arabia.

The RED race represents feeling and touch.
Location: Atlantis and North America (Native Americans).

The YELLOW race represents hearing and sound.
Location: Gobi Desert. The Mongolian land was then fertile (Orientals).

The BROWN race represents smell and the olfactory.
Location: The Andes, the Pacific coast of South America and western USA (Lemurians were brown.)

The BLACK race represents appetites and taste.
Location: Upper Egypt or Africa.

The white and yellow races also entered Egypt, India, Persia and Arabia.

The white race is working with vision and sight. This race seems to need eye glasses to see properly more than other races. The white race is not seeing spiritually as it should.
There is the tendency to be judgmental.
The eyes are the windows of the soul.
Thus, the need in the physical Body for visual aids.

171

> ...the weaknesses in the FLESH are the scars of the soul!
> (275-19)

The red race is very in tune with nature and treats her as their Mother.
They respect animals and treat them as younger brothers and sisters.
The red race is very sensitive to the elemental forces in nature.
They recognize the Spirit that works in and through animals and nature.
They have deep feelings for plants and animals and consider them in a deeper spiritual reality than other races do.

> The entity then was among the people, the Indians, of the Iroquois; those of noble birth, those that were of the pure descendants of the Atlanteans, those that held to the ritualistic influences from nature itself.
> Hence ALL NATURE, all experiences of nature, all natural forces become as a part of the entity's experience.
> (1219-1)

The yellow races are very polite and careful not to offend others as they wish to convey friendship to their HEARERS.
Perhaps they hear things in a deeper manner than we realize.
Some of their music opens the Mind to be able to hear the ancient sounds of flutes and bamboo rustling in the wind.

> ...speech being even three times greater than the sense of hearing or sight; that is the highest vibration we have in the Body at all.
> (5681-1)

The brown race recognizes the use of spices and various odors and incense that have a deep effect on people.

The Readings say that there is no greater influence in a physical Body than the effect or odors upon the olfactory nerves.
Odors can lift one to higher levels of consciousness.
Others can be healing and some are also degrading or can irritate or burn the Body.
With the rising above physical appetites and taste, the black race becomes highly educated in every field and contributes to uplifting all of mankind.

The number five represents the fifth spiritual center, which is the thyroid gland in the Body.

> Q: Why was the number five selected for the Projection of the Five Races?
>
> A: ...is that element which represents man in his physical form, and the attributes to which he may become conscious FROM the elemental or spiritual to the physical consciousness. As the senses; as the sensing of the various forces that bring to man the activities in the sphere in which he finds himself.
> (364-13)

The thyroid gland is the seat of the WILL.
This is where we can choose. "Thy will be done," instead of my will.

> Thy Kingdom come. Thy will be done in Earth, as it is in Heaven.
> Matthew 6:10

The "sixth sense" is intuition which was given to Eve.
Women seem to have more of the "sixth sense" than men.
But spiritual man has the "sixth sense" as well.

Many souls have incarnated in all the races.

Moreover, there are some souls who have had no need to enter each race and have remained in only one race since the beginning.

We enter a different race if we need to work on the sense associated with that race. If we abuse or persecute a race, then we will owe a Karmic debt to that race.

Whatever race we are in, it is by God's Grace and for our development.

> The...entrances of soul-entities into the material experience. As to race, color or sex - this depends upon that experience necessary for the completion, for the building up of the purposes for which each and every soul manifests in the material experience.
>
> (294-189)

> ...there's no races, they are all One – they have either enjoined or have separated themselves, and as has been indicated from times back the environmental influences have made for changes in color, or the food or the activity has produced those various things...
>
> (1260-1)

Four other soul groups besides Adam incarnated in a flesh man/ woman Body type in Four different Races. Their soul forces were divided into a male and female form, as were Adam and Eve. Moreover, some souls retained the androgynous form for longer periods than others did.

Edgar Cayce was given an androgynous incarnation in Atlantis in which both the male and female soul self was contained in the Body of the female.

> ...and in the first Earth's plane as the "voice" over many waters, when the glory of the Father's Giving of the Earth's indwelling of man was both male and female in One.
>
> (288-6)

Adam is the pattern used for the other Four Races.

These were the four souls or soul GROUPS still connected to Amilius in Spirit and part of His group of souls entering the Earth. There is very little known about the four other groups of Adam and Eve.

The Apocalyptic Book 2 Enoch states that God assigned to Adam, "four special stars."

These could refer to the four souls or soul groups who entered the other Four Races.

The Bible goes on to describe one river that went out of Eden and became four separate heads or rivers. This could indicate the locations that could represent the other four races.

> And a river went out of Eden to water the Garden; and from thence it was parted, and became into four heads.
> Genesis 2:10

Rivers are bodies of water and are an important symbol of spiritual influence. The Spirit was manifesting in the Earth into five streams (heads/rivers) of consciousness, in five different branches or races. Five states or levels of consciousness or states of Mind or dimensions were represented.

Five rivers of Life flowing into different areas of the Earth in the Five Races (five psychic centers).

The first river is called Pison which is in the land of Halivah, where there is gold. This river is identified by scholars now with the Nile and the Indus, the Ganges and other rivers.

The second river is Gihon, that encompasses the whole land of Ethiopia.

The third river is Hiddekel, which goes toward Assyria.

The fourth river is the Euphrates (from the Bible).

The Garden of Eden was said to be located between the Euphrates or where the Red Sea and the Dead Sea are now located.

It described the Garden as "the land of the inter-between."
The Garden was in the Caucasian or Carpathian area.
The Caucasian mountain range stretches over 900 miles across central and eastern Europe.

> Q: Where was the Carpathian region?
>
> A: Aarat.
>
> Q: Where is the location?
>
> A: Southern part of Europe and Russia, and Persia and that land. Caucasian mountains.
> (364-13)

The Eden of the Bible was also stated to be between the Tigris and Euphrates rivers which are now in Iraq.
There is a lot of speculation as to where the Garden of Eden is located but no one really knows since the land, rivers, and names have changed; some have dried up in all these years.
The flood of Noah and the destruction of Atlantis must have greatly altered the geography of the Earth.
Some authorities place the Garden of Eden in Turkey near where the headwaters of the Tigris and Euphrates originate.
Others place Eden at the head of the Persian Gulf at the other end of the Tigris and Euphrates.
It is another mystery.

> ...that known in the beginning, or in the Caucasian and Carpathian, or the Garden of Eden, in that land which lies now much in the desert, yet much in mountain and much in the rolling lands there.
> (364-13)

These Projections of souls from Amilius, or the Christ self BECAME what we know as man as they grew into individuals.

There were also other centers that were developing. For in the Projections they began as MANY, and in creating influences they began as five – or in those centers where crystallization or Projection had taken on such form as to become what was called man.
(877-26)

Edgar Cayce's Twin Soul, Gladys Davis Turner, asked a question:

Q: In Atlantis, was I associated with Amilius? If so, how?

A: One as projected by that entity (Amilius) as to a ruler or GUIDE for many, with its associating entity, Edgar Cayce (294).
(288-29)

This was an androgynous incarnation in which both were confined in the Body of the female and they were the ruler of the land in Atlantis, referred to as the Poseidian incarnation.
The time frame for their next incarnation which was not androgynous is in ancient Egypt during the time of the FIRST of the Pharoahs when they separated.
We do not know the time frame for the FIRST period of the Pharoahs but during one of Cayce's Life Readings, there was mentioned a Lifetime during the rule of the Pharoahs which was during the "council of the forty four leaders" or Five Nations meeting in 50,722 B.C.

In that of the Egyptian rule, during the first of the Pharoahs do we find this connection as separated brought to the Earth's plane.
(288-6)

Another Egyptian incarnation was given in Egypt during the time of the SECOND rule in the Ra Ta period (10,500 B.C.)

Many mistake a date given of 12,800 B.C. for their androgynous incarnation. It is not clear to which Lifetime this date refers but it may refer to another Egyptian incarnation before Ra Ta.

> ...we find the entity in the Egyptian land, the Indian land, the lands from which most of those came for one of the branches of the first appearances of the Adamic influence that came as five at once into the expressions in the Earth, or the expression in that now known as the Gobi land.
>
> (1210-1)

There is another Reading on Atlantis that describes the activities and great developments during the time of Amilius and calls it, "The Eden of the world."

> Hence we find in those various portions of the world even in the present day, some form of that as WAS presented by those peoples in THAT great DEVELOPMENT in this, the Eden of the world.
>
> (364-4)

Again the words are used:

> - there WERE those periods when the activities of the physical were as was what would be termed the everyday Life of the SONS of God in the Atlantean or Eden experience...
>
> (364-7)

Eula Allen said that the "Garden of Eden" was in Atlantis in her book (The River Of Time, Page 5). But I think she may have gotten the Eden city in Poseidia mixed up with the Garden of Eden.

> ...in the Atlantean period before the second of the turmoils that separated the islands or broke up the

land into islands; and in the city of Eden in Poseidia
did the entity then dwell.
(390-2)

Adam and Eve were driven OUT of the Garden of Eden and
relocated.
The city of Eden in Poseidia was before the flood of Noah, when it
was broken up into islands during or before the second disruption
of Atlantis.

I believe the early Atlantis period in which Amilius projected Himself
with a group of souls was more on a spiritual level as "Thought
Form" beings.
This was before the First Creation of a Flesh and Blood Body Form
in Adam and in which the Five Races were formed. The Amilius
Atlantis before Adam was more of a spiritual Eden on a higher
dimensional level blending into the third dimension in an attempt
to LIFT it up.
It is stated that Atlantis was the location for the red race.
Yet the Carpathian was said to be Caucasian which represents the
white race.
What race was Adam, red or white?
We always picture him as white.
It is said that Adam means red or ruddy or red Earth.
(Hebrew; adhamah "red soil" or "ground").
Moses and the Israelites were Caucasians, were they not and
descendants of Adam?
There was a lot of racial mixing.

Atlantis was mainly of the red race in the beginning but it could
have been inhabited by all the races after some time.
The white race was in the Caucasian area (Garden of Eden).
But then it is stated that the "PURE" white race was NOT perfected
until the Ra Ta period in Egypt which was at a later time.

Hence, as Ra Ta means and indicates, among – or the first PURE white in the experience then of the Earth.
(294-147)

…Ra Ta, or Ra, was among the first of the men who had been purified to that of the Whole or WHITE.
(1100-26)

For, few of those had arisen to that state in which there were the preparations so as to produce the alabaster or all white…
(2329-3)

Why is the white race referred to as the Whole?
("Purified to the WHOLE or white".)
The white race may have been Light but not yet white in the original creation.

Also those in Caucasia or the Lighter or whiter peoples.
(5748-3)

The people of Mu were the brown race in part of the Pacific Ocean regions and Peru. Many people relocated to western United States before Lemuria sank. The Atlanteans also migrated to many different areas before the final destruction of Atlantis.

There are many legends about the continent of "Mu". There is a 19th century zoological theory that there was an ancient land bridge that connected various areas where the Lemur monkey was found. (Madagascar, Africa, India and Malaysia).
This land bridge is called Lemuria after the Lemur monkey.
Some people believe that the sons of God in Lemuria used the monkey as an experimental pre-Adamic Body form.
Others speculate that the Lemur monkey was used as a form for early man. So, some men may have come from the monkey?

However, the Lemur monkey is very small and I doubt it would have been a suitable choice to be used for that purpose.

The Readings state that man did not descend from the monkey.

It had been said that Lemur also means shadow or ghost. I can identify with the Lemurian period as a land of shadows. Lemuria seems to be a vague recollection in our far distant collective unconsciousness of the memory of that "Thought Form" ghost-like era.

There are stories of a physical Body type in Mu that is both male and female in one Body. The legends seem to indicate that this was more than the androgynous combination of the masculine and feminine spiritual entity but was an actual physical being with male and female reproductive organs in one Body (hermaphrodite).

The red race was called by the Readings the "Mixed Peoples." Does that mean that they were mixed races? Or of the "Mixtures?" The black race is also called "Mixed Peoples."

Atlantis was the home of the "Mixtures" who were a type of being for many centuries.

> Hence coming into that form as the red, or Mixture Peoples – or colors; known then later by the associations as the RED race.
> (364-3)

There is hidden symbolic meaning in the various races in what they can represent to us personally. Each race has one sense to work on as a main theme. Dividing the five senses into various groups may have diminished their Power to influence man.

Having only one main sense to control instead of dealing with all five as a major influence could have been a way for man to gain more control over the senses.

There is a Reading that refers to the "Mysteries of the Races."

> ...we find in the land when the highest civilization existed in that land known as Atlantis.

> The entity then among those who preserved the Laws of the peoples as relating to the Mysteries of the Races. (1629-1)

Note that the word STORY is used to describe the Garden of Eden. This could indicate that the "story" is symbolic, not literal or a combination of both.

It also mentions SECOND incarnation in Atlantis. Does this mean Amilius as the first incarnation and Adam as the second incarnation of the One Son? Or the second incarnation of Amilius in Atlantis?

> Q: The center or beginnings of these Projections was in Atlantis?
>
> A: Was in Atlantis. Hence we have, as from the second incarnation there – or the STORY as is given in Judaism doesn't vary a great deal from that of the Chaldean; neither does it vary at all from that that WILL be discovered in Yucatan; nor does it vary a great deal from that as from the OLDER ones of the Indian (East Indian, of course - as it is from the present.) (364-9)

It could be that all the Four Race locations are referred to as Edens, since each race had its own personal Eden.

There was a city in Poseidia which was one of the last islands of Atlantis that was called Eden; this may have been destroyed when the second destruction broke it up into islands (Noah era).

> There were also other centers that were developing. For in the Projections they began as many, and in creating influences they began as five - or in those centers where crystallization or Projection had taken on such form as to become what was called man. (877-26)

This was a Reading for someone who began in the yellow race in the Gobi Desert.

> ...we find the entity in the Egyptian land, the Indian land,
> the lands from which most of those came for one of the
> branches of the first appearances of the Adamic influence
> that came as five at once into the expressions in the Earth,
> or the expression in that now known as the Gobi land.
> (1210-1)

But the Readings tell us that all the races are one race.

> For they are all One; there's no races,
> they are all One -
> (1260-1)

It is not wise for one race to claim superiority over another for all are equal in God's sight.

> For He hath made of One BLOOD the nations of the
> Earth.
> (3976-24)

The Bible gives the account of God commanding the man, Adam, that of every tree in the Garden he may freely eat but NOT of the Tree of the Knowledge of Good and Evil.
God tells the man that in the day he eats of this tree, he will surely die.
It is interesting to note that God gives this command to Adam BEFORE the woman, Eve, or his feminine nature is taken out of Him.

> And the Lord God commanded the man, saying, "Of
> every tree of the Garden thou mayest freely eat:
> but of the Tree of the Knowledge of Good and Evil,
> thou shalt not eat of it; for in the day that thou eatest
> thereof, thou shalt surely die."
> Genesis 2:16-17

Symbolically, the Garden of Eden is a state of consciousness.

It is a Garden of Paradise that is walled in or protected as an enclosure.

Eden is the consciousness of being centered in the Oneness of God.

Eden is the state of being in companionship and communication with God. Oneness with God protects a soul from being outside of God Consciousness.

Eden is Peace and bliss.

The Garden is a GROWING place (state) full of flowers and fruits.

Paradise has two trees.

A tree is symbolic of the axis of the world. A tree can be a "cross."

Eula Allen taught that the cross was symbolic of man's will at cross purposes with God's will. We crossed God's will and disobeyed, making our own will supreme instead of God's will.

A tree is the shape and symbol of a man with outstretched arms.

Its roots are deep in the Earth and in contact with the underworld or subconscious Mind. The tree's trunk grows into the Light and records TIME by adding a ring to its growth each year.

We are each our own individual Tree of Life. Then we have our Family Trees for each Lifetime.

Branches stretch upward to reach out for the solar energy of the sun (Son). A tree dies in winter and is reborn in spring as a symbol of regeneration, resurrection, and reincarnation.

Wood from a tree that is burned becomes fire which gives warmth; it forms into incense, and smoke as it sends messages (smoke) into the atmosphere and sky (Heaven).

An evergreen tree is symbolic of immortality as it stays green.

Paradise has two trees in its Garden.

The first tree in the Garden of Eden is the "Tree of Life" which is in the center of the Garden and is symbolic of immortality as it gives eternal Life. From the center of the Tree of Life flows a spring or fountain giving rise to four rivers that flow in four directions (forming a cross?). Eternal Life is entrance into the Heavenly state of awareness and Oneness with the Creator.

The second tree is the Tree of the KNOWLEDGE of Good and Evil.

This tree brings duality into consciousness and the separation from Paradise. It causes One to have the WISDOM to see the outcome of choice and to know whether the choice is in God's Oneness and will or not in God's will.

Tasting this fruit brings the knowledge of the DIFFERENCE between Good and Evil.

What is the Tree of the Knowledge of Good and Evil that is forbidden to man?

The tree could represent many trees as in a forest, groups or nations, or various concepts.

It seems that Adam in the Garden only knows Good.

He is in direct communication with God.

He is innocent and obedient to God's will.

Adam is in a state of perfection and is in Harmony with God and His surroundings in the Garden. (Adam is symbolic of the soul that is able to be companionable to God.)

If he partakes of this Tree of the Knowledge of Good and Evil, he will know not only Good but Evil as well. God only wanted Adam to know Good and not to be aware of or experience Evil.

Evil is deviation from the Law of God.

Therefore, the Tree of the Knowledge of Good and Evil must have to do with LAW and obedience or Law and disobedience.

Since the rebellion in Heaven, there are two different influences that began to exist.

We have two influences or choices available to us.

The Angels and celestial beings who were cast out of Heaven were in the Earth influencing matter along with the souls entrapped in the "Mixtures."

The choices of Good or Evil and Light and darkness are the influences in the Garden as well as other realms of consciousness.

Maybe God wanted to protect Adam and Eve from the influences of evil until they had time to adjust to the new bodies and environment of the Earth. They were meant to maintain their direct contact with God.

After all, they were newly awakened into a type of flesh and blood Body for the first time.

This was a new experience.

The First Flesh and Blood Physical Body was made by God for the entire family of mankind to inhabit.

This was a new beginning of a new Root Race for mankind.

The Garden in which Adam and Eve lived was like a paradise.

They needed to learn now to function in their new element.

God was protecting them by forbidding them to know evil.

They were God's own perfect creation and without sin.

However, they did have free will.

They could choose with God or against God.

We need to remember that Adam was on a rescue mission. There were still in the Earth all those part human and part animal "Mixtures" and also beings that the Readings refer to as "Things." I prefer to call them all the "Mixtures." Some of these were only animals with soul influences; whereas, others were souls lost in animal matter. Creation was progressing along evolutionary lines set with the imperfect channels.

There were also the fallen Angels that were a big influence.

Some of them could have been trapped in animal bodies as well.

Adam and Eve did not know the difference between Good and Evil and were surrounded by a lot of influences which were not of God. But they did not need to know evil. All they needed was to trust and obey God since they were in direct contact with Him.

There is a Reading for one of the "Mixtures" that was in the Earth at that time that was referred to as one of the "Things." The "Things" were the Thought Projections infused with animal matter, used by the Atlanteans for workers. Some of the "Things" had souls but most did not but were portions of the soul and cellular Body of their makers or producers (Clones?). The "Things" were robotic and did the main labor for all. They were described as similar to our domestic pets of today.

This "Mixture" or "Thing" had a soul and was named Suz.
This same entity named Suz, in a later Lifetime, was in the Holy Land and knew the Master, Jesus. Her children were among the first blessed by Him.
Suz is one of the souls rescued by Amilius/Adam and later blessed by the SAME soul in Jesus.

> Before that we find that the entity was in the early, early days, when there was the Garden called Eden.
> There we find the entity was among those who looked on the activities of the Mother of Mankind.
> The entity then was among the "Things," and yet was touched in person, was touched in heart, and sought to know the meaning of same, for it saw then fruit, leaves, trees, which had their spiritual meaning in peoples' lives. The name then was Suz.
> (5373-1)

Eula Allen, who wrote Before The Beginning Creation Trilogy, taught us in her creation class (1966-1968) that the Serpent in the Garden was one of the "Mixtures" who was part man and part Serpent. She called him the "Serpent Man."
Allen thought this being was Satan himself who inhabited that snake-man form or one who was part of the Lucifer group or a being that was influenced by evil.

Some say that Satan disguised himself as a snake to deceive Eve. This was a snake being unlike a snake of today as this snake-man stood upright and was very beautiful.
This snake-man was able to talk and appeared to be Wise.

The Readings do mention that Satan influenced Adam in the Garden and also refer to Satan as the Serpent.

> Where is Ariel and who was he? A companion of Lucifer or Satan, and one that made for the disputing of influences in the experience of Adam in the Garden.
>
> (262-57)

> Now the Serpent was more subtle than any beast of the field which the Lord God had made.
> And he said unto the woman, "Yea hath God said, ye shall not eat of every tree of the Garden?"
> And the woman said unto the Serpent, "We may eat of the fruit of the trees of the Garden: But of the fruit of the tree which is in the MIDST of the Garden, God hath said, ye shall not EAT of it, neither shall ye TOUCH it, lest ye die."
> And the Serpent said unto the woman, "Ye shall not surely die.
> For God doth know that in the day ye eat thereof, then your eyes shall be opened, and ye shall be as Gods, knowing Good and Evil."
>
> Genesis 3:1-5

Allen believed that Eve was seduced by the Serpent Man into having sex which was not intended since the Immaculate Conception was the plan for mankind. This changed the format for bringing souls into the Earth to a more animal level.

Unless Adam and Eve had the physical reproductive centers, the participation must not have been physical or sexual on the human Body level.
If they were not intended to have physical sex, then it seems that they would not have had the human sexual organs required.

Or maybe they did have sexual bodies but were to use them at a higher level of functioning to demonstrate a new pattern.

> And that used to gratify an appetite of the Body sets or puts the Body ABOVE the Spirit.
> (2533-7)

The influence must have stimulated desires in the mental-spiritual levels which were damaging to the physical being.
Whatever the influence, it was seducing and evil and got Eve to agree to partake of that which was a command not to do.
Eve broke God's Law. Then she introduced Adam to the "forbidden fruit."
Now they were both in a state of disobedience or sin.

> "Adam's changed status, due to his choice of action had established a new order in the Earth. Though He had come to lead man from their ignorance, He had chosen to use the channel common to Earthlings to bring souls in through the doorway of sex instead of by the immaculate means ...as a sexless Body for Eve. As a consequence souls were not required to come into the Earth under changed conditions."
> Eula Allen

In dream interpretation the Serpent is a symbol of Wisdom, which according to how it is used, results in either Good or Evil.
The Serpent is a symbol of Mind Power, creative energy, and Wisdom.

The Kundalini or Life force of the soul that flows though the endocrine system in the human Body or the seven spiritual Chakras (wheels) is described as a Serpent.

There are twelve spiritual centers in the Body but we are only using seven today. It is the means of communicating between the human self and the spiritual reality.

The Life force is "coiled" in the lower centers of the Body (ready to RISE up and be used to commune with God).

> Just which one is desired to be known? (Reactions of Kundalini forces.)
> There are twelve centers acted upon, each in a different manner, and from the varying Sources from which these vibrations are raised in and through these centers—and for what purposes.
> (1861-11)

Meditation is attuning the physical and mental to the spiritual.
We must first empty ourselves of all that would hinder that contact and communication. This requires purification and prayer.
When one's will is One with God (the thyroid gland represents the will), then the Kundalini force is raised into the higher centers of the pineal gland (Christ/Son) which can lift One into the pituitary (God center) and then overflow into spiritual awareness and Oneness with God. The energy spilling over into the other centers purifies the Body, Mind, and soul.
It is the meaning of, "My cup runneth over."
This is true meditation as it is Communion with God.

The Serpent can represent the spiritual Power associated with clairvoyance and visions. It can mean Wisdom from on HIGH.
The ancient Priests of Egypt wore the sign of the Serpent on their headdress to symbolize the Power of the raised Kundalini force.

Because a snake sheds many skins, it s a symbol of reincarnation, rebirth, and eternity.
The staff of Moses was in the shape of a Serpent.

The caduseus is a winged rod with two Serpents entwined and is used by the medical profession as a symbol of healing.

The dark or evil side of the Serpent represents Wisdom misapplied and used for self glory, self honor, and self indulgences. This Serpent represents the lower self.
The Serpent is associated with deception, temptation, fear, treachery, sneakiness, cunning, devious thoughts and acts, betrayal, and lies.
Poisonous emotions or thoughts can also mean evil intentions like lust, sexual indulgences, and seductions.

A "snake in the grass" is a warning of someone trying to deceive us. The snake hisses and makes the SHHH sound which is full of hidden whispers and evil secrets.
There have been psychological studies done on what attracts men and women.
It seems indicated that men are attracted by what they SEE (images in Mind.)
Women are attracted by what they HEAR
(words can create images that flatter, which can entice.)
The Serpent asks Eve if they are not to eat of every tree in the Garden. Eve replies that they can eat of every tree except the tree in the MIDST of the Garden which they are not to even TOUCH, lest they die.

The Serpent tells Eve that God knows that in the day they EAT of the forbidden fruit, their eyes would be opened and they would be as Wise as Gods, knowing Good and Evil.
Paula Fitzgerald taught that the sin of Adam and Eve was the same as the sin of Lucifer, to be as Gods.
God's concern was that man would be separated from Him.
God has never said that He did not want us to be like Him.
We are as Gods in Him but we are not to be Gods outside of His will and purposes or to glorify ourselves.

And the Serpent said unto the woman,
"Ye shall not surely die."
Genesis 3:4

Eve saw that the TREE was Good for food, pleasant to the eyes as a tree to be DESIRED to make One Wise so she took the fruit thereof and she gave it to her husband who was also WITH her.

> And when the woman saw that the tree was Good for food, and that it was pleasant to the eyes, and a tree to be DESIRED to make One Wise, she took of the fruit thereof, and did eat, and gave also unto her husband WITH her; and he did eat.
> Genesis 3:6

Eve believed what the Serpent told her.
She was seduced by what she HEARD.
She should have trusted God and questioned the Serpent.
Eve liked the idea of being as Wise as a God.
The thought was pleasing to Adam as well.

Once Eve TOUCHED the tree, it created DESIRE in her.
Evidently Adam was WITH her at the time so he might have observed the act or felt the vibration of her disobedience and self indulgence.
What Adam SAW attracted Him to also partake of the forbidden tree.

The tree in the midst of the Garden has many different ways of interpretation.
The tree in the midst of the Garden is the Life force center or the Kundalini.
It is the Tree of Life in the Garden of the physical Body consciousness.
The Kundalini force or "élan vital" is our creative energy Source.
The path or shape of the Kundalini energy is in the shape of a raised cobra or Serpent and/or a shepherd's staff.

This is the force we raise when we center our will in God's will and meditate to commune with the divine within the Temple of the Body. When the Kundalini force is raised continually within the Body, there is no need or desire for sexual expression.

> The Spirit and the soul is within its encasement, or its Temple within the Body...
> With the arousing, it rises along that which is known as the Appian Way, or the pineal center, to the base of the BRAIN, that it may be disseminated to those centers that give activity to the Whole of the mental and physical being. It rises then to the hidden eye in the center of the brain system (pituitary), or is felt in the forefront of the head...
> (281-13)

The fall of Adam and Eve was not that they chose to disobey God but instead to partake of knowledge without Wisdom.

> When...a soul, uses a period of manifestation to its OWN INDULGENCIES, then there is need for the lesson, or for the soul understanding or interpreting, or to become aware of the error of its Way.
> What, then, was the FIRST Cause of this awareness?
> It was the EATING, the partaking, of knowledge; knowledge without Wisdom – or that as might bring PLEASURE, SATISFACTION, GRATIFYING – not of the soul but of the phases of expression...
> Such manifestations become as PLEASING to the EYE, PLEASANT to the Body APPETITES.
> (815-7)

The Readings are telling us that the First Cause of this awareness was eating or partaking of that pleasant to bodily appetites which did not uplift the soul. It was feeding the animal nature over the spiritual nature.

> ...he who uses knowledge for his own personal aggrandizement DOES so to his OWN undoing...
> (3976-16)

> In the day ye eat or use the knowledge for thy own aggrandizement, ye shall DIE.
> (3976-29)

Here we have the evil influence working again to prevent the soul from being One with God.

> Who, what INFLUENCE, caused this, ye ask?
> It was that influence which had, or would, set itself in opposition to the souls remaining, or the entity remaining, in that state of At-Onement.
> (815-7)

What is the first thing that happens to Adam and Eve when they partake of the forbidden tree?
They lose their singleness of purpose and become double Minded. The Oneness is broken.
Their physical eyes are opened and they realize that they are naked. (They are looking at themselves from a human, physical viewpoint instead of as souls.)
Their sin is now exposed in Body, as well as in Mind and in Spirit. They feel unlovely to look upon.

They are ashamed, so they try to hide themselves in Body and in Mind from the presence of God. They hide themselves from the Oneness that they had with God because their conscience put fear into them once they knew they had disobeyed God.

They make fig leaf aprons to hide their psychic centers.
Why would they hide their Body parts if their sin had not involved something related to them? Whether they had sexual Body parts or not, they had misused the spiritual Life force within their bodies.

When God asks Adam if He has eaten of the tree He commanded Him not to eat, Adam blames Eve. To eat means to FEED upon. Eating is partaking of an influence that translates into One's self and forms into an actual part of the self. It is absorbed into the self.

> And the man said, "The woman whom thou gavest to be with me, she gave me of the TREE, and I did eat."
> Genesis 3:12

When Eve is asked what is it she has done, she blames the Serpent.

> And the Lord God said unto the woman, "What is this that thou hast done?" And the woman said, "The Serpent BEGUILED me, and I did eat."
> Genesis 3:13

Beguile means to charm, to bewitch or morally seduce. Beguile means to divert one's attention in a pleasant way from work or something more worthwhile.

Adam and Eve blamed each other instead of asking for forgiveness and accepting responsibility for their mistake.
Fear had entered into them both.

The Serpent Man is cursed above all animals because of his EVIL influence in the Garden.
The Serpent had fallen as well as Adam and Eve.
He will no longer walk upright but will slither along on his belly.
He will eat dust. (Snakes eat flesh so this must refer to something else).
There is nothing lower than having dust come up into your face and mouth all the time.
Thus the expression, "Eat my dust."

The Serpent Power in the Body is now fallen from the higher centers into the lower centers (Kundalini).
God awareness has shifted into self awareness.

The roots of the Life force tree are in the Lyden Center (cells of Leydig) which is the gland that seats the soul. It is also the center of temptation.
The result of this disobedience means procreating through the sexual center which will result in painful suffering in childbirth.

The husband will rule over the woman which means equality is lost.
The man will no longer have all his food provided for him.
When the Kundalini force was always raised, the Body was sustained by that spiritual force.
Now man will have to toil, sweat, and work the soil for his food and nourishment.

God adds the green herb to their diet for healing as now mankind will need purification.
The perfect diet given to man was vegetarian.

> And God said, "Behold, I have given you every herb bearing seed…and every tree, in the which is the fruit of a tree yielding seed; to you it shall be for meat."
> Genesis 1:29

Eating meat was forbidden until after the flood, according to the Bible.

> Every moving thing that liveth shall be meat for you; even as the green herb have I given you all things.
> Genesis 9:3

The bodies of Adam and Eve were very Light and gelatinous and not solidified or as hardened as ours of today.
I am not sure if they had the actual physical sexual centers as we do now.

If they were meant to procreate on a higher level, then there was no reason to have sexual reproductive centers except to demonstrate to the fallen ones the ability to be in a sexual Body and still be able to conceive spiritually. But the sexual center is part of the Kundalini force in the Body we have today.

I think that the coats of animal skins that God made for Adam and Eve at this time was the addition of the physical, sexual Body since they were spiritually and mentally partaking of it already.

> Unto Adam also and to his wife did the Lord God make coats of skins, and clothed them.
> Genesis 3:21

Matter is an energy vibration, and its substance can vary, according to the level in which it is vibrating. I think that after their indulgence in the "forbidden fruit," God made them into sexual beings as they had chosen it in their disobedience.

> ...all force in nature, all matter, is a form of vibration - and the vibratory force determines as to what its nature IS...
> (900-448)

> Each atom of the Body-physical is an expression of a spiritual import. That is how matter comes into being.
> (264-45)

All the souls who projected themselves into matter as "Thought Forms" originally did not have any sexual parts as none exist in Spirit. They had to enter into the animal Kingdom to experience sex and eventually the animal parts and instincts became part of them and grew out of them as well as from within them.

Amilius and his group of souls had entered in a more pure form to show the souls who were trapped in animals the way out of this entanglement.
The Readings stated that the Adamic Body was the most ideal Body yet created as it was designed by God.
It had the "all seeing eye" which could be moved about in the Body. This "eye" held the divine image and enabled continual contact with God. The "eye" finally became stationary as the pituitary gland which is still the entrance of the "Holy of Holies."
Or unto the Father.
But it is a trespass against God to enter it without going through the Son or Christ center of the pineal gland.

The following Reading is usually attributed to the Atlantean "Thought Forms" before Adam but this statement is made right after saying that the ideal form was during the time of Adam when he appeared as five in One. God did not make coats of the skins of animals for the "Thought Forms" but for the Adamic group.

> In this the physiognomy was that of a full head, with an extra EYE-as it were-in those portions that became known as the EYE. In the beginning these appeared in WHATEVER portion was desired by the Body for its use!
> As for the dress, those in the beginning were (and the Lord made for them coats) of the skins of animals.
> These covered the parts of their person that had become, then, as those portions of their physiognomy that had brought much of the desires that made for destructive forces in their own experience.
> (364-11)

Adam and Eve experienced a sort of virtual dreaming experience of tuning into a lower physical vibration in thought and in feeling without its actually being their own but it felt as if it were their own while commingled in the process.

The continuation of the virtual dream caused them to lose their self awareness and to become the dream.

This is very similar to what happened to the first souls that fell into matter earlier. Adam and Eve's partaking of the Tree of Knowledge was more a problem of lowering their ideals into that which was self centered, instead of God centered, than just a physical act.

Their Life force was lowered, now fallen into the lower centers from which they would have to function.

They partook of some type of selfish or sexual imagery, emotion or energy, a virtual dream which changed their mental and spiritual state and it affected their physical bodies. It was carnality of MIND. Now they had carnal knowledge. Desire was created for that which was forbidden. Cayce said the gratification of Body appetites that were not soul related brought separation from God through self indulgences.

They used spiritural forces for material appetites.

They now had knowledge of sexual activities and desires that needed to be controlled. These new desires interfered with their Communion with God. The desires of the flesh war against the motivations of the Spirit. They had been told to keep SEPARATE but they disobeyed and partook of carnality of Mind and Body.

Selfishness took the place of Love in their act of disobedience.
The carnal Mind is enmity against God.
There is Body, Mind, and Spirit.

Amilius fell in the Spirit in Atlantis, now as Adam He has fallen in the Mind and Body.

> ...for were He not the SON of the living God made manifest, that He might be the companion in a made world, in material manifested things, with the injunction to subdue all, BRING all in the material things under subjection – all UNDER subjection - by

that ability to project itself IN its way? KNOWING itself, as given, to be a portion OF the Whole, in, through, of, by the Whole? In this desire, then, keep - as the injunction was-thine self separate: OF that seen, but NOT that seen. The apple, then, that desire for that which made for the associations that bring carnal-Minded influences of that brought as sex influence, known in a material world, and the partaking of same is that which brought the influence in the lives of that in the symbol of the Serpent, that made for that which creates the desire that may be ONLY satisfied in gratification of carnal forces, as partake of the world and its influences about same – rather than of the spiritual emanations from which it has its SOURCE. Will control - inability of will control...
(364-5)

The entity was among the Children of the Law of One that succumbed to the wiles – it may be WELL interpreted in the answer recorded in the Holy Writ—"Ye shall not SURELY die; that it is pleasant for the moment and for the satisfying of longings within." Thus did the entity begin to USE the spiritual forces for the satisfying of material appetites.
(2850-1)

For to be carnally Minded is death:
But to be spiritually Minded is Life and Peace.
Because the carnal Mind is enmity against God:
For it is not subject to the Law of God, neither indeed can be.
Romans 8:6-7

I think that knowing they would need more animal type bodies to function as sexual beings, that God changed their bodies (coats) which hardened their skins or exterior bodies as well.

The coat is often a symbol of the Body or form we must wear to enter an incarnation in the Earth. On the soul level, our coat is our countenance, which radiates out our energy patterns formed by thought and experience.

Our clothes are our inner-most thoughts and deeds. A cloak is a covering which hides our sins of selfish thoughts and motives.

Maybe Adam and Eve needed tougher skins.

Their bodies were now animal skins or coats.

> As for the dress, those in the beginning were of the skins of animals. These covered the parts of their persons that had become, then, as those portions of their physiognomy that had brought much of the DESIRES that made for destructive forces in their own experience; and these (coats) then were of those (animals) about them.
>
> (364-11)

> ...Adam and Eve, the knowledge of their position, or that as is known in the material world today as desires and physical bodily charms, the understanding of sex, sex relationships, came into the experience. With these came the natural fear of that as had been forbidden...
>
> (364-6)

Adam and Eve were expelled from the Garden because God did not want them to eat of the Tree of Life and live forever in their "fallen - from – Grace" state of consciousness.

So, they were sent forth from the original Garden and now have to work soil that will bring forth thorns and thistles.

The thorns and thistles are the difficulties and trials that make their Life one of toil but they are appointed for man's Good as a form of training needed to uplift him again.

Remember, there are flowers on the thistles and that the thorns are covered with beautiful fragrant roses in a variety of colors.

Everything God does is in Mercy and with His loving kindness to help the created man and never to harm or punish him.

The Serpent told Adam and Eve that they would not surely die.

The Bible says that Adam lived for nine hundred and thirty years. The Readings give a different age number for Adam's Life span which was only about 600 years.

> Yet the Tempter said, "Not surely die," for it may be put off; and it was - six hundred years - and yet death came, the pangs of the loss of self.
> (3188-1)

> …"In the day ye eat thereof ye shall surely die."
> In the day thou sinneth, ye have destroyed, then that something in thine consciousness that must be paid, that must be met in thyself.
> (3028-1)

> And with error (sin) entered that as called DEATH, which is only a transition - or through God's other door - into that realm where the entity has builded, in its manifestations as related to the knowledge and activity respecting the Law of the universal influence.
> (5749-3)

There is the possibility that Adam and Eve could have lived as long as they remained in a state of Oneness with God.

There are a couple of Readings that state that death is the result of their disobedience.

But physical Life in a flesh and blood Body was never intended to be eternal. Physical death existed from the beginning in the animals. Flesh and blood cannot inherit eternal Life.

For to create One must die?

To create we must lose our self or give up One's self?

We must die to the desire to create out of God's will.

God was not referring to death of the Body but a break in the contact with Him which was the loss and SEPARATION of At-Onement in Spirit.

> ...as man's concept became to that point wherein man walked not after the Ways of the Spirit but after the desires of the flesh, sin entered - that is, away from the Face of the Maker, see? And death then became man's portion, SPIRITUALLY, see? For the physical death existed from the beginning; for to create one must die, see?
>
> (900-227)

> For the wages of sin is death; but the Gift of God is eternal Life through Jesus Christ, our Lord.
>
> Romans 6:23

> Q: What did the Angel mean when he said, "I will tell thee the mystery of the woman, and of the beast that carrieth her?"

> A: That which is understood by those that follow in the Way of the Lamb, that come to know how man separates himself through the DESIRES to become as the PROCREATOR in the BEASTS; which made the necessity of the shedding of blood for redemption, for it brought sin IN the shedding – and only through same may there be the fulfilling; and as given, the

> Heavens and the Earth may pass but His Law, His
> Love, His Mercy, His Grace, endureth for those who
> will seek to know His will.
>
> (281-16)

According to the Readings, the evil influence in the Garden of Eden
was none other than Satan, the Devil, the Serpent, who is often
called the Prince of this world. Rebellion.

> For that desire to procreate in self, or to hold to selfish
> interests, has grown - grown - until it IS- what did He
> give? The PRINCE OF THIS WORLD; the Prince of
> this world (Satan)!
> Know that He who came as our director, as our
> Brother, as our Savior, (Jesus) has said that the Prince
> of this world has NO part in Him nor with Him.
> Then as we become more and more aware within
> ourselves of the answering of the experiences, we
> become aware of what He gave to those that were
> the First of God's Projection – not man's but God's
> Projection into the Earth; Adam and Eve.
> And then in their early days they were tempted by the
> Prince of this world, and partook of same.
>
> (262-115)

> Hereafter I will not talk much with you; for the Prince
> of this world cometh, and hath nothing in me.
>
> John 14:30

> Even as the Dragon represents the one that separated
> self so FAR as to fight with, to destroy WITH, those
> that would make of themselves a KINGDOM of
> their own.
>
> (281-16)

Man had the ability to procreate within self and to become a procreator in/with the BEASTS which he chose over being a co-creator with God in loving kindness.
The flesh became more Powerful than the Spirit.

> Thou hast been in Eden, the Garden of God; every precious stone was thy covering, the sardius, topaz, and the diamond, the beryl, the onyx, and the jasper, the sapphire, the emerald, and the carbuncle, and gold:
> The workmanship of thy tabrets and of thy pipes was prepared in thee in the day that thou wast created.
> Thou art the anointed Cherub that covereth; and I have set thee so: Thou wast upon the Holy mountain of God; thou hast walked up and down in the midst of the stones of fire.
> Thou wast perfect in thy Ways from the day that thou wast created, till iniquity was found in thee.
> Ezekiel 28:13-15

Sin came into God's creation by the misuse of the creative God force in the bodies of Adam and Eve at the sexual level but this is only the physical result of the mental and spiritual disobedience.
The God force was misused in the Garden of Eden.
Adam realized that He must become the Savior of the world.

> Q: When did the knowledge come to Jesus that He was to be the Savior of the world?
>
> A: When He fell in Eden.
> (2067-7)

The Only Begotten Son of God fell as the soul of Amilius and then He fell again as Adam. He took it upon Himself to be our pattern. He would continue in the Earth through as many incarnations as it took to totally function in perfect Harmony with God's will.

He would bear the burden of all sin and pay the Karmic debt for all souls, that we through Him might have access to the Father.
He would not fail again.
As in Adam we all die, so in Jesus Christ we are all made alive.

> For, know that He - who was lifted up on the cross in Calvary - was...also He that first walked among men at the beginning of man's advent into flesh! For He indeed was and is the First Adam, the last Adam; that is the Way, the Truth, the Light!
> (2402-2)

> Q: What is meant by "As in the First Adam sin entered, so in the last Adam all shall be made alive?"

> A: Adam's entry into the world in the beginning, then, must become the Savior of the world, as it was committed to His care, "Be thou fruitful, multiply, and subdue the Earth!" Hence Amilius, Adam, the First Adam, the last Adam, becomes – then - that that is GIVEN the Power over the Earth, and - as in each soul the first to be conquered is self-then all things, conditions and elements, are subject unto that self!
> (364-7)

The original sin of Adam and Eve changed all of mankind.
The fall of Adam and Eve is symbolic of the fall of all the sons/ daughters of God who entered with the Amilius group into the Five Races of mankind in the new Root Race with a flesh and blood Body. These bodies of the Adamic race are not like the ones we have today as ours are much firmer.

> ...the sons of Adam that had joined themselves with the sons of God, and as the sons of Adam that – with Amilius – had made the records of those things

whereby there might be the cleansing of the Body from the pollutions of the world, or of the animal Kingdom.

(884-1)

As given in the Scripture, there was breathed into man the soul. Biologically, man makes himself as an animal of the physical; with the desires that are as instinct in animal for the preservation of Life, for the development of species, and for food.
These three are those forces that are instinct in the animal and in man.
If by that force of will man uses these within self for the aggrandizement of such elements in his nature, these then become material desires – or are the basis of carnal influences, and BELITTLE the spiritual or soul Body of such an individual.
If the Mind is dwelling upon or directed in that desire towards the activities of the carnal influences, then it becomes destructive in such a force.
"Let thy will, O God, be my desire!
Let the desire of my heart, my Body, my Mind, be thy will, O Father in the experiences that I may have in the Earth!"

(262-63)

God gave sex to the animal Kingdoms and we, as souls, stole it from them. Then spiritual beings of Light inhabited animal fleshly bodies in the Earth and as animals, they had to co-exist with the sons of Adam. The human Body has a consciousness separate from the soul. Therefore, there must be a blending and a training/control of the animal Body by the soul Body.

What was the great attraction?
I think it provided a temporary reconnection to the Oneness once known in Spirit with God. Memory of a state of bliss.

There is a mystery in all of this yet to be revealed to us.

Mankind must now learn that sex is a biological urge in the Body which is like that of the animal Kingdom. The main purpose of sex was originally for procreation in the animal Kingdom.
Now all of mankind would know that animal sex could be seeking self gratification, which is innocent for the animal Kingdom but unworthy of celestial beings.
Mankind would need to learn to spiritualize desire in sex with pure Love which is unselfish.

Man is more than just animal as he is soul and made in the spiritual image of God. His human Body contains within it psychic spiritual centers to enable him to reconnect to his spiritual Source.
This is the creative force in the Body THAT CAN, THAT MUST be spiritualized by pure creative LOVE. It is the creative force that connects us to our awareness of and in God.
It is the creative force that can infuse two separate beings into the Oneness of companionship that is acceptable to God.

Mankind has the ability to procreate. It is a pattern of the divine that man/woman can have offspring from himself/herself.
It is an opportunity to provide a channel for another soul to enter into the Earth as well as an expression of their Love and devotion to one another.

The God force in man can be directed into higher levels and used for art, healing, and the benefit of all Life.
The sexual center is like the furnace (fire) in the basement; when lit it can travel into the higher centers and connect us to our true identity and reunite us with the Light of God again.
If we waste our energy in the lower centers, we never grow up or come into our spiritual natures as souls with a purpose and a mission nor can we have a personal relationship with the Christ.
Many souls live their lives never using their energy in the higher realms as intended. They dissipate their energy at the lower levels.

Once again there are the two choices for Good or Evil now in the
Body of flesh as well as in the Body of Mind and Spirit.
How will mankind use this creative force in the Body?
In Love or in selfishness?
In Oneness or in fragmenting the Oneness?
Creatively or non-creatively?
In God's will or out of God's will?
As an animal or as a being of Light?

> Each as an entity is a miniature copy of the universe,
> possessing a physical Body, a mental Body, and a
> spiritual Body. These bodies are so closely associated
> and related that the vibrations of one affect the other
> two. The mental especially partakes of the other two,
> in the physical as the conscious Mind and in the
> spiritual as the superconscious Mind.
> (262-10)

In the Earth we have third dimensional human consciousness
which does not exist in the higher levels of Mind. When absent
from the physical Body, at death, our subconscious Minds become
our conscious Minds and our super-conscious or spiritual Mind
becomes the unconscious Mind.

> Q: What happens to the conscious Mind forces and
> physical forces at death?

> A: The conscious Mind forces either are in the soul's
> development, and in the superconsciousness, or left
> with that portion of material forces which goes to
> the reclaiming, or remoulding, of physical bodies, for
> indwelling of spiritual entities.
> (900-17)

The human conscious Mind does not go with us when we leave the Earth although all our experiences are recorded by the subconscious Mind so we retain the memory.

This does not mean that we are not aware of ourselves as individuals. It is more of a total self awareness which includes memories from all of our Lifetimes and soul experiences as One Whole entity. This requires adaptation which is why Cayce recommended prayer for the dead since it is like a birth into another realm of consciousness.

> Hence God prepared the Way through flesh whereby all phases of Spirit, Mind and Body might express.
> (1567-2)

Mankind can participate in creation by having offspring. Understanding the parental Love and nourishing needed to raise a child who is part of his or her own Body is teaching us about God's Love for us who are a part of the Christ soul.

The type of Body we give a soul to enter into depends on the level of our creative energy used at the time of conception.

Are we praying to be a channel worthy for a spiritual soul to enter? Will we give birth to a Frankenstein or a Saint?

The "seventh sense" is the awareness of Good and Evil.

> ...that (Adam and Eve) were bestowed with the very Power of God, yet not aware of right and wrong. For they were IN a world ruled by the Prince of selfishness, darkness, hate, malice, jealousy, backbiting, uncomely things; not of the beauties, but that self might be taking ADVANTAGE in this or that Way or manner.
> (262-115)

The Readings discuss the consecration of physical desire by the Virgin Mary who had been the Eve of the Garden in being able to immaculately conceive the vessel for the Son of God, Jesus, to inhabit. The seed of the Virgin Mary is Jesus Christ who overcomes death, sin, and evil, or Lucifer, Satan, and the Serpent, by crushing his head.

> ...know that the message is ONE; for the Lord thy God is One, and that Jesus IS the One who was promised from that day, "...and her SEED shall bruise thy head."
> (2067-1)

> And I will put enmity between thee and the woman, and between thy seed and her seed; it shall bruise thy head, and thou shalt bruise his heel.
> Genesis 3:15

> Q: Does this mean that the world will evolve into bringing souls into the world in the manner that Mary did? (Immaculate Conception).

> A: Souls will evolve into the manner to be able to bring into the world souls, even as Mary did.
> And these may come as the souls of men and women become more and more aware that these channels, these temples of the Body are INDEED the Temple of God and may be used for those communications with God, the Father of the souls of men!
> (1158-5)

This is an affirmation given by the Readings:

> Lord, thou art my dwelling place! In thee, O Father, do I trust. Let me see in myself, in my brother, that thou would bless in thy Son, thy gift to me that I might know thy Ways!
> Thou hast promised, O Father, to hear when thy children call! Harken, that I may be kept in the Way

that I may know the glory of thy Son as thou hast promised in Him, that we through Him might have access to thee! Thou, O God, alone, can save! Thou alone can keep my ways!

(262-73)

For ye are all His, bought not only with the birth of the God-Child into flesh but with the death – that ye might know that He, thy brother, thy Savior, thy Christ, has been and is the WAY to the Father in this material plane.

(262-103)

...the Christ-Child was born into the Earth as man; One born in due season, in due time... that man might have a PATTERN of the personality and the individuality of God Himself.

(5758-1)

The Adamic nature that is within us all must be overcome by the Christ within us.

Christ prepared the Way for us to return to God through Himself.

CHAPTER VII

AFTER THE FALL OF ADAM

As in the First Adam sin entered, so in the Last Adam all shall be made alive.
(364-7)

...the First Man, Adam, was made a living soul; the Last Adam was made a quickening Spirit.
The First Man is of the Earth, Earthy:
The second man is the LORD from Heaven.
I Corinthians 15:45 & 47

All flesh is not the same flesh...
I Corinthians 15:39

All flesh (is) not one flesh. Flesh being that it has MERITED by its development in its plane of existence.
(900-70)

There were Five Race groups functioning on the Earth in five different locations. They were as a part of the collective Mind in Spirit at first but began individualizing into complete separate individuals during the time of Amilius and now consciously awakened in human physical bodies as the Adamic man/woman.

Many had divided into male and female bodies and were procreating as Adam and Eve, who are the original pattern in Spirit.

There were some souls who had not separated as yet into male and female and were contained together in one Body of either the male or female.

Eula Allen taught us that Cain was the son of Eve's union with the Serpent Man who was one of the "Mixtures."

The Serpent Man was Satan or the influence of evil.

If this is true on a physical level, then Eve must have had the reproductive center in her Body at the fall to be able to produce an offspring on a sexual level.

We need to keep thinking of this "story" as if it has meaning on more than one level at a time.

Cain could represent a thought pattern that developed when Eve ate the "forbidden fruit" as well as representing the individual. Cain can represent the ego or lower nature of self centeredness and rebellion.

Edgar Cayce told his Sunday school class that the Serpent must have made himself very desirable to Eve so that she forgot God's commandment. He mentions the interesting thought that God had given the command to Adam and that Eve probably only heard it "second hand." Remember the command was given to Adam BEFORE Eve was taken out of Him.

Cain could have been fathered by the Serpent or he could have been the offspring of Adam and Eve. Perhaps Cain entered without any physical doorway needed just from the mental-spiritual Projection of their union or desire.

Cain is symbolic of a destructive, self centered thought pattern that formed when Eve disobeyed God's commandment not to eat the fruit of THAT tree.

Cain represents man in his fallen state of consciousness.

Is Cain symbolic of the EGO?

When we look at the genealogy of Adam In the Bible, we find that Cain is not mentioned. Cain's genealogy is mentioned separately. (Two separate race lines? Results of different choices?)

There is the thought that Cain and Abel might have been fraternal twins, which means they came from two separate bags of water. Water is Spirit and this might indicate the Spirit of God and the Spirit of disobedience to God's Law.
They were very different in character and this could support the "two Father"
theories or be symbolic of the two choices of Good or Evil available to us all.

> In this the Children of God are manifest, and the children of the Devil: Whosoever doeth not righteousness is not of God, neither he that loveth not his brother.
> For this is the message that ye heard from the BEGINNING, that we should Love one another.
> NOT as CAIN, who was OF that WICKED ONE, and SLEW his brother.
> And wherefore slew he him? Because his own works were evil, and his brother's righteous.
> 1 John 3:10-12

The above scripture says that Cain was of that "wicked one" indicating Satan or the Dark Forces.

We need to keep in Mind that all flesh is not the same flesh.
There were two forms of Body creations going on all over the Earth.
First, there were the souls trapped in animal bodies, the "Mixtures," and "Things" called the sons and daughters of men or the Children of Belial who served Beelzebub. This is a creation out of God's will. But nevertheless loved by God who sent His Only Begotten Son to rescue them, too.

Joan Clarke

Additionally, there were those bodies of the sons and daughters of God coming through Adam and Eve and also the bodies coming from the other Four Race locations which are created by God.
They were called the Children of God or the Children of the Law of One or Children of the Lord which had been established by Amilius earlier.

Abel was a keeper of sheep and Cain was a tiller of the ground. Cain brought the fruit of the ground as an offering to God. Abel brought the firstlings of his flock and the fat thereof. (Amilius had established offerings as a symbol of devotion and worship to God to help man keep in contact with the divine.)
God had respect for Abel's offering but not for Cain's.
Cain fell in countenance and was angry. God told Cain that if he did well he would be respected and if not, "Sin lieth at the door."

This scripture always bothered me since I have a lot of humanitarian tendencies; I personally felt the fruit of the Earth was a better offering than killing an innocent animal.
But I was not seeing the whole picture.

Because the offerings represent a symbol of inner personal sacrifice and self will control more than the items that are sacrificed or offered.
Abel was sacrificing the animal or lower nature within and was presenting his Body, Mind, and soul as the living sacrifice to God.
The animal offered was symbolic of the necessity of presenting the Body as a living sacrifice to God daily.
The lower nature must be under submission to the higher nature of the soul for him to remain in contact with God.

It was also symbolic of the Atonement of Christ with the shedding of blood for the remission of sin.

> For on that day shall the Priest make an Atonement
> for you, to cleanse you, that ye may be clean from all
> your sins before the Lord.
> Leviticus 16:30

Cain was not controlling his lower nature or God would not have
told him that "Sin lieth at the door."
Cain could not have murdered Abel in a jealous rage if he were in
Harmony with God. It was not the outer offering but the inner one
that was important to God.

The real Gifts we lay before our Creator are our inner most feelings,
thoughts, and motivations to serve others and to love God.

Cain kills his brother Abel.
The lower self kills out the higher self.
Then when God asked Cain where his brother is, Cain lies and says
that he does not know.

"Am I my brother's keeper?" Cain asked.
This is a most famous quote and is used repeatedly in the Readings
which affirm that we ARE our brother's keeper!

> "Am I my brother's keeper?" (YES!) Who is thine
> neighbor? He that is in need of understanding! He
> who has faltered, he who has fallen by the Way. HE is
> thine neighbor, and thou must answer for him!
> (3976-8)

Next in the story, God tells Cain that his brother Abel's BLOOD is
crying from the ground.
The blood is demanding to be heard. This is a Powerful thought.
The Life and the soul identity (DNA) is carried in the blood.
When a person reincarnates, could the DNA contain all the patterns
and memories of all the Lifetimes one has lived?

> And He said, "What hast thou done?
> Thy voice of thy brother's blood crieth unto ME from
> the ground."
>> Genesis 4:10

God tells Cain that now the Earth will not yield her strength when he tills the soil and he will be a fugitive and a vagabond in the Earth. Cain feels that his punishment is greater than he can bear and that anyone finding him will kill him.
God places a MARK on Cain lest any finding him might kill him.
Many have speculated on what this mark on Cain might be.
One story says he had horns like one of the animal people or "Mixtures."
The Bible states that Cain is OF the "wicked one."
It also says that Cain's offering was evil.
Cain is symbolic of the lower nature or ungodly self that needs to be spiritualized.

The flesh Body is a result of that merited by the soul incarnating in it. Often problem bodies when born were for the parents as well as the soul of the child, both being given as an opportunity to undo a past Karmic situation or pattern.

There are those bodies of the sons and daughters of God coming through Adam and Eve and also the bodies coming from the other Four Race locations which are created by God.

Then we still have the old conditions existing in which the "Mixtures" are procreating and having offspring that are part animal and part human. We also have the "Things" which are laborers or workers that are projected by a soul using its own soul essence, which is like a separate extension of itself.
Some of these "Things" have souls, some do not, but are a part of the soul essence of its overseer or producer.
"Suz" was mentioned earlier as one of the "Things" who had a soul. Most of the "Things" were like automatons or robotic and some

were similar to our domestic pets. Therefore, they must have been lovable and important to many of us who cannot abide cruelty to animals or mistreatment to any lesser being.

Many of the sons of God had chosen mates from the daughters of men or from the "Mixtures."

Some of the bodies of the "Things" were found attractive by souls looking for a form to enter matter. Souls entered the "Things" and more offspring came in.

This complicated the already bizarre situation in the Earth even more.

At some point in time it became forbidden for anyone to enter a Body in the Earth unless lighted by the Christ. It was a Law that was established.

Some people believe this was at the Adamic period and others say the Law came in after the period of the Noah flood when most of the "Thought Forms" were abolished. I think this Law was with the beginning of the new race of mankind in the Adamic Flesh Body.

No longer could entities jump into animals or subhuman beings.

They had to come in through the right doorway which is the Light of Christ. Every baby born of a woman in the Earth is given the Gift of Life and breath from the Christ Light/Life personally.

> That was the true Light, which Lighteth every man that cometh into the world. He was in the world, and the world was made by Him, and the world knew Him not.
> John 1:9-10

There are still disembodied entities (ghosts) who seek to possess a Body that does not belong to them but they cannot just jump into an innocent Body without their permission or without a doorway opening for them to enter.

Fallen Angels do not need a fleshly Body to influence.

But some of the Angels could have been living in the "Mixtures" or have been "Thought Forms."

There were TWO major lines of flesh developing in the Earth and both are manifesting into male and female expressions.

The purpose of the Adamic Root Race was to provide a clean birth channel for ALL souls to enter.

The "Mixtures" would have a higher vibration of Body to help them become what they were created to be without all the animal influences and appendages to hinder.

The "Mixtures" were referred to as the sons and daughters of men. These are the sons and daughters of Belial, which are the souls in rebellion. They were not created in flesh by God but they projected their Spirits into animals. When the sons of God mated with these Children of Belial, some of their offspring were giants.

Not all of these rebellious souls were animal and human "Mixtures." Some were very much like our bodies of today.

They must have been very beautiful because the sons of God looked upon the daughters of men and found them very fair and chose wives from them. This happened during the Adamic fleshy mankind incarnations as well as in the Amilius era earlier.

In Atlantis there were still the same two groups functioning throughout the three periods of destruction.

> Then those souls who entered through a channel made by God – not by thought, not by desire, not by lust, not by things that separated continually – were the sons of God, the daughters of God.
> The daughters of men, then, were those who became the channels through which lust knew its activity...
> And the sons of God looked upon the daughters of men and saw that they were fair, and LUSTED!
> (262-119)

> ...in the Atlantean land... when there were the
> divisions between those of the Law of One and the
> sons of Belial...(or) ...the offspring of what was the
> Pure Race and those that had projected themselves into
> creatures (beasts) that became as the sons of men...
> (1416-1)

Cain is symbolic of the followers of the Belial groups.

It is written in the Bible that Cain went out from the presence of God to dwell in the land of Nod in the east of Eden.

Cain was no longer allowed to be with his parents but was an outcast.

The land of Nod has been symbolic of sleep, unconsciousness or unawareness when the conscious Mind is dull to the inner realities.

There is a Reading that refers to the "land of Nod" as the "land of Night."

> ...and the entity would do well to study even the Book
> of the Dead...rather the Book of Life; or it represents
> that which is the experience of a soul in its sojourn not
> only in the Land of Nirvana, the land of Nod, or the
> land of Night...
> (706-1)

Here Cain finds a wife. Since the other Four Races created by God that have manifested were in distant areas, it seems that the wife of Cain might have been one of the daughters of the sons of man ("Mixtures").

Cain is the ancestor of the first practitioners of the main vocations in Earth, agriculture and the raising of cattle, the arts, as the harp and organ, and science and warfare and instructor in brass and iron artifices.

There are a couple of Readings for descendants of Cain.

> ...she also bare Tubal-Cain, an instructor of every
> artificer in brass and iron...
> Genesis 4:22

However, the Readings mention other souls in Atlantis during the time of Amilius that were developing these same vocations at an earlier time as well.

This Reading was given for a person who had been a seven year old girl named Su-Su-Lu, a companion of Tubal-Cain. She also knew Eve in the Garden. Su-Su-Lu made overtures to Eve on behalf of those who were wounded. She was helping the souls of the "Mixtures" who were suffering.

> Before that we find the entity lived in that period when there were those in the land of the inner-between, or that between the Euphrates, or where the Red Sea and Dead Sea NOW occupy - was the entity's dwelling land.
> There we find the entity was an associate and a companion of one Tubal-Cain, the first of the sons that had been made perfect to become an associate with those of OTHER activities in the Earth.
> The entity withdrew, and made for those activities that brought that which is the cry of those that are wounded in Body, wounded in Spirit, wounded in soul.
> Then in the name, Su-Su-Lu, though it was a trying and testing experience, the entity gained.
> For the entity made overtures to those of the daughters of Eve (in person - that Eve of the Garden, that Eve who made for the activities).
> Though the entity was the seventh, tenth generations, it made overtures in PERSON – in the age of those periods.
> (1179-2)

It seems that Tubal Cain was the first son of Cain that was born perfect. Because Tubal Cain was perfect, he could associate with either the OTHER more Godly activities in the Earth or the less Godly.

Being perfect could mean without appendages or animal parts.

It could mean birth by the Immaculate Conception or refer to being in perfect accord with God's will.

The other activities could mean the "Mixtures," which were forbidden to mate or join with by the Adamic group.

It may mean that because of his perfect Body that Tubal Cain was more accepted by the Adamic group (The Children of God or the Law of One group from which Cain was expelled from association when he killed Abel.)

The purpose for Adam coming in to Earth was to provide a Way of escape for them but they were to keep separate from mingling the blood of the Pure Race with the impure blood of the "Mixtures."

However, the "Mixtures" who were ready to incarnate again could enter through a CLEAN birth channel and have an opportunity to develop on a higher level.

There is another Reading for a thirteen year old boy who was born an invalid from birth. He was told his condition was of Karmic origin going all the way back to the time of Lamech.

(There were two Lamech's in the Bible. One is the sixth generation descendant of Cain and is the one being referred to in the Reading. His father was Methusael.)

Lemech was the first one to have more than one wife.

He also told his wives that he, like Cain, had also slain men.

> And Lamech said unto his wives,
> Adah and Zillah, "Hear my voice:
> …For I have slain a man to my wounding and a young
> man to my hurt."

> If Cain shall be avenged sevenfold, truly Lamech
> seventy and sevenfold.
>> Genesis 4:23-24

During this period, the sons of God were taking wives of as many as they chose of the daughters of men and the Pure Race was intermingling with the animal people or the "Mixtures."

> We find the entity was in the period when there
> were those changes in the sons of Tubal-Cain, when
> Lamech made for those choices of the first beginnings
> of when MAN as man partook of those things that
> made for the multiplicity, or when polygamy first
> began among those peoples. This brought to the entity
> during the experience that of disorder, disturbance,
> the unfavorable expressions of many about the entity;
> and bringing those experiences that have builded for
> disorders in the experience.
>> (693-3)

The reason for keeping a Pure Race was because it needed to be of a high enough vibration for the eventual entrance of the Only Begotten Son of God to enter as the Savior of mankind. Plus the fallen souls needed clean Body channels to enter into to lift them up in consciousness.
During the Noah period many of the sons of God began to choose mates from the daughters of men or from the "Mixtures."
This is the period when God intervened by sending the flood that cleansed the Earth of most of the "Thought Forms."

The sons of God looked upon the daughters of men and took wives of them. Some of their offspring were giants.

> There were giants in the Earth in those days; and also
> after that, when the sons of God came in unto the
> daughters of men, and they bare children to them, the

same became mighty men which were of old, men of renown.

Genesis 6:4

When was the period of the flood?

The date that was given as the time for the flood of Noah was 22,006 B.C. (which was in only one Reading).

There are Readings that consistently confirm the flood date was around 22,000 to 25,000 B.C. The Noah flood was before the ancient Egyptian era of Ra Ta. This flood occurred during the "second destruction or eruption of Atlantis". (28,000 B.C.)

It could be that Atlantis in this period was more than several thousand years in breaking up, thus the various dates given.

There are several methods of calculating time and it depends on which one is used.

> Q: In relation to the history of Atlantis as presented, at what period did the flood as recorded in the Bible in which Noah took part, occur?
>
> A: In the second of the eruptions, or – as is seen – Two Thousand – Twenty Two Thousand and Six (22,006?) - before the Prince of Peace.
>
> (364-6)

The second period of disturbance in Atlantis was said to be some 28,000 years before Christ entered as Jesus, which was 22,500 years before the Egyptian activity covered by Exodus.

> ...the entity was in Atlantis when there was the second period of disturbance – which would be some twenty-two thousand, five hundred (22,500) before the periods of the Egyptian activity covered by the Exodus; or it was some twenty-eight thousand (28,000) before Christ.
>
> (470-22)

For as has been given, the deluge was not a myth (as many would have you believe) but a period when man had so belittled himself with the cares of the world, with the deceitfulness of his own knowledge and Power, as to require that there be a return to his dependence wholly – physically and mentally - upon the creative forces.

(3653-1)

We know that God repented that He had made man because man had become so wicked.

And God saw that the wickedness of man was great in the Earth, and that every imagination of the thoughts of his heart was only evil continually.
And it repented the Lord that He had made man on the Earth, and it grieved Him at His heart.

Genesis 6:5-6

...for as has been said, Repent that man was ever made. Why? For the purpose and intent of Man is to satisfy Earthly DESIRES of the FLESH rather than that of the manifesting of My Spirit in the Earth's plane.

(139-9)

...and man with his natural bent - not only attempted to subdue the Earth - but to subdue one another...

(3976-8)

Noah and his family were of the Pure Adamic Race line through Seth, that had not mixed or intermarried with the sons of Belial.

But Noah found Grace in the eyes of the Lord.

Genesis 6:8

It is indicated that only ONE group or race line was saved. We can assume that the other Four Race lines also had warnings and were provided means of escaping the deluge.

The Bible relates that Noah was five hundred years old when he had his sons, Shem, Ham and Japheth and six hundred years old when the flood occurred.

But it was at this period that the Life span of mankind was decreased due to the sins of man.

People lived such long lives back then that time was counted differently.

> And the Lord said, "My Spirit shall not always strive with man, for that he also is flesh: Yet his days shall be an hundred and twenty years."
> There were giants in the Earth in those days; and also after that, when the sons of God came in unto the daughters of men, and they bare children to them, the same became mighty men which were of old, men of renown.
> Genesis 6:3-4

> What was the length of Life then? Nearly a thousand years. What is your Life today?
> ...first from a thousand years, to a hundred and twenty, then to eighty. Why? Why? The sin of man in his desire for SELF-GRATIFICATION.
> (3976-29)

Edgar Cayce told his Bible class, when he was asked HOW Noah was to get the wild animals into the ark...

> "Animals are much closer to God in Spirit than we are. They sense when any great change is imminent. Perhaps they just came to him."
> (Edgar Cayce)

I think Edgar Cayce was correct, Noah was able to "call" the animals, psychically.

Another point that is worth mentioning is that Noah was commanded by God to take SEVEN pairs of the CLEAN animals and only ONE pair of the UNCLEAN animals.

He did not take any of the "Mixtures" or "Things" but he did take one pair of the animals that were unclean or polluted by the influences of evil. (Moses gave lots or dietary Laws of certain foods considered "UNCLEAN" and unfit for human consumption.)

Perhaps those animals had habit patterns and influences not worthy to build into the Body of a soul serving God.

Cayce also said the Ark of Noah landed on Mount Ararat after there was a cleansing of the Earth. This is when most of the "Mixtures" and "Thought Forms" were destroyed.

Remember the rainbow is God's promise to man.

> ...the promises of the divine that were and are written in the rainbow of the sky, when the cloud has passed, are the same as written in the lives of individuals; that they, too, may see their sign, their colors, and KNOW whereunto they have attained in THEIR relationship with creative energies or God.
> (1436-2)

Before the final sinking of Atlantis many were gathering in Egypt during the Ra Ta period which was about 10,500 B.C.

> Why Egypt?...might be the least disturbance by the convulsive movements which came about in the Earth through the destruction of Lemuria, Atlantis, and - in the LATER periods - the flood.
> (281-42)

The above Reading tells us of another flood that came AFTER the sinking of Lemuria and after a sinking of Atlantis.

Is this a later period than the Noah flood?
Or is it the first Egyptian period before the Noah flood?
This may be a different flood from Noah which was the time of
22,000 B.C. or it could be indicating that this area of Egypt was a
safety land during the earlier flooding.
Surely there must have been flooding after each destruction of
Atlantis. Each Atlantean period lasted thousands of years.

There were three different periods of destruction of Atlantis. The
first destruction was around the time of the meeting of the Five
Nations to discuss the enormous prehistoric monsters roaming the
Earth that were threatening mankind.
There were huge monster like beasts that were multiplying in the
Earth and hindering mankind. These prehistoric beasts were not
destroyed until God shifted the poles creating an ice age, although
man tried to destroy them with explosives. The date of 50,722 B.C.
was given for this meeting during the Adamic period as the Five
Nations, (races) were called to discuss this problem.
The Adamic race (FIVE RACES) was BEFORE this time, so the
date has to be at least 60,000 B.C.
Forty four (44) important people came from the main Five Race
nations to plan how to destroy these animals.
Cayce describes these important ones as "MEN" and not "Thought
Forms."

> And the gathering of those that heeded, as would be
> the scientific Minds of the present day, in devising
> ways and means of doing away with that particular
> kind or class of menace.
> (262-39)

> The entity was among those who were of that group
> who gathered to rid the Earth of the enormous animals
> which overran the Earth, but ICE, the entity found,
> nature, God, changed the poles and the animals were

destroyed, though man attempted it in that activity of the meetings.
(5249-1)

...or MEN, then - began to cope with those of the beast form that OVERRAN the Earth in many places.
(364-4)

This was the first time that explosives, the "death ray", and atomic energy were used for destructive purposes.

...the ways and means devised were as those that would alter or change the ENVIRONS for which those beasts were needed...And this was administered much in the same way as there were sent out from various central plants...termed in the present the "death ray" or the super-cosmic ray...
(262-39)

...then began in that period when there were the invasions of this continent (Atlantis) by those of the animal Kingdoms that brought about the meeting of the nations of the globe to PREPARE a way and manner of disposing of (prehistoric animals) else they be disposed of themselves by these forces.
With this coming in, there came then the FIRST of the destructive forces as could be set and then be meted out in its force or Power. Hence that as is termed, or its first beginning of, EXPLOSIVES that might be carried about, came with this period when MEN began to cope with those of the beast form that OVERRAN the Earth in many places.
(364-4)

Man built machines of destruction that sailed through the air and under the water attempting to get rid of the beasts that threatened them but also caused the first destruction of Atlantis.

> ...when the entity builded those that made for the carrying of those machines of destruction that sailed both through the air and under the water...
> (1735-2)

> In Atlantis, just preceding the first breaking up of that land, when there was the use of the many influences that are again being discovered, that the sons of Belial turned into destructive forces those things that were intended for benefits of individuals; as the use of transportation and communication.
> (2560-1)

> ...in the Atlantean land, during those periods when there were the first of the rebellions that brought the misapplication of the knowledge; or the forces that might have been used constructively but were used in destructive activities. The entity then joined with the sons of Belial that brought about destructive forces in the attempts to destroy the animal Life that in other lands overran same.
> (1378-1)

> In the Atlantean land, during those periods of the FIRST destructions or separations of the land during the FIRST destruction...who aided in the preparation of the explosives, or those things that set in motion the FIRES of the inner portions of the Earth...
> (621-1)

The second period of disturbance in Atlantis was said to be caused by tuning of the Crystals too high which was around 28,000 B.C. This caused Atlantis to be broken up into islands.

Many people, from various places in the world migrated to Egypt when there were the warnings of the final destruction of Atlantis. The Atlanteans realized the coming dangers and also entered Egypt.

Poseidia was given as one of the first main cities of Atlantis that later became one of the last islands of Atlantis when it sunk. Poseidia was a very highly developed civilization throughout all periods which was far more technologically advanced than ours today.

> ...just before the breaking up of Poseidia (Atlantis), the entity controlled those activities where communications had been established with other lands, and the flying boats that moved through air or water... ...then joined in with those movements for the preparation of people for the regeneration of the bodies of the THINGS in that period.
> (3184-1)

The final sinking of the last three islands of Atlantis, which were Poseidia, Aryan and Og, happened during the time of Ra Ta in Egypt.

The last period of the destruction of Atlantis was caused from the warring between the Children of Belial and the Children of the Law of One. This was around 10,400 B.C. in the Ra Ta period.
All three destructions involved the selfish motives and actions of the sons of Belial.

> ...the entity was in the Atlantean land, during those periods when there were those activities that brought about the last destruction of same through the warrings between the Children of the Law of One and the sons of Belial.
> (1599-1)

...the entity was in the Atlantean experience when there was the breaking up of the land itself, through the use of SPIRITUAL truths for the material gains of physical Power.

(1152-1)

There was a Temple of Isis in Ancient Egypt that Ra Ta discovered (uncovered) that stood during the Noah flood.
It was upon this site that the Sphinx was built.

We see this Sphinx was builded as this: The excavations were made for same in the plains above where the Temple of Isis had stood during the DELUGE, occurring some centuries before, when this people (and this entity among them) came in from the north country, setting up the FIRST DYNASTY, also in the second dynasty of Araaraart when those buildings were begun.

(195-14)

It is not clear why there were so many "Mixtures" and people with animal entanglements like feathers in the Ra Ta period if most of them were wiped out earlier in the Noah flood.
Perhaps the "Mixtures" that were left were flesh and blood and not "Thought Forms" but the offspring of the "Thought Forms."
There are Readings that refer to one of the "Things" as PARTLY "Thought Form" which indicated it was a "Mixed" being and a "Thought Form" as well.

The purpose of the Adamic race was to provide a clean birth channel for ALL souls to enter.
The "Mixtures" would have a higher vibration of Body to help them become what they were created to be without all the animal influences and appendages to hinder soul development.
The "Mixtures" were referred to as the sons and daughters of men.

This is the Belial group which was inhabited by the souls in rebellion. They were NOT created in flesh by God but had created their own forms often by projecting their Spirits into animals.

The same two groups continued to function in Atlantis throughout all three destructions.

Cayce was said to have come into being or individual consciousness when the Earth was being created. There are Readings that indicate that the souls who had NOT fallen began to individualize at this time.

It is possible that Edgar Cayce could have been part of the original Projections of the Five Races which settled in Atlantis.

The Readings state that this is their first incarnation in flesh.

They could have had incarnations as "Thought Forms" during the time of Amilius but that is NOT given in the Readings, if it is true.

With their very next incarnation in the flesh, they separate into male and female bodies in the Egyptian period, during the FIRST of the Pharoahs. No date is given for this period.

Atlantis was one of the locations for the other Four Races and where the largest development of mankind was gathered.

Edgar Cayce and his Twin Soul were as One person or an androgynous soul incarnating in the female Body and as a ruler and guide for many people. Why does the Reading specify "female" if they were still joined in Spirit?

Evidently the two are as One but IN a female flesh Body together.

This soul of Edgar Cayce and Gladys Davis Turner were One Whole soul, not split apart, but living in a female Body and referred to as "THEM."

It is stated that together:

"The desire remained in the One, for which the Oneness was created."

> We find in the beginning that they, these two (which
> we shall speak of as "they" until separated), were as
> One in Mind, soul, Spirit, Body; and in the Earth's
> plane as the voice over many waters, when the glory
> of the Father's Giving of the Earth's indwelling of man
> was both male and female in One.
>
> In FLESH form in Earth's plane we find the FIRST
> in that of the Poseidian forces, when both were
> confined in the Body of the female; for this being the
> stronger in the then expressed or applied forces found
> manifestations for each in that form.
>
> ...These two were the Giving of the spiritual
> development in the land (Atlantis), and the Giving of
> the uplift to the peoples of the day and age.
>
> ...the desire remained in the One, for which Oneness
> was created.
>
> (288-6)

The names given were as Aczine and Asule.

Asule was the feminine and was Gladys Davis Turner, the secretary who recorded the Readings. (Her Reading # is 288.)

Edgar Cayce was within the female Body as the male aspect of their soul named Aczine. They were not as yet cosmically severed into two beings but functioned as one person in the female Body. The female Body enabled a stronger and more pure expression of their complete Spirit at that time.

We do not know what year this was but if it were their FIRST incarnation in FLESH, it would seem it may have been as one of the Five Race Projections or during the period of the Adamic race entrance. The red race began in Atlantis.

The time frame for this Root Race in Adam is not clear but some Cayce writers say it was during the second disturbance in Atlantis which was 28,000 years before the entrance of Jesus as the Christ. This would make the Noah date of the flood of 22,006 B.C. more accurate but still does NOT fit.

Other writers claim the date of the Adamic Races is only about 12,000 B.C. This is not correct!

The reason the above date is disputed is because the meeting of the Great Congress, in which an all-world broadcast was sent out to help rid the Earth of the enormous prehistoric animals roaming the Earth. This was in 50,722 B.C.

which was after Adam was in the Earth. The Adamic period had to be before 50,722 B.C.

We know the Noah flood happened centuries after Adam's entrance. There were three disturbances in Atlantis and all could have caused floods. Each destruction could have been a series of disturbances lasting many years before completion.

I have found Readings that state that the flood of Noah was BEFORE the Ra Ta period in ancient Egypt of 10,500 B.C.

> ... the entity was in Atlantis when there was the SECOND period of disturbance – which would be some twenty two thousand, five hundred (22,500) before the periods of the Egyptian activity covered by the Exodus; or it was some twenty-eight thousand (28,000 years) before Christ, see?
> (470-22)

Excavations of old tombs were found to be from the period of the flood of Noah DURING Ra Ta's time.

In the first androgynous Lifetime of Gladys Davis and Edgar Cayce, (in the same Body of the female in a flesh form), they ruled giving the spiritual development to uplift the people of that land in Atlantis.

> In that fair country of Alta, or Poseidia, when this entity was in that FORCE that brought the highest civilization and knowledge that has been known to the Earth's plane...
> (288-1)

What does it mean that the entity was in that FORCE that brought the highest to mankind?

This same entity (Gladys) asked if she knew Amilius in Atlantis and was told that she and Edgar Cayce were PROJECTED by Amilius.

Amilius, who projected into the new Root Race in the flesh and blood Adamic bodies, was a group soul FORCE of Light that was the Christ Spirit in the early world. These souls were the individual selves or companions in/of the Christ in Spirit.

In this incarnation Asule and Aczine were envied because of their androgynous state of being. Yet to them, it brought the need to separate in order to give of self to the other which happened in their next incarnation. (Egypt/first period.)

It is stated that Edgar Cayce and Gladys were among the FIRST to inhabit the Earth in the new flesh and blood Adamic form in that Atlantean incarnation.

> ...in the first, when the forces in flesh came to dwell in the Earth's plane. The entity was among the first to inhabit the Earth in that form, and was from that of the beginning in Earth's plane, when referred to as the human form dwelling in the Earth's forces. In this we find the larger development in the entity, for then (the soul was) able to contain in the Oneness of the forces as given in the sons of men, and realizing the Fatherhood of the Creator.
> (294-19)

In their beginning Edgar Cayce and Gladys Davis were able to be sons of mankind in a flesh form yet maintain their Oneness with God and still remember and have their relationship with the Creator. They kept their companionship with God. However, just like Adam and Eve, they were enticed into having a sexual relationship with one of the "Mixtures" which resulted in a comatose condition.

Remember that the "Mixtures" and the "Things" were the offspring of the subhuman beings who had animal characteristics. Many of these beings were the result of generations of genetic experiments by the Atlanteans.

> The desire came for the bodily connection of coition with one of lower estate, and through this TREACHERY of one not capable of understanding it brought physical defects in the limbs of these then contained in the One Body in physical form.
> Hence in COMA, and KARMA exercised in coma, there was brought the separation, as given in the injunction from the Maker: "I have this day set before you Good and Evil. Choose the Light or the darkness."
> With this desire of self's aggrandizement there was brought separation (into male and female bodies) in the next plane.
> (288-6)

Evidently the Adam and Eve pattern of disobedience was experienced by all of the Five Races. Separation in the next plane could mean in the spiritual forces of the planetary realms and not an incarnation in flesh.

The Readings state that they separated into male and female in Spirit and in their next incarnation appeared in separate bodies yet bound together in their affections.

This incarnation was during the Egyptian rule of the first Pharoahs. There we find them again as the Priest and Lawgiver, though separated now as male and then again as female. A date of 12,800 B.C. is given in this Reading but it is unlikely that it is for this appearance. We know it is not the Ra Ta period as that was later. Also it mentions sexual desires between the two developing and counted for righteousness. There again, a sexual relationship cannot have existed between the two entities in the Ra Ta era as the Gladys soul was Ra Ta's daughter separated from him at birth and kept in Egypt when Ra Ta was in exile. The child died at 4 years old.

A Reading is given stating that Cayce was Asapha during an Egyptian period when the forty four persons were called from all the nations of the Earth to get rid of the enormous animals.

This would have been 50,722 B.C. I think this is the incarnation of the first Pharoahs mentioned.

During the Ra Ta period in ancient Egypt (10,500 B.C.), there were many "Mixtures" being operated on to remove an extra gland that they had which the Adamic humans did not have in the leg or thigh which still exists in some animals today.

> Thus in the experience for the first time there was found the eradication of that indicated in the flesh of the animal, in the lower or hind limbs or legs, that does not exist in the human being.
> (1223-6)

It took surgery and several generations to transform a "Mixture" with animal parts into a totally human form which resulted in an offspring later.

Getting rid of the appendages (feathers, hair, tails, claws, paws, etc.) did not happen in one Lifetime although much help was given and changes begun.

The Cayce Readings tell us that the records of the "Mixtures" are now only found in legendary tales.

Greek mythology is filled with myths of Gods and Goddesses and many "Mixtures" who may have been from Atlantis.

> ...the entity was in that land known as the Atlantean, during those periods when there were the questions arising much as may be termed in the land today, in a local section, as the acknowledgement of the castes in

> a land where the untouchables are considered as but
> DOGS among the higher castes.
> The entity was in that position then of attempting to
> gain for the untouchables an approach for their own
> self-development during that period.
>   (333-2)

Ra Ta was another incarnation of Edgar Cayce given in the Earth.
The Readings usually ONLY gave the incarnations bearing on the
current Lifetime and they are NOT all given in order of appearance
but at different periods when the time is right or the person is ready
to absorb the information.
There are Readings that mention an incarnation of Cayce during
the time of the meeting of the Five Nations (50,722 B.C.) in which
the Master Jesus also has an incarnation or influence. It seems clearly
indicated that Cayce was Asapha.

> Or, as in those days as Asapha, indicating that Joseph
> and Asaph were one and the same...
>   (364-8)

> We find that the entity Uhjltd was an incarnation of
> Asapha...
>   (294-142)

A list of incarnations is upcoming in Chapter VIII for the Master
soul of Jesus, when He has walked and talked with men. The name
of AFFA is given as being in those periods when the counsels of the
many nations sought to save the world from the wild beasts taking
over. Juliet Brook Ballard says this is an incarnation of Jesus. I agree
with her.

The Cayce & Gladys incarnations are difficult to discern as it appears
that several are lumped into one paragraph. This is how I interpret it
but feel free to disagree. These are only the early incarnations:

Aczine and Asule in Atlantis in the beginning as rulers in the first flesh form Adamic bodies (androgynous).

Asapha of Egypt; the meetings of Five Nations (again as the Priest and Law Giver). During the first Pharoahs. (50,722 B.C.)

In 12,500 B.C., we find them together, the sex desire between the two for developing, counted as righteousness in both, one in the Priest craft, the female brought destruction early and in a few years the other (died).

Ra Ta in Egypt 10,500 B.C. -
Gladys was the daughter of Ra Ta who lived only four and a half years.

The son of a daughter of Zu, Ra Ta was said to be not begotten. He was an Immaculate Conception.

> The entity chose rather the peoples that were to enter in the land, and was the son of a daughter of Zu...that was not begotten of man.
> (294-147)

This unusual birth and the white skinned son who had a prophetic anointing made the mother unpopular among her tribe. He was called Ra Ta due to his hair which was golden like the sun and because of his white skin.
They left the tribe of Zu and joined with the people of Ararat and were treated well, especially Ra Ta who was recognized as a Prophet.
Ra Ta was instructed by God to lead the King, his household and son, and 900 people to Egypt which would be the center of the world when Atlantis sunk.

Ra Ta became the High Priest or spiritual authority in Ancient Egypt. The King's young son (age 16) became the King, named Araaraat.

In Egypt there was still the one language spoken; whereas, only in Atlantis were the divisions of tongues into the various languages.

> ...for the understandings were of one tongue!
> There had not been as yet the divisions of tongues in this particular land. This was yet only in the Atlantean or Poseidian land.
> (294-148)

Ra Ta taught the Law of One and established families in private homes where as before there was a group separation of the sexes and mating was chosen for the benefit of the race by the King. The offspring was taken from the mother at three months of age to be raised by those so trained. This was an effort to prevent the reproduction of any more "Mixtures."
Most of the native Egyptians had feathers.

> These...were exhibited as feathers on the limbs of the native Egyptians...
> (585-12)

There were NO merchants as one common storehouse was for all. The land was prosperous and all people benefited.
There was no poverty and no competition among the people.
Competition did exist among some of the rulers and the various Priests.

Ra Ta also established two temples: The Temple Beautiful and the Temple of Sacrifice.
Ra Ta sought to speed up evolution of lower caste beings like the "Mixtures" and also the "Things" as well as the local natives who were uneducated.
The Temple of Sacrifice was like a hospital.
Its objective was to purge the mental and physical Body of carnal influences and help the individual to make contact with the God force of Light within.

It required a great deal of self-sacrifice to be cleansed of the animal instincts and entanglements.

Those who were purified were next sent to the Temple Beautiful for vocational and spiritual training.

Bodies without blemishes from the animal Kingdoms were highly valued.

The Temple Beautiful trained people to manifest the Light of Truth in their lives for the benefit of mankind.

The Priest was able to lead individuals into the "Holy of Holies."

> ...the Priest who gave the entrance into the Holy of Holies to the King and then gave the rule to the people...
> (341-9)

The religious teaching of this period became the foundation of the teachings of Jesus Christ thousands of years later.

In the Temple Beautiful, people were trained in vocations of service, such as in art, science, music, dietary rules and cooking, medicine, or as a Priest or Priestess. These vocations always were intended to be constructive and purposeful and to manifest the nature of God.

The tenants of the Law of One were:

> As ye would have another be, that be yourself.
> Do not ask another to do that ye would not do yourself.
> Make concessions only to the weak.
> Defy the strong if they are in the wrong.
> (1336-1)

While Ra Ta was setting up these higher standards there were those other Priests who taught animal worship who came in from the Arabian land. The sons of Belial crept in from Atlantis before it sank and attempted to continue with their self indulgences.

While Ra Ta was away, some of these lower concepts sneaked into the temples he had set up.

Ra Ta and his associates continually traveled to many countries and back and forth to Poseidia and Og before they sank.

> The entity made many trips to and from Egypt to Poseidia, where the activities...had brought a high order of civilization...
> (423-3)

These Priests were able to cause Ra Ta to be banished for a time of nine years. The cause of his banishment was that he was tricked into breaking his own Law of having only one mate or wife.

There was a beautiful dancer who was the favorite of the King. She was perfect in Body and since Ra Ta was trying to perfect the all white, perfect Body, it was suggested that he mate with her to help lift up the race by creating another perfect human form.

Since one of the Five Races in the beginning was the white race, it is not clear why there were no other white people at this time, except for Ra Ta and a few others. Some speculate that the races mingled by intermarrying and the white race was lost.

There is a Reading which describes different areas of the Earth that were overrun with the beasts.

At that time (50,722 B.C.), Egypt was relatively less disturbed than the rest of Earth by the beasts but mentions those in Caucasia were disturbed and mentions them as the lighter or whiter peoples.

> ...the indwelling of those many beasts whom man had to defend self against. Also those in Caucasia, or the lighter or whiter peoples.
> (5748-3)

Ra Ta was experimenting in changing skin color to reintroduce the white race.

It was stated that the Devil knows the weakness men have for woman. Then, men get laughed at for this fault!

> ...and there were sought various ways and manners in which there might be fault found...saying, "When the Devil can't get a man any other way, he sends a woman for him."...divisions arose even unknown to Ra Ta, for he trusted all - as it were - for the time the Gods laughed at his weakness!
> (294-148)

Ra Ta was very trusting and believed the plan was Good, not realizing it was a trap. The King was upset as this dancer was his favorite, not only because of her beauty, but inwardly he sensed that she was his Twin Soul. (According to the Readings, the young King was correct. The King was an incarnation of Cayce's son, Hugh Lynn.)

The offspring from that union of Ra Ta and Isis was an incarnation of Gladys Davis Turner. A fair skinned, blonde haired child with blue eyes who only lived to age four and a half, she was held in captivity and wasted away while the Priest was banished.
Ra Ta and the group with him thrived well in banishment as well as the natives in the area and great things were accomplished.

> With the entering into the Nubian land, there came such a change that there were the bettered conditions in every term that may be applied to human experience; ...as the Priest in this period entered more and more into the closer relationships with the creative forces, greater were the abilities for the entity or the Body (of) Ra Ta to be able to make or bring about the MATERIAL manifestations of that relationship.
> Hence, the Peace that was enjoyed by the peoples, not only with the Priest but (with) all those of that land.
> (294-150)

Upon the end of his banishment, the Priest returned to Egypt. He was called Ra; his wife, Isis. The name of the capital city Luz (Light) was changed to Bethel, which means, "Silence is golden if you are in the presence of God."

> And in that land did the entity then make for that indeed as Bethel means, "Silence is golden, if thou art in the presence of God!"
> (991-1)

Ra was over a hundred years old and went through a period of regeneration to restore his health and youth.

Ajax from Atlantis, Saneid from India, Yak from Carpathia, and Tao from Mongolia or the Gobi land were among the many prominent spiritual leaders from all the various countries of the known world deeply influenced by the advanced teachings of Ra from his relationship and Oneness with God.

> ...the entity became one who carried to those of many lands the correlating influence from those teachers; as Ra Ta in Egypt, Ajax the teacher from Atlantis, Saneid from India, Yak from Carpathia, Tao from Mongolia.
> The teachings of these were combined....
> (991-1)

(The Tao philosophy was not recorded for many centuries, but evidently it existed during this period.)

There are Readings for people who were able to change to white skin.

> Five feet four inches in height. Bronze when beginning in the service, the pure white when cleansed, in color.
> (275-38)

> For the entity was among those who had the ability
> to change the color, change the activities, through the
> vibrations of stone as well as the odors, as were about
> the Body.
> (1616-1)

Ra Ta attempted to speed evolution of the Body by over emphasizing
the perfect Body with a standard of white skin and blue eyes which
was not necessarily God's will.
He was also able to regenerate his own Body by reversing the aging
process which was also not in keeping with the Whole Law.
Many people were changed physically but had not changed within
to match their outer appearance.

> For, the Priest had not interpreted in himself that
> even that being attempted was a matter of spiritual
> evolution. Thus, as many an individual, the Priest had
> attempted to HURRY the process, or to placate God's
> purposes with individuals.
> In this the Priest had also regenerated self, as to turn
> back time – as it were – in his own Body.
> This too, as will be seen in part, was not in keeping
> with the Whole Law of spiritual evolution.
> (2390-7)

Ra Ta did much to solidify the present Fourth Root Race which was
in the stages of confusion as it got mixed up with animal influences.
He was divinely inspired and instructed as to how to separate the
human and soul forces from those of the animal.
Ra Ta was used by God to reintroduce the present WHITE race
into being as it was almost extinct at that time.

> Let's remember that it is in this period when the
> PRESENT RACE has been called into being – and
> the INFLUENCE is reckoned from all experiences of

Ra Ta, as the effect upon the Body physical, the Body mental, the Body spiritual, or soul Body…
(294-150)

After his banishment when he returned to Egypt, Ra Ta with Hermes as the architect, built the Great Pyramid. This took one hundred years.
(Hermes was indicated as an incarnation of the Master, Jesus.)
The Great Pyramid was intended as a Temple of Initiation into Truth and Light which was called the "Temple of Understanding."
It is an astronomical observatory built with precise solar measurements and contains a sacred record of all the events of mankind up to the Second Coming of Christ and the Fifth Root Race.

All changes that came in the religious thought in the world are shown there, in the variations in which the passage through same is reached, from the base to the top – or to the open tomb AND the top. These are signified by both the layer and the color in what direction the turn is made.
(5748-5)

…the records of the manners of construction of same are in three places in the Earth, as it stands today: In the sunken portions of Atlantis, or Poseidia, where a portion of the temples may yet be discovered, under the slime of ages of sea water - near what is known as Bimini, off the coast of Florida. And (secondly), in the temple records that were in Egypt, where the entity later acted in cooperation with others in preserving the records that came from the land where these had been kept. Also (thirdly) the records that were carried to what is now Yucatan in America, where these stones (that they know so little about) are now – during the last few months - being uncovered.
(440-5)

The Sphinx which is called the "Mystery of the Ages" is a symbol of the mixture of man and beast that existed at one time. This mixture was being cleansed and purged in the temples of Ra Ta.

Much of the animal instincts and entanglements had already been purified in Atlantis but not in Egypt until Ra Ta.

The Atlanteans also brought many "Things" as workers with them when they relocated in Egypt that Ra Ta wanted to uplift in consciousness.

Most of the "Thought Forms" had been wiped out in Noah's flood.

The Styx, mermaid, satyr, centaur and half human and animal beings who had set themselves up as Gods were now gone.

But their offspring were beings with animal parts.

Most of the native Egyptians had feathers on their legs but otherwise were souls with human bodies.

The Sphinx was founded upon ruins discovered by Ra Ta during archaeological research where there had been a monument in earlier times before the deluge or flood of Noah.

Cayce said those mounds were left by the beginning people most of which had tails. This Reading is often misinterpreted and thought to be during the time of Ra but it means BEFORE as it is about the ancient mounds Ra found of an earlier civilization in Egypt.

> The beginnings of these mounds which were as an interpretation of that which was crustating in the land (See, most of the people had tails then!)
> In those BEGINNINGS these were left.
> When there was the entrance of Arart and Araaraart, they began to build upon THOSE MOUNDS which were discovered through research.
> (5748-6)

Ra Ta had been in ancient Egypt in an earlier Lifetime as Asapha and had past Life recalls of where many of the earlier temples were buried.

The Sphinx has the face of the chief counselor of the King who was named Asriaio. The Sphinx is set as a guard over the undiscovered Temple containing the Hall of Records of mankind.

> He arranged then for the first monuments that were being restored and builded in those places, being then the founder of now that "Mystery of Mysteries," the Sphinx.
> (195-14)

The Sphinx reminds us of the time when the sons of God made man a BEAST as part of his consciousness and it manifested in the flesh as the "Mixtures."

> The entity aided in those activities, being among the Children of the Law of One from Atlantis; AIDING the Priest in that preparation, in that manner of building the Temples of Records that lie just beyond that enigma (Sphinx) that still is the "Mystery of Mysteries" to those who seek to know what were the manners of thought of the ancient sons who made man - a beast - as a part of the consciousness.
> (2402-2)

There is another pyramid, called the Tomb, that was sealed and not as yet uncovered or discovered that is said to be between the Sphinx and the "Pyramid of Records."

> ...and for the preservation of the data, that is yet to be found from the chambers of the way between the Sphinx and the Pyramid of Records."
> (1486-1)

There is said to be an entrance chamber to the Hall of Records from the right paw of the Sphinx.

...there is a chamber or passage from the right forepaw to this entrance of the Record Chamber or Record Tomb.
(5748-6)

The Readings stress the fact that these hidden records of the past will not be opened until the time is right and the consciousness of those in the Earth have higher spiritual motivations.

> As for the physical records, it will be necessary to wait until the full time has come for the breaking up of much that has been in the nature of selfish motives in the world.
> (2329-3)

> This may not be entered without an understanding, for those that were left as guards may NOT be passed until after a period of their regeneration in the Mount, or the Fifth Root Race begins.
> (5748-6)

It was during this period that the Library of Alexandria was founded.

> And, as will be seen from those that may yet be found about Alexandria, the entity may be said to have been the first to begin the establishment of the Library of Knowledge in Alexandria; ten thousand three hundred (years) before the Prince of Peace entered Egypt for His first initiation there. For read ye, "He was crucified also in Egypt."
> (315-4)

> Q: Please describe Jesus' education in Egypt in Essene schools of Alexandria and Heliopolis, naming some of His outstanding teachers and subjects studied.

> A: Not in Alexandria – rather in Heliopolis, for the period of attaining to the Priesthood, or the taking of the examinations there – as did John. One was in one class, one in the other.
>
> (2067-7)

When the Great Pyramid was completed, Ra Ta felt that his mission in Egypt had come to an end.

The Readings state that he "ascended into the Mount and was borne away." Could this mean translated into the spiritual realms as not to experience death? Or that he was consciously able to exit the physical Body and enter into the Spirit? It states that Ra Ta ascended INTO the Mount. This may indicate that he ascended within the self to the Christ Mount or Light inside.

I have never heard this Reading explained, although everyone quotes it.

> ...and there came then that period when all the Pyramid or memorial was complete, that he, Ra, ascended into the Mount and was borne away.
>
> (294-152)

> But the entrance into the Ra Ta experience, when there was the journeying from materiality – or the being translated in materiality as Ra Ta - was from the infinity forces, or from the sun; with those influences that draw upon the planet itself, the Earth and all those about same.
>
> (5755-1)

It would seem that Ra Ta's exit from Earth was just as unusual as his entrance. Many nations were aided by Ra Ta as this Egyptian period was that time when the present Fourth Root Race was called into being.

The Readings state that the Ra Ta Egyptian time was...

>...as one of the most momentous occasions or periods
>in the world's history...
>(900-275)

There is a prophetic Reading which predicts the next Lifetime of
Edgar Cayce and his Twin Soul as liberators of the world coming
into material manifestation in 1998.

There are people claiming to channel Edgar Cayce and also to be a
reincarnation of him. The sure way to tell imposters is to determine
if they are Jesus Christ centered. Cayce is very closely knit in and
with the Christ soul and after such a Lifetime as Edgar Cayce, he
would surely be even more Christ centered in today's time.

Those making Cayce claims who do NOT have personal relationships
with Jesus are NOT Cayce.

>Is it not fitting, then, that these must return? As this
>Priest may develop himself to be in that position, to
>be in the capacity of a LIBERATOR of the world in its
>relationships to individuals in those periods to come;
>for he must enter again at that period, or in 1998.
>(294-151)

There are people involved with the Cayce work who have spent a
Lifetime studying the information about ancient Egypt and many
books have been written about that period based upon the Readings.
I have only touched upon some of the major points to provide a
glimpse into that era.

CHAPTER VIII

THE INCARNATIONS OF THE SOUL WHO BECAME JESUS, THE MASTER

...God, who gave self in the Son that man might approach that Throne in a Way that all may be One in Him, knowing self to be a portion of that Whole, yet individual in the Gift of the Creator that made each THEMSELVES, yet can make themselves a portion of the Whole.
(31-1)

...all Power is of a First Cause, but that Light which was the Light of the world from the beginning is crystallized in the entity known as Jesus of Nazareth, who passeth by today for thee, and unless ye take hold upon Him, ye must falter.
(5265-1)

For He is the beginning and the end of all things.
(5322-1)

Know there was not anything made that was made
that did not pass through Him.
(2441-4)

For He, thy God, thy Christ, is conscious of and hath
need of thee...
(5064-1)

He, the Son, was in the Earth-Earthy even as we- and
yet is of the Godhead.
(1567-2)

Consider, for the moment, that the Master was the
Creator, the Maker of all that was...
(1561-18)

We know that the Christ, who is the Only Begotten Son is the part
of the Godhead that manifests in Earth and in the Heavens.
All Life flows through Him.
We as Lights in Him are as His individual selves or souls.
Becoming an individual soul in Spirit is the pattern for us all,
therefore,
He was the first to demonstrate the Way as our pattern to follow.

It took thirty incarnations for the soul of Jesus to be able to express
perfect Oneness with God and demonstrate the divine nature of the
Christ Consciousness while in the Earth.

Here is the list given by Cayce of some of these incarnations:

AMILIUS: A spiritual being who was a soul expression of the Only
Begotten Son before the creation of Adam in flesh. ("The Lamb
that was slain before the foundation of the world.")

ADAM: The first physical form created by God for soul inhabitation.
The establishment of the Adamic race line.

ENOCH: A Prophet who warned of the flood and was translated (absorbed into his spiritual Body) so as not to experience physical death because He pleased God.

MELCHIZEDEK: A Priest of God who blessed Abraham and was the founder of an everlasting Priesthood, called the "White Brotherhood." Melchizedek had no mother or father and did not die, yet was a human being in flesh.

JOSEPH: Favored son of Jacob who was a dream interpreter. Sold into slavery by His brothers.

JOSHUA: Aide & "mouthpiece", a spiritual adviser to Moses. Committed all Laws of Moses to writing. Established the twelve tribes in the "promised land."

ASAPH: Psalmist & musician to David and Solomon.

JESHUA: High Priest who was a leader of the first return from Babylon to Jerusalem to rebuild the temple. A scribe who translated the rest of the Bible written up to that time.

Other incarnations:

MU: From Lemuria as sage and Prophet and ruler.

HERMES: Who designed and built the Great Pyramid.

ZEND: Who was the father of Zoroaster.

UR: Indicated as a prehistoric person and a city.
There is a Cayce Reading given for the Individual #870 who had been the son of a King of Persia. It is mentioned that under the ruins of the third city in UR may be found many of the records made by him.

Note by Gladys Davis Turner: "Perhaps Ur was a prehistoric person who established Ur of the Chaldees."

> Ur was rather a land, a place, a city – and the thought, or intent, or the call was from Ur. Ur, then, as represented in the experience of Jesus, as one that impelled or guided those thoughts in that period, or experience.
> (364-9)

Amilius was the first soul incarnation mentioned of the Master.

> In the beginning as Amilius, as Adam, as Melchizedek, as Zend, as Ur, as Enoch, as Asaph, as Jeshua, -Joseph-Jesus.
> (364-7)

In the beginning all souls who had not fallen existed in Amilius as a group or collective consciousness like wheels of Light within Him ("for in Him we live and move and have our being.")

> These (sons of God) were all together in Amilius.
> (288-29)

> For in Him we live, and move, and have our being; as certain also of your own poets have said, for we are also His offspring.
> Acts 17:28

We do not know how long Amilius ruled in the Earth but we know that the Christ Spirit has been involved in all creation since before the beginning.

There is a whole chapter on the Amilius period in Atlantis so there is no need to repeat it again. Amilius is the higher self or soul who became Adam.

Joan Clarke

It seems possible that the Amilius soul could have had other soul
involvements in the earlier times of Lemuria.
In every period of history the Christ Spirit has been an influence for
Good, presenting the Truth of the Oneness and Love of God.

> In all those periods that the basic principle was Oneness
> of the Father, He (the soul of Jesus) has walked with
> men.
> (364-8)

> ...the entity (Jesus) as an entity – influenced either
> directly or indirectly all those forms of philosophy or
> religious thought that taught God was One.
> (364-9)

There is a Reading about an entity that might have been an
incarnation of the Master in Lemuria. Mu, who was the father of
Muzuen was described as a sage, Prophet, Lawgiver and the ruler of
Lemuria.

> ...the son of Mu or Muzuen came in that experience.
> The land was among those in which there was the first
> appearance of those that were as separate entities or
> souls disentangling themselves from material or that
> we know as animal associations. For the Projections
> of these had come from those influences that were
> termed Lemure, or Lemurian, or the land of MU.
> This then we find as the period when there was the
> choice of THAT SOUL that became in its FINAL
> Earthly experience the Savior, the Son in the Earth
> indwellings, or of those as man sees or comprehends
> as the children of men.
> The land under those influences of MU became
> as what would be termed in the present as among
> or the highest state of advancement in material
> accomplishments for the benefit or conveniences for

man's indwelling, or the less combative influence of the elemental or of that man knows as nature – in the raw.

These activities then included those things known as colonies or groups that were gathered for a common purpose, and submitting themselves to an order as might be proclaimed by one of their own number.

Or MU, the ruler, the sage, the Prophet, the Lawgiver, was of this particular group.

(877-10)

I believe that this Reading indicates Mu as an incarnation of the same soul who became Jesus in His final incarnation.

This presents a possibility of two incarnations; before Adam, one as Amilius, and one as Mu.

The next incarnation was as Adam (Adamic line), the first form deemed worthy to incarnate in flesh which was made by God. The Readings state that Adam was the Spirit of Light.

After Adam, the Christ soul incarnates as Enoch.

There is a lot of mystery and mysticism surrounding Enoch.

Remember those forms which have been given.

First, He was created – brought into being from all that there was in the Earth, as (Adam) an encasement for the soul of an entity, a part of the Creator; knowing separation in death.

Then He was made manifest in birth through the union of channels growing out of that thought of the Creator made manifest, but so expressed, so manifested as Enoch as to merit the escaping of (physical) death – which had been the result as the Law of Disobedience.

Joan Clarke

> Again it (the soul who became Jesus) was manifested
> in Enoch, who oft sought to walk and talk with that
> divine influence...
> (2072-4)

> By faith Enoch was translated that He should not see
> death; and was not found, because God had translated
> Him; for before His translation He had this testimony,
> that He pleased God.
> Hebrews 11:5

> Thus all the days of Enoch were three hundred and
> sixty five years:
> And Enoch walked with God, and He was not; for
> God took Him.
> Genesis 5:23-24

Enoch was said in the Readings to have warned the people of the
deluge or flood of Noah.

> ...Enoch as he warned the people.
> (3054-4)

Enoch preserved the records of the Law of One before the flood.
Legends say that Enoch was taken into Heaven. While there he
became an Archangel who also became a Heavenly scribe. The Book
of Enoch is considered as a sacred text.
Enoch and Hermes are thought to be the same soul by some people.
However, Hermes lived after the flood, not before it.
Remember the Sphinx was built at the same time as the Great
Pyramid and temple ruins were uncovered there that were left over
from the deluge many centuries earlier.

> The excavations were made for same in the plains
> above where the temple of Isis had stood during the
> deluge, occurring some centuries before...
> (195-14)

Since Edgar Cayce does not confirm the legends of Enoch as Truth, I am not going to get into them.

Many popular metaphysical groups were said by the Readings to contain some Truth but from their own viewpoints and not necessarily true from the Christ viewpoint.

Hermes, the architect who designed and built the Great Pyramid with Ra Ta, was an incarnation of the soul who was Jesus.

> ...it would seem to be implied that Jesus had an incarnation in Egypt at the time of Ra-Ta under the name of Hermes.
> (281-10)

The Readings make references to Hermes being the Master but not a lot of detail is given.

They do mention what the "teacher of teachers" taught in Egypt.

Most Cayce writers accept Hermes as a valid incarnation of Jesus.

> Then, with Hermes and Ra...there began the building of that now called Gizeh...that was to be the Hall of Initiates of that sometimes referred to as the White Brotherhood.
> (5748-5)

> Q: What was the date of the actual beginning and ending of the construction of the Great Pyramid?
>
> A: Was one hundred years in construction. Begun and completed in the period of Araaraart's time, with Hermes and Ra.
>
> Q: What was the date B.C. of that period?
>
> A: 10,490 to 10,390 before the Prince (of Peace) entered into Egypt.
> (5748-6)

Melchizedek was a Priest of God Most High and also the King of Salem in ancient Jerusalem. This was a human incarnation without father or mother in the Earth during the period of Abraham.
This was one of the most spiritual incarnations of the Master.
This Lifetime was so perfect a manifestation that neither birth nor death was required.

This tells us clearly WHO this soul is, the Christ, the Only Begotten Son, the part of the Godhead that manifests.

> For as those experiences, (when) Jesus...came into the Earth, the FIRST that were of the sons of God to enter flesh, there the FIRST and ONLY begotten of God. Again, as names would say, Enoch walked with God, became aware of God in His movements – STILL that entity, that soul called Jesus – as Melchizedek, without father, without mother, came - STILL the soul of Jesus; the portion of God that manifests.
> (1158-5)

> ...the entity (Jesus) was that One who had manifested to Father Abraham as the Prince, the Priest of Salem, without father and without mother, without days or years but a living human being made manifest in the Earth from the desire of Father God to prepare an escape for man...
> (5023-2)

> Again there may be drawn to self a parallel from the realm of spiritual enlightenment of that entity known as Melchizedek, a Prince of Peace, One seeking ever to be able to bless those in their judgments who have sought to become channels for a helpful influence without any seeking for material gain, or mental or material glory; but magnifying the virtues, minimizing the faults in the experience of all...
> (2072-4)

The Readings state that the Lifetimes of Enoch and Melchizedek are "in the perfection."

> First (Adam), in the beginning, of course; and then as Enoch, Melchizedek in the perfection. Then in the Earth as Joseph, Joshua, Jeshua, Jesus.
> (5749-14)

We are not sure exactly what "in the perfection" means. We do know that they were in perfect accord with God's will and that they did not experience death.

I have pondered the meaning of "in the perfection" about Enoch and Melchizedek for many years.

"In the perfection" could mean functioning from the spiritual Mind or the super-conscious or soul self.

First of all, Adam died but Enoch and Melchizedek were translated into Heaven without dying. Their human bodies were able to be spiritualized into their Spirit forms. We know that flesh and blood cannot enter into the higher realms. Their flesh bodies were translated (absorbed) into their spiritual bodies.

Adam, Enoch and Melchizedek were functioning on a higher level of awareness which was from the super-conscious level of their being. They were able to walk and talk with God.

Melchizedek was a very Christ-like manifestation of that soul.

Melchizedek is responsible for two acts that became important religious rites. The payment of tithes is one as Abraham gave Melchizedek a tenth of everything. Additionally, Melchizedek brought out bread and wine to give thanks to God with the victorious Abraham. (Symbolic of the redemption of mankind through the blood and body of Jesus Christ. Today's communion is an example.)

Melchizedek is the founder of an everlasting Priesthood called the White Brotherhood.

Joan Clarke

> (Jesus) called of God a High
> Priest after the order of Melchizedek.
> Hebrews 5:10

Cayce said that the Book of Job was written by Melchizedek and that it was more symbolic than literal.

> For, as the sons of God came together to reason, as recorded by Job, WHO recorded same? The Son of Man! Melchizedek wrote Job!
> (262-55)

Another important fact to be noted that is unusual is that Edgar Cayce was one of the spiritual messengers (Angels) sent to warn Lot of the destruction of Sodom. This seems to be a supernatural manifestation, not physical.
There was a dream that Cayce had about fleeing the city of Sodom while it was raining fire and brimstone with a companion, and Lot, Lot's wife, and their two daughters. A Reading was given which confirmed the dream as a true experience.

> In this particular vision this is rather as an experience through which the Body passed with those at the period; for the Body then, the entity, was one that accompanied these bodies in this experience...
> (294-136)

The next incarnation of Jesus given is as Joseph, known to have the coat of many colors as well as prophetic dreams. He was the son of Rachel and Jacob.
Joseph was the first incarnation we know of in which the functioning was in the conscious Mind, which is of the physical human realm.
We lose our conscious Mind when we die as it is more of the Earth and of the individual Body of the present incarnation.
The Life of Joseph often parallels the Life of Jesus.

The Joseph incarnation was later in time than the Ra Ta ancient Egyptian era.

> Before that we find the entity was in the Egyptian land, during that period when there were sore distresses being brought about by the sins of the peoples, - and when Joseph was in the land.
>
> (2067-1)

A teenage Jewish girl was told in a Reading that she had been the daughter of the High Priest and was the wife of Joseph.

> ...the entity was in the land now known as Egypt, when there were those turmoils that arose with those activities just before the periods of the famines in the land.
>
> There the entity was the one whom Joseph chose as the companion, of all the peoples that were a part of his experience – the daughter of the High Priest of Heliopolis.
>
> Thus we find that the entity came under those tenets, those truths which were so much a part of her companion.
>
> In the experience the entity gained throughout; in the abilities to make adjustments for the peoples of various beliefs, various activities – that brought Peace and Harmony throughout the sojourn in that land.
>
> With the entrance of Joseph's father, the entity, Asenath – studied what had been a part of the customs of the early patriarchs – Isaac, Abraham – who had been those that brought such satisfaction, such an awareness.
>
> Hence, as has been indicated, the deep convictions of Spirit as may make alive in materiality are innate in this entity; and with deep meditation, these may be aroused to mental AND material activity in the entity's relationship to others – as a helpful influence to all.
>
> (2444-1)

There were other Readings given for people that were greatly influenced for Good from the association with Joseph in His Lifetime. It seems that wherever the Master soul is, the understanding of the Oneness of God is expanded among the people.

I will relate a couple of these Readings.

This is a Reading for a lady who was a lecturer and gives insight into the vision and the teachings of Joseph at that time.

> ...the entity was in the Egyptian land, in that period when there were the preparations for the peoples of another land entering – or the days when Pharoah of that period was aroused to activity by the voice of Joseph, the wanderer in that realm.
>
> There we find the entity was among the daughters of that Pharoah – in the name Kotapet.
>
> In the experience the entity gained much through not only the mental application of those tenets of that messenger who came to save, as it were, a people as well as Himself, but- as that entity was the messenger of the living God among those in a disturbed world - the entity caught that vision of the universal Love as might be exemplified in the relationships of a people, of a nation – and not as in self-indulgences or self-aggrandizement for the passing appetites, or for those things that made for the laudation or the enslavement of any that material blessings might be in the experience of a FEW.
>
> Hence we find again the entity giving of self in giving the expressions of MERCY and GRACE among a people disturbed by those activities which had been as of a RACE consciousness in that sojourn.
>
> In the present from the experiences in that sojourn, then, we find the great abilities in Giving in Word, in messages – that may be a part of the mental

consciousness of the many – those things that will
bring UNIVERSAL PEACE, UNIVERSAL LOVE
within the hearts and the realms of those who may
take heed by the mental experience of this entity.
(1837-1)

This is a Reading for a lady who was a Princess at the time of Joseph.
She became a worshipper of the One God through her association
with Joseph.
She was devoted to helping the lower caste or classes.
Later she had a Lifetime in the early Christian period.

...the entity was in the land now known as the
Egyptian, during those periods when there was
the understanding gained by the ministrations and
activities in the days when Joseph ruled in that land.
The entity then was among the Princesses of Egypt,
and of that King who made for the establishing of
that closer relationship to those who had chosen to
SERVE the living God, rather than to serve their
own selves.
For the entity was acquainted with and oft associated
with Joseph, the incarnation of HIM whom the entity
later served so well in Thessalonica!
There the entity gained through the experiences in
aiding who were of the low degree, or caste to become
acquainted with the forces and Powers that brought
the greater comprehension and activities of the people
in that sojourn.
Hence we will find in the present experience a lesson
in the Life of Joseph that is no where else gained in the
writings of the Old Testament.
Then the entity was in the name of Zerlva.
(1825-1)

Edgar Cayce taught in his Bible class that he believed that Joseph had a premonition about His descendants going into bondage which is why He requested that they take His Body with them after He died. Centuries after His death, the children of Israel still carried the Body of Joseph during the forty years in the wilderness.

> And the bones of Joseph, which the children of Israel
> brought up out of Egypt, buried they in Shechem...
> Joshua 24:32

The father of Joseph was Jacob who was later reincarnated as John the Beloved, Jesus's disciple. Benjamin, the younger brother of Joseph, returned as Saul who became the King of Israel.

> But it was a channel that EVENTUALLY brought
> the material made manifest in Saul, an incarnation of
> Benjamin.
> (281-48)

Another incarnation of the soul of Jesus was as Joshua.

> ...Joshua the Prophet, the mystic, the leader, the
> incarnation of the Prince of Peace.
> (362-1)

> For Joshua was the interpreter through whom the
> message was given to Israel.
> (3645-1)

> ...the patient Joshua, the One who followed closely in
> the Way that would give to the individual (who would
> study) the Life and interpretation of the Son of Man.
> These in the Earth activity were much alike (Joshua
> and Jesus) not as combative, as in the warrings, but in
> Spirit, and in purpose, in ideals, these were One.

Thus...may ye use the Son of Man, Jesus, the Master, as the ideal in the present, and find a new meaning – if there is the studying and the paralleling of the Life of Jesus and of Joshua.

(3409-1)

Joshua is also famous for the affirmation:

Choose you this day whom ye will serve;
...but as for me and my house, we will serve the Lord.

Joshua 24:15

Joshua was responsible for the miracle of the walls, in the city of Jericho, which came tumbling down. Joshua defied physical Laws by commanding the sun and moon to stand still.

And there was no day like that before or after it, that the Lord hearkened unto the voice of a man...

Joshua 10:14

A young girl was given a Reading which stated that she was the betrothed of Joshua but died young. Joshua did marry, as a comment was made briefly in a physical Reading for someone who had been His wife.

...the entity was in the Egyptian land when there were the activities in the preparations for the exit from Egypt to the favored land, the people through whom was chosen the hope of the world.

The entity was then the close friend of Joshua.

Yes, one of those to whom Joshua was engaged, as would be called in the present, and of the daughters of Levi, not the same as Moses and Aaron but rather of Korah.

There we find the entity beautiful, lovely, beloved of Joshua and yet weak in Body, because of conditions under which the entity had in a portion of its experience

labored, and thus weak-lunged, passing away during
the period of the journey to the Holy Land.

But to have been beloved by Joshua was sufficient to
have builded, into the personality, that individuality
of the entity, that which still makes the entity beloved
of all who know the entity best, loved by all its
companions, its associates, just as in those experiences
with the great leader who was to carry the Children of
Promise into the Holy Land.

The name then was Abigal.

(5241-1)

In the mental and spiritual Body, keep in self the
ideals that were set by self in much of its association
through the various periods in the Earth; as was seen,
especially as the wife of Joshua -as a close association
with the Master:

"Let others do as they will or may, but as for ME and
my house we will serve a living God."

(573-1)

One of the Lifetimes of the Master soul was Asaph. Gladys Davis
Turner notes that, according to Psalm 81:5, Asaph and Joseph were
the same soul.

This He ordained in Joseph for a testimony, when He
went out through the land of Egypt: Where I heard a
language that I understood not.

Psalm 81:5 (A Psalm of Asaph)

Asaph was the psalmist, and chief musician in the courts of David
and Solomon. He also acts in the capacity of one of the Priests who
ministers before the Ark.

One of the duties of Asaph was prophecy as He was a seer to the
King.

> ...and Asaph, and Heman, and Jeduthun,
> the King's seer...
> 2 Chronicles 35:15

He is said to be the author of some of the Psalms.
Cayce did not mention much about Asaph.
The Christ soul is involved with recording the Bible throughout history either directly or indirectly.

Jeshua is another incarnation of the Master but about whom there is very little information.
Jeshua was a scribe who translated the rest of the Bible written up to that time. He was also a High Priest who was a leader of the first return from Babylon to Jerusalem to rebuild the temple.

> First find thyself. Apply thyself in such a Way and manner as to know what ye will do with this man, Jesus of Nazareth, Jeshua of Jerusalem, Joshua in Shiloh....
> (3054-4)

Zend was the father of the first Zoroaster.
This is an interesting Lifetime to note as this Zend was the son of Gladys Davis and Edgar Cayce during their incarnation in the "City of the Hills and Plains" in Persia or the Arabian lands which was (according to Davis) about 8058 B.C.

Cayce was named Uhjltd. (Pronounced Yew-ult).
There are several Readings for individuals who were healed by Uhjltd.
"The Brotherhood of Man and the Fatherhood of the ONE God" was the teaching instituted by Uhjltd.

Gladys Davis Turner was named Ilya. She was the niece of the King.
This was during the period of first and second Croesus.

> The entity (Ixelte) then was among the keepers of the treasury during the first and second Croesus; for this was among the EARLY experiences, being some seven to ten thousand years B.C.
> (962-1)

The City of the Hills and Plains established by Uhjltd was first a small stopping place for caravans but it became an oasis.

It was a peaceful center for those tribes who were continually at war and sought freedom. The mysteries of Egypt and India were available there for those with spiritual depth and many forms of healing were used for the sick.

Diet, farming and cleanliness were considered important factors in health.

This city became a place of refuge for those seeking spiritual development and Peace.

The City of the Hills and Plains was said to have been in a place now known as Shustar, Persia, or Arabia. (See 956-1)

Zend, who was a mystic and a Prophet, is said to have developed an elaborate system of religious thought which is embodied in what later became the Zend-Avista.

> There is the One approach to the Father through the Son, who manifested in the Earth through the activities which were later, in the son of Uhjltd (Zend) the manifestations of that which eventually became the consciousness in the Nazarene.
> (2982-4)

> Zan (Zend) not in the Earth's plane in the present. Came again as those that were the Sons of Man, and the Savior of the World.
> (538-32)

Zoroaster, the son of Zend, was a Prophet who reformed the religion of the Iranians. Zoroaster is the Greek spelling of the Iranian Zarathushtra. History gives the much later dates of late 7th and 6th centuries B.C. However, Cayce gave the date of Zend's father, Uhijltd, who was the grandfather of Zoroaster as 7,000 to 10,000 B.C.

So many dates seem confusing with a difference of several thousand years in a time frame due to the changes in the way we measure and have measured time throughout history. It is unclear as to which method is being used here.

There were many different leaders who may have used the Zoroaster name, as during the centuries, religious beliefs spread which may account for some of the time differences.

> Q: Are the Truths given by San (Zend) to the people included in the Zend-Avesta?

> A: They were these!
> (288-29)

According to Cayce the forerunners of Zoroaster taught the Oneness of God and the Brotherhood of man. God was the One universal force in all Life that created all that is Good and constructive.

All that is false and destructive is the result of the evil, called the lie. We must daily choose between the Truth and the lie which is the universal struggle that has been going on since before Earth was created. Good will eventually win over evil but it is man's responsibility to choose.

Many of the tenets and rituals passed down through this religion are similar to pre-Christianity.

Their prophesies included the coming of a Messiah, who would be born of a virgin with visitation from the Magi. The Magi would predict His birth by astrological and numerological means.

Cayce indicated that the Magi who arrived in Bethlehem came because of such predictions and that they were familiar with Zoroastrian.

> For the entity was the keeper of the Records for what became the Zoroastrian religious purposes...the entity should use those religious experiences as comparative experiences in the present – but know that these also came from that same One who gave, "I am the Way, the Truth and the Light."
> (3685-1)

> Q: In the Persian experience as San or Zend, did Jesus give the basic teachings that became Zoroastrianism?

> A: In all those periods that the basic principle was the Oneness of the Father, He has walked with men.
> (364-8)

I would highly recommend Robert Krajenke's books, one of which is Edgar Cayce's Story Of The Old Testament for detailed information from the Readings on those who lived during Biblical times.
Paula FitzGerald taught that the incarnations of Jesus in the Bible were: Adam, Enoch, Melchezedek, Joseph, Joshua, Jeshua, Asaph, and Jesus. She also taught that His incarnations found in the Sacred Books Of World Religion are: Brahma in Brahmaism, Tao, as in Taosim, and Zend as the father to Zoroaster in Zoroasterism.

> For the Master, Jesus, even the Christ, is the pattern for every man in the Earth, whether he be Gentile or Jew, Parthenian or Greek. For all have the pattern, whether they call on that name of not; but there is no other name under Heaven whereby men may be saved from themselves.
> (3528-1)

CHAPTER IX

THE LIFETIME OF JESUS

For, did the Master Jesus come by chance? Or was it not according to the preparation made from the very foundations of the world?

...without Him there was not anything made that was made.

(3645-1)

For what is the pattern? He gave up Heaven and entered physical being that ye might have access to the Father.

(5081-8)

...that JESUS, the MAN WAS the Son, WAS the Savior, IS the manifestation of the God-Consciousness in materiality!

(1527-1)

...all Power is of a First Cause, but that Light which was the Light of the world from the beginning is CRYSTALIZED in the ENTITY known as JESUS of Nazareth.

(5265-1)

>...reaching the FINAL cross with ALL Power, ALL knowledge, in having overcome the world – and of Himself ACCEPTED the cross. Hence doing away with that often termed Karma (ours) that must be met by all.
>
> (262-36)

> For He, the Maker, the Creator, came into a Body, flesh and blood, that it might be shown man – yea, might be shown the entity – as to what ideal manner to meet every experience.
>
> (1440-2)

The Lifetime of Jesus is familiar to most people; therefore, I am not going to repeat it all but instead present some aspects of His Life only found in the Readings.

We know that the Only Begotten Son knew that He must be the Savior of the world when He fell in Eden as Adam.
He had thirty Lifetimes in which He had completed His own personal Karma and was perfected in all the planetary realms before entering as Jesus.

> When the soul (Jesus) reached that development in which it reached Earth's plane, it became in the flesh the model, as it had reached through the developments in those spheres, or planets, known in Earth's plane, obtaining then One in all.
> As in Mercury pertaining of Mind.
> In Mars of madness.
> In Earth as of flesh.
> In Venus as Love.
> In Jupiter as strength.
> In Saturn as the beginning of Earthly woes, that to which all insufficient matter is cast for the beginning.
> In that of Uranus as of the psychic.

In that of Neptune as of mystic.
In Septimus (Pluto) as of consciousness.
In Arcturus as of the developing.
In this man called Jesus we find a Oneness with the Father, the Creator, passing through all the various stages of development. In mental perfect, in wrath perfect, in flesh made perfect, in Love become perfect, in death become perfect, in psychic become perfect, in mystic become perfect, in consciousness become perfect, in the greater ruling forces becoming perfect, and is as the model, and through the compliance with such Laws made perfect, destiny, the pre-destined, the fore-thought, the will, made perfect. The condition made perfect, and is an example for man, and only as a man, for He lived only as man. He died as man.
(900-10)

We know that the original mission of the soul of Amilius was to provide a Way for mankind to return to God.
After reaching His own perfection in God again, He was ready to enter in again to become the Way for mankind.

Q: Should Jesus be described as the soul who first went through the cycle of Earthly lives to attain perfection, including perfection in the planetary lives also?

A: He should be. This is as the man, see?

Q: Should this be described as a voluntary mission of One who was already perfected and returned to God, having accomplished His Oneness in other planes and systems?

A: Correct.
(5749-14)

> In the illustration of this, we find in the man as called
> Jesus. This man, as MAN, makes the will the will of
> the Father, then becoming One with the Father and
> the model for man.
>
> (900-10)

In only one incarnation since Adam did the soul who became Jesus
come without going through the birth channel of a woman and that
was Melchizedek (Adam was not born of a woman but created by
God.)

The doorway for souls to enter into the Earth is through a woman,
a mother.

Not just any woman would have a high enough vibration to build
the Body suitable for that pure, sacred soul who came from the
Throne of God to express the nature of God through that Body as
a pattern and Savior for all of mankind.

A lovely virgin girl named Mary was the chosen vessel.

The Readings tell us that Mary, Joseph, and John the Baptist were
all members of a strict religious sect called the Essenes.

The Essenes prepared the Way for the birth of the Messiah. Essene
means "expectancy" as they were preparing for and expecting
the Messiah. The Essenes were involved with the "School of the
Prophets" established by Elijah. They studied astrology, astronomy,
numerology, reincarnation, and ancient prophetic manuscripts.
They lived strict lives filled with prayer and self discipline and were
on special diets.

They were persecuted by the Sadducees who did not believe in
reincarnation or the immortality of the soul.

Cayce predicted that the writings of this sect would be discovered
near the Dead Sea. His prediction proved correct; the Dead Sea
Scrolls written by the Essenes were found in 1947.

They were a Jewish group who took in gentiles as well.

Women were considered as equals with men.

Hence there was the continued preparation and dedication of those who might be the channels through which this chosen vessel might enter – through choice – into materiality.

Among them was Mary, the beloved, the chosen One; and she, as had been foretold, was chosen as the channel.

Thus she was separated and kept in closer associations with and in the care or charge of this office.

(5749-7)

Mary was visited by the Angel Gabriel who told her that she had found favor with God and would have a Son conceived by the Holy Spirit.

Q: How old was Mary at the time she was chosen?

A: Four; and, as ye would call, between twelve and thirteen when designated as the One chosen by the Angel on the stair.

Q: Describe the training and preparation of the group of maidens?

A: Trained as to physical exercise first, trained as to mental exercises as related to chastity, purity, Love, patience, endurance...

Q: Were they put on special diet?

A: No wine, no fermented drink ever given. Special foods, yes. These were kept balanced according to that which had been first set by Aran and Ra Ta.

Q: In what manner was Joseph informed of his part in the birth of Jesus?

A: First by Mathias or Judah. Then as this did not coincide with his own feelings, first in a dream and then the direct voice.

And whenever the voice, this always is accompanied with odors as well as Lights; and oft the description of the Lights is the vision, see?

Q: How old was Joseph at the time of the marriage?

A: Thirty six.

Q: How old was Mary at the time of the marriage?

A: Sixteen.
(5749-8)

After her marriage to Joseph, there were groups of Essenes that were selected to protect, to travel with, and to proceed and follow them on their journey to Bethlehem to register to be taxed, and later into Egypt.

A girl named Josie was chosen by the White Brotherhood to be a handmaiden and companion to help Mary.

Thus this entity, Josie, was selected or chosen by those of the Brotherhood...as the handmaid or companion of Mary, Jesus, and Joseph, in their flight into Egypt.
(1010-17)

There has to be a human Body prepared for a soul to enter into the Earth. What is it that determines the quality of Body that a soul in Spirit can choose to enter that particular Body?

The moment and purpose of conception determines the type of Body that will be formed and if it is suitable for the soul seeking to incarnate.

How was the Body of Jesus conceived?

It was an Immaculate Conception by the Holy Spirit.

Mary was also an Immaculate Conception.

> Then, the Immaculate Conception is the physical and mental so attuned to Spirit as to be quickened by same.
> Hence the Spirit, the soul of the Master then was brought into being through the accord of the "Mother" in materiality that ye know in the Earth as conception.
>
> Q: Was Mary immaculately conceived?
>
> A: Mary was immaculately conceived.
> (5749-7)
>
> Q: Is the teaching of the Roman Catholic Church that Mary was without original sin from the moment of her conception in the womb of Ann, correct?
>
> A: It would be correct in ANY case. Correct more in this...
> In the beginning Mary was the Twin-Soul of the Master in the entrance into the Earth!...
> There was no belief in the fact that Ann proclaimed that the child was without father. It is like many proclaiming today that the Master was immaculately conceived. They (others) say, "Impossible!" They say that it isn't in compliance with the natural Law. It IS a natural Law, as has been indicated by the Projection of Mind into matter and thus making of itself a separation to become encased in same – as man did.
> Then, that there has been an encasement was a beginning. Then there must be an end when this must be broken; and this began at that particular period with Ann and then the Master AS the Son; but the ONLY begotten of the Father in the flesh AS a Son OF an immaculately conceived daughter!

Q: Neither Mary nor Jesus, then, had a human father?

A: Neither Mary nor Jesus had a human father. They were One SOUL so far as the Earth is concerned; because (otherwise) she would not be incarnated in flesh, you see.
(5749-8)

But when the fullness of time was come, God sent forth His Son, made of a woman, made under the Law, to redeem them that were under the Law, that we might receive the adoption of sons.
Galations 4:4-5

The inn was not considered a safe place for the birth due to the large number of people gathered there to be taxed. Therefore, the grotto which was called a stable, was chosen.

Q: When and where in Palestine was Jesus born?

A: In Bethlehem of Judea, in that grotto not marked in the present but called a stable...
(587-6)

The innkeeper's wife and daughter were selected as helpers for the birth.

For no inn, no room, could contain that as was being given in a manifested form!
(262-103)

The innkeeper's daughter (Sara), on her way to the grotto, saw His star and heard with the shepherds, the Angels proclaim, "Peace on Earth Good Will to men."

But as the entity walked into the open upon that eve, the brightness of His Star came nearer and nearer. And the entity heard, even as the shepherds, "Peace on Earth Good will to men."
(1152-3)

The Readings state that the star seen was Arcturus which is described as "His star." One wonders how it was able to move that close to Earth to proclaim His birth.

...and the star that led the entity - that source from which and to which it may gain so much of its strength in the present; ARCTURUS, the wonderful, the beautiful!
(827-1)

All were in awe as the brightness of His star appeared and shone, as the music of the spheres brought that joyful choir, "PEACE ON EARTH! GOOD WILL TO MEN OF GOOD FAITH."
All felt the vibrations and saw a great Light, - not only the shepherds above that stable but those in the inn as well.
Just as the midnight hour came, there was the birth of the Master.
(5749-15)

God so loved His creation, or the world, as to give His Only Begotten Son, for their redemption.
(3744-5)

And there were in the same country shepherds abiding in the field, keeping watch over their flock by night.

And, lo, the Angel of the Lord came upon them, and the glory of the Lord shone round about them; and they were sore afraid.

And the Angel of the Lord said unto them, "Fear not; for I bring you good tidings of great joy, which shall be to all people.

For unto you is born this day in the city of David a Savior, which is Christ the Lord.

And this shall be a sign unto you; ye shall find the babe wrapped in swaddling clothes, lying in a manger."

And suddenly there was with the Angel a multitude of the Heavenly host praising God and saying, "Glory to God in the highest, and on Earth, Peace, Good will toward men."

    Luke 2:8-14

Few can conceive of the Body through which the Prince of Peace manifested – the Son, the First and the Last Adam – as having been a channel for material desire, when considered as a Body so purified as to bear that Perfect One.

    (281-51)

They stayed in Bethlehem until the time of purification was past, which was twenty nine days, in which time there was the circumcision.

For, through the period of purification the Mother remained there, not deeming it best to leave, though all forms of assistance were offered; not leaving until there was the circumcision and the presenting in the Temple of the Magi…

    (5749-15)

There was more than one visit of the Wise Men. One is a record of Three Wise Men. There was the fourth,

as well as the fifth, and then the second group. They came from Persia, India, Egypt, and also from Chaldea, Gobi, and what is NOW the Indo or Tao land.
(2067-7)

The Bible records the visit of the Three Wise Men.

> Then Herod, when he had privily called the Wise Men, enquired of them diligently what time the star appeared.
> Matthew 2:7

> ...they (Wise Men) represent in the metaphysical sense the three phases of man's experience in materiality: Gold, the material; frankincense, the ether or ethereal, myrrh, the healing force as brought with same, or Body, Mind, soul...
> (5749-7)

After the return of the Mother and Joseph to Nazareth, there was the presenting of the child to the Lord in the temple.
Then came the mandate to kill young children.

> When with the return of the Mother and Joseph to Nazareth - there was the edict that all children up to two years of age were to be destroyed.
> (5749-16)

> There was not the proclamation of the Wise Men... that this new King was to replace Rome! It was to replace the Jewish authority in the land!
> (1472-3)

A group of Essene supporters went with the Holy Family as they had to flee into Egypt; this was a very difficult journey for a young mother and baby. They all settled near what was Alexandria.

> The entity then chose to join with the Holy family,
> and acted in the capacity of the handmaid to the
> Mother, the child, Joseph…
> (1010-12)

Two different time frames are given for the years spent in Egypt but
one could include the travel time to and from Egypt (two and one
half to five years).
When they did leave Egypt for political reasons, it was decided to go
to Capernaum, not Nazareth.

Because of the purity of the Body of the young Christ child, His
garments were said to be healing influences to other children.

> - the apparel brought more and more the influence
> which today would be called a lucky charm…
> (2067-7)

> …the nature and the character that would be a
> part of the experiences to those coming in contact
> with the young child; as to how the garments worn
> by the child would heal children. For the Body
> being perfect radiated that which was health, Life
> itself. Just as today individuals may radiate…that
> vibration which is destruction to dis-ease in any
> form in bodies.
> (1010-17)

A woman named Judy, who was a leader in the Essene community,
was chosen to be the teacher and to oversee the development of the
Christ child. Judy the teacher, Prophetess, healer and recorder for all
these groups, was said to be the "feminine of Sampson."

> Q: Please describe Judy's personal appearance,
> her dress, her personality, her faith.

A: Draw upon the imagination for these. As would be the dress of Samson, making it feminine.
(2067-11)

Jesus studied in the home of Judy until his teen years when she sent Him to Persia, India, and Egypt to learn more...that He may have the more perfect understanding and Wisdom from all those ancient teachings of higher knowledge.

> For the entity (Judy) sent Him to Persia, to Egypt, yea to India, that there might be completed the more perfect knowledge of the material ways in the activities of Him that became the Way, the Truth!
> (1472-3)

Jesus was the cousin of John the Baptist and they took their initiations together in the Great Pyramid in Egypt.

> ...when John first went to Egypt - where Jesus joined Him and both became the initiates in the pyramid or temple there.
> (2067-11)

> Q: From what period and how long did He stay in Egypt?

> A: From thirteen to sixteen. One year in travel in Persia; the greater portion being in the Egyptian.
> In this, the greater part will be seen in the records that are set in the pyramids there; for HERE were the initiates taught.

> Q: In which pyramid are the records of Christ?

> A: That yet to be uncovered.
> (5749-2)

Jesus was in a human Body with a conscious Mind which had to be trained just like we are.

The human brain is like a blank page waiting to be written upon.

The human Mind has to learn to process information and to even learn how to talk, then to read and to write, etc.

We are all born with amnesia from our soul level of self.

The subsconscious and superconscious aspects of the soul impress upon the human Mind, images, past experiences, patterns and knowings, or Truth.

It is up to the choice of the individual what intuition will be accepted or rejected.

We have to awaken to who we are and why we are here.

We need outside studies to remind us of what we already know within.

Was He aware of His mission and did He have memories of other Lifetimes?

The Readings state that Jesus was the greatest psychic that ever lived; therefore, we can be assured that He did have past Life recall and was very aware of spiritual Truth.

> No greater psychic lived than Jesus of Nazareth.
> (2630-1)

He was in constant contact with God as His Father because His will was always to do the will of God. Even as a child, He stated that He must be about His Father's business.

> Remember and keep in Mind, He was normal, He developed normally. Those about Him saw those characteristics that may be anyone's who wholly puts the trust in God! And to every parent might it not be said, daily, dedicate thy Life that thy offspring may be called of God into service − to the glory of God and to the honor of thy name.
> (1010-17)

> And Jesus increased in Wisdom and stature, and in favor with God and man.
>
> Luke 2:52

His first trip did not last long as He was called home at the death of Joseph.

> From Persia He was called to Judea at the death of Joseph, and then into Egypt for the completion of the preparation as a teacher.
>
> (5749-7)

After Jesus was ten years old, Mary and Joseph decided to have children of their own. A Reading states that this was the desire of them both.

> Only, you see, until Jesus went to be taught by others did the normal or natural associations come; not required – it was a choice of them both because of their OWN feelings.
>
> ...ten years then they came in succession: James, the daughter (Ruth), Jude.
>
> (5749-8)

According to the Readings, the Great Pyramid in Egypt is a monument built as a temple to stand for all of time containing records from creation to Christ.
Jesus and John the Baptist were initiated into the White Brotherhood of the Essenes, together in the temple (or pyramid) in Egypt.
When the Great Pyramid was first opened (1800s) there was no Body found in the sarcophagus.
This empty coffin symbolizes the victory over death when Jesus was to be resurrected which broke the Life and death cycle that had existed since the time of Adam and Eve. Only Jesus as the Christ was able to break this pattern.

>...as indicated by the empty tomb, which has NEVER been filled, see? Only Jesus was able to break same, as it became that which indicated His fulfillment.
>(2067-7)

After the studies were mastered, Jesus returned and was baptized by John in the wilderness.

>...John seeth Jesus coming unto him, and saith, "Behold the Lamb of God which taketh away the sin of the world."
>John 1:29

The baptism of Jesus is the beginning of His ministry as He is commissioned by God in public.

>And Jesus, when He was baptized, went up straightway out of the water; and lo, the Heavens were opened unto Him, and He saw the Spirit of God descending like a dove, and lighting upon Him.
>And lo a voice from Heaven saying, "This is my beloved Son, in whom I am well pleased."
>Matthew 3:16-17

After the baptism, Jesus is led by the Spirit into the wilderness to be tempted by the Devil (Satan).
The Readings state that He must face that which was His undoing in the beginning. (Was that a misuse of spiritual Power?)

>And there, as the initiate, He went out - for the passing through of the initiation, by fulfilling - as indicated in the baptism in the Jordan; not standing in it or being poured or sprinkled in it either! As He passed from that activity into the wilderness to meet that which had been His undoing in the beginning.
>(2067-7)

After a fast of forty days, Jesus was hungry.

The first test was on the physical level, to use the Power of His creative energy to turn the stones into bread to feed the Body.

Jesus refused to be tempted and tells the Tempter, "Man shall not live by bread alone, but by every word that proceedeth out of the mouth of God." (See Matthew 4:4). He quoted scripture in His defense.

The second test is on the mental levels when He is taken up to the Holy City and set on the pinnacle of the temple and told to throw Himself down if He is the Son of God which will prove who He is. God will not allow Him to be harmed and will send Angels to protect Him, the Tempter tells Him.

The third test is Spiritual as Jesus is told to bow down to Satan and receive the Gift of all the Kingdoms of the world for self glorification and Power.

Jesus refused, knowing that the Power of God must not be used for self, but only to aid others.

Jesus passed the tests on the physical, mental, and spiritual levels, and then Satan departed. Angels were sent to minister to Him.

> In the Life, then, of Jesus we find the Oneness made manifest through the ability to overcome ALL of the temptations of the flesh, and the DESIRES of same, through making the WILL ONE WITH THE FATHER.
> (900-16)

> All Powerful - yet never using that Power, save to help, to assist, to give aid, to give succor to someone who is not in the position to help or aid self, see?
> (900-147)

> For in that He Himself hath suffered being tempted, He is able to succour them that are tempted.
> Hebrews 2:18

> ...calling the name - Jesus, the Christ, the same yesterday, today and forever! This will bring the

conviction within self as it did to Him when He withstood the temptations of the Body, the temptations of the Mind, the temptation of purpose in the Earth - and Angels ministered unto Him.

(3357-2)

It was at this time that Jesus was ready to begin His ministry.
Shortly after He returned from the temptation in the wilderness, John the Baptist was put into prison.
Jesus was not given permission to rescue John due to a Karmic situation being fulfilled (when John was Elijah).

For, John was more the Essene than Jesus. For Jesus held rather to the Spirit of the Law, and John to the letter of same.

(2067-11)

The first miracle recorded is turning the water into wine at a wedding. The bride was a cousin of His Mother, Mary, who prompted Him to do something about the lack of wine.

Mary felt, knew, was convinced within herself that here again there might be such an experience, with her son returning as a man starting upon His mission.
This might be called a first period of test.
For, had He not just ten days ago sent Satan away and received ministry from the Angels?

(5749-15)

...when water saw its Master, blushed and became wine even by activity! Remember, only as it was poured out would it become wine.
...no wine would have filled those conditions where embarrassment was being brought...

(3361-1)

292

Then there was the healing of Simon Peter's wife's mother, of a fever. It was one of the few healings performed among His own people, among His own kindred.
(5749-16)

The healings and miracles which happened during the ministry of Jesus are well known, so I will not repeat them.
According to the Readings, sickness is the result of breaking Laws. Jesus was not only able to heal the Body, but to forgive sins.

> Respecting the miracles of healing, there were many instances where individual healings were as the nature to be instantaneous - as that when He said to him sick of the palsy, "Son thy sins be forgiven thee."
> When the questionings came, (as He knew they would), He answered, "Which is it easier to say, thy sins be forgiven thee, or arise, take up thy bed and go into thine house?"
> IMMEDIATELY, the man arose, took up his bed and WENT into his house! Here we find it was not by the command but by His own personage. For, the question was not as to whether He healed but as to whether He had the Power to forgive sin! The recognition was that sin had caused the physical disturbance.
> (5749-16)

Sins are of commission and omission. Sins of commission were forgiven, while sins of omission were called to Mind - even by the Master.
(281-2)

...HIM, who is the God of the storm, God of Peace, God of the wind, God of the rain, yea the Lord of the Earth of whom the disciples said, "What manner of man is this, that even the wind and the rain, the sea and the elements obey his voice?"
(5276-1)

> And they feared exceedingly, and said one to another,
> "What manner of man is this, that even the wind and
> the sea obey Him?"
> Mark 4:41

Jesus lived and died as a man which demonstrates that we, as in mankind, can live in perfect Harmony with God in a human vessel of flesh and blood if our will is centered in Christ.

> Jesus is the man—the activity, the Mind, the
> relationships that He bore to others. Yea, He was
> mindful of friends, He was sociable, He was loving, He
> was kind, He was gentle, He grew faint, He grew weak
> – and yet gained that strength He has promised, in
> becoming the Christ, by fulfilling and overcoming the
> world! Ye are made strong - in Body, in Mind, in soul
> and purpose—by that Power in Christ. The POWER,
> then, is in the Christ, the pattern is in Jesus.
> (2533-7)

Even though Jesus was Christ before He was born, He had to BECOME the Christ in the human Body by being totally at One with God in will and purpose.
He lived as a man that was in flesh and blood, yet always keeping the communion with God in ideal and purpose, choosing ONLY that which was companionable with God's will in the Earthly choices, as well as the mental and the spiritual.

> As man found himself out of touch with that complete
> consciousness of the Oneness of God, it became necessary
> that the will of God, the Father, be made manifested,
> that a pattern be introduced into man's consciousness.
> Thus, the Son of Man came into the Earth, made in the
> form, the likeness of man; with Body, Mind, soul. Yet the
> soul was the SON; the soul was the LIGHT!
> (3357-2)

Jesus was able to manifest the pure Christ Spirit and Power while in a human Body. Therefore He became that which He already was in Spirit by manifesting that perfection of the Christ Love and Light while in the Earth.
Jesus was man but He was also God incarnate.
We do not worship the man but the Spirit of God He manifested.

> ...He took Peter and John and James, and went up into a mountain to pray.
> And as He prayed, the fashion of His countenance was altered, and His raiment was white and glistering.
> And, behold, there talked with Him two men, which were Moses and Elias.
> Who appeared in glory, and spake of His decease which He should accomplish at Jerusalem.
> Luke 9:28-31

> For He made Himself of no estate, though He came into a world created by His very breath.
> (1158-5)

> There is set an example, and by THAT example should one ever measure one's efforts as related to God or man; for HE, being BOTH God AND man, can be TRULY the example for men to pattern their activities, their going in, their coming out.
> (311-5)

He is not just one of the original souls who made it back home to God again. He IS that FIRST Begotten through, IN and BY, which all the other souls were created and are contained within.
The pattern is in Jesus and the Power is in the Christ Spirit.
God gave Himself in the Son that we might return home.

God gave self in the Son that man might approach
that Throne in a Way that all may be One in Him,
knowing self to be a portion of that Whole, yet
individual in the Gift of the Creator that made each
THEMSELVES, yet can make themselves a portion
of the Whole.
(31-1)

But each son, each daughter, through these very acts of
the Only Begotten, of the Son of Mary, of the first in
the Earth, - becomes then as the elder Brother to all who
are BORN in the Earth, as the Maker, as the Creator, as
the first, as the last; as the beginning, as the end of man's
soul's experience through the Earth and throughout the
spheres of consciousness in and about the Earth.
Thus is He the Only Begotten, the Firstborn, the first
to know flesh, the first to purify it.
(1158-5)

Jesus identified Himself with the "Son of Man" which was a term
known to indicate the many past Lifetimes He lived and indicative
of being the expected Messiah.
Jesus's humanity cried out loudly as he wept outside the tomb of his
friend, Lazarus, then He manifested His divinity when He raised
him from the dead.

Jesus deeply loved little children and taught that the Kingdom of
God was achieved by us when we can become like little children.

...unless you are as forgiving, unless ye are as generous,
unless you are as dependent as little children - these
become in their deeper sense the meaning, the
influence that arises in the experience of the entity.
(1532)

> Though He were in the world, He was not of the
> world; Yet subject to the Laws thereof, of materiality.
> (1504-1)

Some people have tried to present a romantic relationship between
Jesus and Mary Magdalene but the Cayce Readings said that this is
NOT true.

> Mary, the sister of Martha, was an harlot – until the
> cleansing; and not one that Jesus would have loved,
> though He loved all. The closer associations brought
> to the physical or filial Love, were with the children -
> and not with those the same age of the Master.
> (2067-7)

Edgar Cayce had been one of the seventy disciples of the Master
that was sent out, known then as Lucius of Cyrene. There is some
confusion of mixing him with Luke who was his mother's brother.
Lucius was not easily accepted by the other disciples as he had a
common-law wife named Vesta and two children and was also
closely associated with Paul.
Vesta became active in the ministry later in Life.

> With the acceptance of Lucius by Paul…Lucius
> determined - with his companion (Vesta) - to return
> to the portion of his own land…and there to establish
> a church; to be the Minister, to be the active force in
> those portions of the land.
> (294-192)

We know that the disciples taught conflicting doctrines at times and
had a lot of problems to resolve among themselves.
However, Lucius wrote the Book of Luke and was Bishop over
Laodicea.

> Luke was written by Lucius, rather than Luke; though a companion with Luke during those activities of Paul...
> (1598-2)

Lucius took a Jewish bride named Mariaerh whose parents were associated with Elizabeth, the mother of John the Baptist.

> And yet there had been the making of the agreements, or the marriage contract for Lucius. Yet, this has little to do with the associations of these two, or their companionship...during that experience the marriage took place (Lucius and Mariaerh).
> (1523-16)

Due to Paul's teaching on celibacy, Lucius and Mariaerh did not have children at first, but the wife longed for a son and sought the help of Mother Mary who was sympathetic to her case. Mariaerh eventually was given her wish.

> - there was a son born to the entity (Mariaerh), that grew in Grace and in favor with all of those not only in the first church but those who had been closely associated with the activities that preceded the coming of the Master, and the teachings of the Essenes.
> (1468-3)

I met the lady (Mariaerh) in this Lifetime when I went to lunch with Jess Stearn who interviewed her. She did not seem to remember anything of that Lifetime nor was she interested in it. Her main topic was the Ministry she had been involved with in this Lifetime. I went to visit her several times later with Paula Fitzgerald. The lady (Mariaerh) was a senior citizen who lived in the Ghent area of Norfolk. I regret that she died a tragic death (the victim of a murder).

There is a reference in the Readings that needs to be mentioned.

> Yet were He the Son, He learned obedience by the
> things which He suffered.
> (25-5)

I believe that Jesus came into the Earth for His own development as well as to be our Savior.

First, we have the already perfected soul who gave up Heaven to enter the Earth as a "ransom" and Savior of mankind.

Yet, He also seems to have something of His own to complete.

I think that He already learned obedience through His suffering in His other Lifetimes but had to continue to submit to God's will and learn them over again. In every new Body we inhabit, we have to learn to walk and talk and read and write all over again.

We have to relearn what we already know within so we can apply it in our Life again.

We have to apply each principle over again for it to belong to us in each new Lifetime.

His suffering was mainly for us as we ARE His OWN.

As far as His own development goes, His mission was to rescue us. He was the lamb slain from before the beginning of the world. We are His OWN individual selves. He needed to be the mediator between us and God providing a Way through Himself for us to return to our Christ selves as individuals in Him.

> For, He only is that approach. There is NO name
> under or in Heaven whereby men may be saved but
> Him, who has known the Whole Way through. For,
> He is the Maker; He is the Life; He has purchased
> each soul with that He has suffered in Body, Mind
> and Spirit, that men may have the perfect approach
> to the Father.
> (378-42)

299

But when the Prince of Peace came into the Earth for the completing of His OWN development, He overcame the flesh AND temptation. So, He became the first of those who over came death in the Body...
(1152-1)

Though He were a Son, yet learned He obedience by the things which He suffered; and being made perfect, He became the author of eternal salvation unto all them that obey Him.
Hebrews 5:8-9

For He manifested in flesh that the evil forces, as manifest in the relationships of individuals as one to another, may be eradicated from the experiences of man.
(1293-1)

This is part of a Reading for the Last Supper that describes what Jesus looked like.

The Lord's Supper – here with the Master—see what they had for supper— boiled fish, rice with leeks, wine and loaf. One of the pitchers in which it was served was broken, as was the lip to same.
The whole robe of the Master was not white, but pearl gray – all combined in one – the gift of Nicodemus to the Lord.
The Master's hair is mostly red, inclined to be curly in portions, yet not feminine or weak - STRONG, with heavy piercing eyes that are blue or steel gray.
His weight would be at least a hundred and seventy pounds. Long tapering fingers, nails well kept.
Long nail, though, on the left little finger.
Merry – even in the hour of trial. Joke – even in the moment of betrayal.

The sack is empty. Judas departs.

The last is given of the wine and loaf, with which He gives the emblems that should be so dear to every follower of Him.

Lays aside His robe, which is all of one piece - girds the towel about His waist, which is dressed with linen that is blue and white. Rolls back the folds, kneels first before John, James, then to Peter - who refuses.

Then the dissertation as to, "He that would be the greatest would be the servant of all."

...and now comes, "It is finished."

They sing the ninety-first Psalm- "He that dwelleth in the secret place of the Most High shall abide under the shadow of the Almighty. I will say of the Lord, He is my refuge and my fortress; my God; in Him will I trust."

He is the musician as well. for He uses the harp.

They leave for the Garden.

(5749-1)

And as they were eating, Jesus took bread and blessed it, and break it, and gave it to the disciples and said, "Take eat, this is my Body."

And He took the cup, and gave thanks, and gave it to them saying, "Drink ye all of it; for this is my blood of the New Testament which is shed for many for the remission of sins."

Matthew 26:26-28

At the Last Supper, Jesus revealed what was to come but they all did not understand the meaning.

...Father, the hour is come; glorify thy Son, that thy Son also may glorify thee.

301

As thou hast given Him Power over all flesh, that He
should give eternal Life to as many as thou hast given
Him.
And this is Life eternal, that they might know thee, the
only true God, and Jesus Christ, whom thou hast sent.
I have glorified thee on the Earth;
…And now, O Father, glorify thou me with thine own
SELF with the glory which I had with thee before the
world was.
John 17:1-5

They leave for the Garden of Gethsemane knowing that the time
is at hand.
It was a long road from the Garden of Eden to the Garden of
Gethsemane.

…My soul is exceeding sorrowful, even unto death:
Tarry ye here, and watch with me.
Matthew 26:38

The real trial of Jesus was in the Garden of Gethsemane when He
knew He must face not only His own death but all our deaths and
all the sins of mankind which must be met on that cross.
He, who was without sin, must bear the sins of the world.
It was a long, lonely night in which Jesus would sweat blood in His
anguish as the human self in flesh wanted to avoid the crucifixion;
He pleaded with God to "Take this cup from me."
But the will of His soul was to do the will of God regardless of the
suffering required. He knew it was a bitter cup to drink.

…He knows the heartaches of fear – even as He
prayed, "If it be possible, let this cup pass from me –
not my will, O God, but thine be done."
(602-7)

...study what happened in the Garden when His disciples - even His closest friends – slept while He fought with self...
(262-100)

...though He sighed with the very blood of His Body in Gethsemane...
(1158-5)

The real test was in the Garden when in the realization that He had met every test and yet must know the pang of death.
(5277-1)

Rather spiritualize the physical desires as He did in the Garden. What there is shown thee as to how the physical, the spiritual, fought...one with another.
"Father, let this cup pass from me."
This is as every experience in the physical man when there is the fear of the loss in this or that direction. There is the constant (cry), "Father, save me from this- from this."
Yet...If there has been builded in thine experience as was in His experience – offering Himself for the world – then thou must pass through same, in making the physical desire and the will of the Father as One...
(262-64)

...yet He overcame that cross in Gethsemane's meditations...
(1213-1)

...surrendering all Power unto Power itself, surrendering all will unto the will of the Father; making of self then a channel...
(1152-1)

After Jesus was at Peace in doing God's will, an Angel came.

> And there appeared an Angel unto Him from Heaven, strengthening Him.
>
> Luke 22:43

Jesus awakens the sleeping disciples, then Judas arrives with a group of soldiers to take Him.
Judas is referred to as the "son of perdition."

> And supper being ended, the Devil having now put into the heart of Judas Iscariot, Simon's son, to betray Him.
>
> John 13:2

The question was asked Cayce in a Reading if Judas sought to force the Master into asserting Himself to bring in His Kingdom.

> Q: Was Judas Iscariot's idea in betraying Jesus to force Him to assert Himself as a King and bring in His Kingdom then?
>
> A: Rather the desire of the man (Judas) to force same, and the fulfilling of that as Jesus spoke of same at the supper.
>
> (2067-7)

Jesus surrendered the self in the Garden. It had been self will over God's will that was the fall in the earlier Garden of Eden. Now He has the victory of having God's will be the real will of the individual soul which rules.
Peter smote the High Priest's servant and cut off his ear when they came to take Jesus. But Jesus healed him.

> Then said Jesus unto Peter, "Put up thy sword into the sheath: The CUP which my Father hath given me, shall I not drink it?"
> John 18:11

Jesus knew the bitter cup He was to drink but now He was accepting what lay ahead because He was ready to fulfill the scriptures and to give Himself as the ransom for mankind. He is letting us know that He is well aware that He must die on our behalf in order to save us. For this reason He came into the world.

He had the Power to wither the hands of those that slapped Him but forgave them instead. Jesus was mocked and endured many insults, harsh beatings without complaint, and then the crown of thorns was placed upon the King of the Jews.

> Know that even as the Christ, even as the Jesus - had He WITHERED the hands of those that smote Him because it was in HIS POWER, He could NOT be, He would NOT be, thy Christ, thy Savior, thy Lord!
> (1440-2)

> The trial – this was not with the pangs of pain as so oft indicated, but rather glorying in the opportunity of taking upon self that which would RIGHT man's relationship to the Father – in that man, through his free will, had brought sin into the activities of the Children of God. Here HIS SON was bringing REDEMPTION through the shedding of blood that they might be free.
> (5749-10)

Jesus had told His disciples what He must suffer throughout His Ministry and that the scriptures must be fulfilled but most of them did not remember or understand until later.

The disciples fled before the crucifixion, except for John.

While Jesus was on the cross, He was mindful of Mother Mary and committed her care unto John. He had the Power to come down from that cross but He embraced it.

> He had the Power within Himself to come down from the cross, though He had the Power to heal, though He had Power to rid the very taking HOLD upon death, it had no claims upon Him. Why? QUICKENED by the Father because the Life LIVED among men, the dealings among men brought ONLY hope, ONLY patience, ONLY Love, ONLY long suffering!
> This then being the Law of God made manifest, He BECOMES the Law by manifesting same before man...
> (1158-12)

Psalm 22 is a prophecy about Jesus' crucifixion.
This is a quote from Psalm 22:1 indicating that scripture was being fulfilled.
As Jesus hung on the cross, He asked:

> My God, my God, why hast thou forsaken me?
> Psalm 22:1

In the same Psalm, the scripture says:

> They part my garments among them, and cast lots upon my vesture.
> Psalm 22:18

The human Body is still a separate vessel from the soul which inhabits it and it has a Mind of its own. The flesh has survival instincts to live.
Remember Jesus was a man in a human form as well as the soul who was the Christ incarnating in it. This is a very difficult concept

to grasp but we need to comprehend the humanness of Jesus as well as the divine. (Traditional Christians have a problem seeing the humanness of Jesus and New Age philosophies have a problem seeing His divinity.)
The Cayce Readings say the flesh cries out with its own voice when it suffers.

> Why did He (say), "Father, why hast thou forsaken me?" Even when the world was being overcome, the flesh continued to rebel...
> (281-3)

Christian theology states that God turned His back upon the sin (ours) that was upon Jesus and that is why He felt forsaken as the presence of God had left Him alone.
I do not like the concept that God turned His back upon Jesus.

> ..."My God, my God! Why hast thou forsaken me?"
> This came, as He promised, that that anguish, that despair may not be in thy experience.
> It was a fulfilling; that the trials, the temptations might be shortened in the days of expression, that the very elect might not be disturbed in their search for Him.
> (2072-4)

Jesus showed us how to live in the flesh and how to die to it.

We cannot fathom what it meant to experience, to bear the sins of mankind in one's own soul, Body, Mind and Spirit.

> Who His own self bare our sins in His own Body on the tree, that we, being dead to sins, should live unto righteousness...
> 1 Peter 2:24

> Christ hath redeemed us from the curse of the Law,
> being made a curse for us; for it is written, "Cursed is
> every one that hangeth on a tree."
> Galations 3:13

No wonder the human self felt forsaken (that of His own BEING crucified in flesh).

> As indicated in the expression that God moved within
> HIMSELF and then He did not change, though did
> bring to Himself that of His own being crucified even
> in the flesh.
> (5749-14)

The Lamb of God has been a symbol since the creation of Adam and Eve when God provided a covering of animal skins over them after they had sinned.

> Then Moses called for all the elders of Israel, and said
> unto them, "Draw out and take you a lamb according
> to your families, and kill (it for) the Passover."
> Exodus 12:21

> All we like sheep have gone astray; we have turned
> every one to his own Way; and the Lord hath laid on
> Him the iniquity of us all.
> Isaiah 53:6

> And Abraham lifted up his eyes, and looked, and
> behold behind him a ram caught in a thicket by his
> horns: And Abraham went and took the ram, and
> offered him up for a burnt offering in the stead of his
> son.
> Genesis 22:13

Every selfish act or thought that all of mankind ever committed or would commit had to be washed clean in the blood of the sacred Lamb who was without sin.

Then throughout the Old Testament, we find many symbolic references to the blood sacrifice of the Lamb.

> For this is my blood of the New Testament, which is shed for many for the remission of sins.
> Matthew 26:28

> For the Life of the flesh is in the blood...
> Leviticus 17:11

> For the blood as of the perfect man was shed, not by reason of Himself but that there might be made an offering once for all...
> (1504-1)

> And there are three that bear witness in Earth, the Spirit, and the water, and the blood: And these three agree in One.
> I John 5:8

> And having made Peace through the blood of His cross, by Him to RECONCILE all things unto Himself; by Him, I say, whether they be things in Earth, or things in Heaven.
> And you that were sometime alienated and enemies in your Mind, by wicked works, yet now hath He reconciled.
> In the Body of His flesh through DEATH, to present you Holy and unblamable and unreprovable in His sight.
> Colossians 1:20-22

...without the shedding of blood there was no remission of sin. For Love is Law – Law is Love, in its essence.

And with the breaking of the Law is the making of the necessity for Atonement and FORGIVENESS, in that which may take away error to or what has been brought in the experience of the individual.

(262-45)

In the blood of the Christ as was shed, Karma is met, and then it becomes the Law, not of cause and effect, but being justified by faith in Him.

(2828-5)

How much more shall the blood of Christ, who through the eternal Spirit offered Himself without spot to God, purge your conscience from dead works to serve the living God?

And for this cause He is the mediator of the New Testament, that by means of death, for the redemption of the transgressions that were under the First Testament, they which are called might receive the promise of eternal inheritance.

Hebrews 9:14-15

I think that sin separates us from the presence of God; therefore, where there is evil or selfishness, then God is not present, in that God is all Good and all Love and all Light and LIGHT cannot participate in the darkness. It's a Law!

Jesus agreed to accept the cross knowing that He would experience the abandonment of the Light as He embraced the darkness of our sins. He spiritualized them all with His Love.

Before Jesus died, He cried out in a loud voice giving His Spirit to God. I think it is important to note that being forsaken was not the last moment but returning to God was the real issue.

...Jesus knowing that all things were now accomplished, that the scripture might be fulfilled, saith "I thirst."

Now there was set a vessel full of vinegar; and they filled a sponge with vinegar, and put it upon hyssop, and put it to His mouth.

When Jesus therefore had received the vinegar, He said, "IT IS FINISHED"; and He bowed His head, and gave up the ghost.

John 19:28-30

And when Jesus had cried with a loud voice, He said, "Father, into thy hands I commend my Spirit;" and having said thus, He gave up the ghost.

Luke 23:46

Jesus was dead.

The creation had crucified its Creator.

Not only was He dead in Body, but the soul was separated from that Body. As all phases of man in the Earth are made manifest, the physical Body, the mental Body, the soul Body became as each dependent upon their own experience. Is it any wonder that the man cried, "My God, my God, WHY hast thou forsaken me?"

(5749-6)

For He hath made Him to be sin for us, who knew no sin; that we might be made the righteousness of God in Him.

2 Corinthians 5:21

He that spared not His own Son, but delivered Him up for us all...

Romans 8:32

...hath He appeared to put away sin by the sacrifice of Himself.

Hebrews 9:26

There was an eclipse of the sun, an earthquake, and the veil in the temple was rent in two. The veil symbolically represents the separation between man and God.

That day when the sun was darkened and NOT by an eclipse alone, and when the Earth shook and the temple veil was rent...
(333-2)

According to Cayce, Jesus was lifted as between the Earth and sky at this time.

...and again far off when the day arose that He was lifted as between the Earth and sky, so that those who looked, those who beheld, might know that they - themselves - must pass along that road, CRUCIFYING in their bodies that which would make for the gratifying of desires...
(897-1)

...when the Earth was darkened, and the foundations of the deep were broken up; for the Son of Man, the Son of God, was suspended between Earth and the sky.
(518-1)

Some Spirits appeared at His death.

And the graves were opened; and many bodies of the saints which slept arose.
Matthew 27:52

The Body of Jesus was placed in a new tomb by a friend, Joseph of Arimathea.

> And he bought fine linen, and took Him down, and wrapped Him in the linen, and laid Him in a sepulcher which was hewn out of a rock, and rolled a stone unto the door of the sepulcher.
>
> Mark 15:46

A Reading was given for a lady who helped prepare the linens that went about the head of the Body of Jesus.

> ...aided in preparing...the wrappings for the last of the anointing of the Body of the Holy One-rather the wrappings than the spices, for Magdalene and Mary and Jose and the Mother of the Lord prepared these. The napkins that were about His head, and with those seals that were later made as raised figures, did the entity prepare.
>
> (649-1)

Also there was a Reading for a lady who prepared the seals.

> ...(she prepared) the seals of the Holy One, as the seals of the Son of David; the pear with the bell, with pomegranates on either side.
>
> (649-2)

He was in the tomb for three days before the resurrection. During these three days, He was in the spiritual realms, cleansing them. It is said that He descended into Hell, Hades, or Sheol, meaning the place of the dead or the place of the departed, not the Hell of the damned. Cayce says He preached to those souls there.

> Did not the Son of Man descend even from the presence of the Father into the Earth, and then into

313

Hell itself, that all might know He walks and talks
with thee…
(295-9)

…He descended into Hell, as interpreted in Mark,
Matthew and John, to preach to those there.
(452-6)

For Christ also hath once suffered for sins, the just
for the unjust, that He might bring us to God, being
put to death in the flesh, but QUICKENED by the
Spirit: By which also He went and PREACHED unto
the Spirits in prison.
1 Peter 3:18-19

Without the resurrection, all the suffering would have been without
merit for the Law of DEATH must be overcome which was begun
at the disobedience of Adam in the Garden.

And with error entered that as called DEATH, which
is only a transition - or through God's other door…
(5749-3)

But we see Jesus, who was made a little lower than the
Angels for the suffering of death, crowned with glory
and honor; that He by the Grace of God should taste
death for every man.
Hebrews 2:9

The period of resurrection – here we find that in which
ye ALL may glory. FOR WITHOUT THE FACT
OF HIS OVERCOMING DEATH, the Whole of
the experience would have been as naught.
(5749-10)

...the man Jesus, who became the Christ through the things which He suffered, and through demonstrating in the Earth the abilities to overcome DEATH, the LAW of death.

(1877-2)

...He broke the bonds of death; proclaiming in that act that THERE IS NO DEATH when the individual, the soul, has and does put its trust in HIM.

(5749-13)

But by One man (Adam) sin came into God's creation. By One man death came. By that same man death was overcome.

(2784-1)

At sunrise on the morning of the third day, Mary Magdalene and others came to finish the burial ceremonies but found that the stone had been rolled away.

Hence when those of His loved ones and those of His brethren came on that glad morning when the tidings had come to them, those that stood guard heard a fearful noise and saw a LIGHT, and – "The stone has been rolled away!" Then they entered into the Garden, and there Mary first saw her RISEN Lord. Then came they of His brethren with the faithful women, those that loved His Mother, those that were her companions in sorrow, those that were making preparations that the Law might be kept that even there might be no desecration of the ground about His tomb. They, too, of His friends, His loved ones, His brethren, SAW the Angels. How, why, took they on form? That there might be implanted into their hearts and souls that FULFILLMENT of those promises.

(5749-6)

Jesus told Mary not to touch Him as He had not as yet ascended unto His Father. Why was it difficult to recognize Him? He must have appeared somewhat different in the glorified Body than before. Jesus ate fish and honey to prove to His followers that He could eat material food in His GLORIFIED Body.

> "Children, have ye anything here to eat?" This indicated to the disciples and the Apostles present that this was not transmutation but a regeneration, recreation of the atoms and cells of (the) Body that might, through desire, masticate material things - fish and honey were given.
> 2533-8

He wanted them to see that He was not just a Spirit.

> ...so He overcame death; not only in the physical Body but in the Spirit Body...
> (5749-6)

Once Jesus was resurrected, His Body was a pattern of Jesus but I do not think it was a human Body as before. The glorified soul-self was made bodily visible. It bore the pattern, the marks of the crucifixion of the human Body which was absorbed into the soul Body. I think it was a metamorphosis like at the Transfiguration. My own viewpoint of it is that this is another mystery.

Cayce was asked if the Resurrection were a transmutation from human flesh to divine flesh. He said it was not but rather a creation. This is a very difficult concept to grasp.

> There is no mystery to the transmutation of the Body of the Christ. For having attained in the physical consciousness the At-Onement with the Father-Mother-God, the completeness was such that with the disintegration of the Body – as indicated in the

manner in which the shroud, the robe, the napkin lay – there was then the taking of the Body-physical form. This was the manner. It was not a transmutation, as of changing from one to another.

Just as indicated in the manner in which the Body - physical entered the Upper Room with the doors closed, not by being a part of the wood through which the Body passed but by forming from the ether waves that were within the room, because of a meeting prepared by faith.

(2533-8)

And their eyes were opened, and they knew Him; and He vanished out of their sight.

Luke 24:31

Not transmutation of flesh but creation, in the pattern indicated.

(2533-8)

For death hath no sting, it hath no Power over those that know the Resurrection...

(1158-5)

For as He gave, without His death – yea, without His Resurrection – there is NO HOPE in man's estate.

(1152-5)

According to the Cayce Readings, Resurrection can transform a body and a soul.

Flesh and blood cannot inherit eternal Life.

(262-78)

...even as thou hast seen and hath known, as thou hath heard, how the Resurrection had brought to the

consciousness of man that Power that God hath given to man, that may reconstruct, resuscitate, even every atom of a very sick Body, that may resurrect even every atom of a sin-sick soul, may resurrect the soul so that it lives on and on in the glory of a resurrected, a regenerated Christ...
(1148-5)

Q: Will you please give more information on the Resurrection of the Body?

A: ...He, thy pattern, resurrected the Body, QUICKENED the Body. So within thine own self must come that which through Him may overcome death, overcome that transition, overcome that which is the change...
(262-88)

The Readings state that there were about five thousand who saw and heard Jesus speak after His Resurrection.

...the entity was present when there were about five thousand who saw and heard the words of the Master after the Resurrection...
(1877-2)

After joining with God as One, and after several meetings with His disciples, He told Thomas, who had doubted, to touch the scars in His hands and side.

The Body that formed that seen by the normal or carnal eye of Mary was such that it could not be handled until there had been the conscious union with the sources of all Power, of all force.
But afterward – when there had been the first, second, third, fourth, and even the sixth meeting – He THEN

said, "Put forth thy hand and touch the nail prints in my hands, in my feet. Thrust thy hand into my side, and BELIEVE." This indicated the transformation.

(2533-8)

Now this separation symbolically represented by the veil no longer existed as Jesus, the MEDIATOR, gave us direct access to God by resurrecting.

Jesus opened the doorway for mankind to enter directly into the Holy of Holies within through prayer and meditation.

The old Law was replaced by the new Law.

Some Spirits appeared after His Resurrection.

Many dead souls arose and appeared to a lot of people.

> And the graves were opened; and many bodies of the Saints which slept arose, and came out of the graves after His Resurrection, and went into the Holy City, and appeared unto many.
> Matthew 27:52-53

There were about five hundred people who saw the Ascension of Jesus when He was lifted into Heaven and heard the words of the Angels.

> The entity was among the five hundred who beheld Him as He entered into glory and saw the Angels, heard their announcement of the event (Second Coming) that must one day come to pass – and will only be to those who believe, who have faith, who look for and expect to see Him as He is.
> (3615-1)

> ...He was received up into Heaven, and sat on the right hand of God.
> Mark 16:19

I AM the Resurrection, the Life.
(1747-3)

...I Am the Resurrection, and the Life: He that
believeth in me, though he were dead, yet shall he
live.
John 11:25

...to the heart and soul He brought a Light that faileth
not, a water that is living, a home that is eternal, a
bread that is INDEED a staff of Life!
For HE IS that Life - that LIFE!
(1152-4)

Christ can no longer be separated from Jesus.
The Body that was Jesus which ascended into Heaven is no longer
human as it is now a divine, glorified soul Body. But it is still the
same Body He occupied in Galilee. Jesus and Christ are ONE
forever. He is the mediator between God and mankind. He is each
soul's pattern.

...all Power in Heaven, in Earth, is given to Him who
overcame. Hence He is of Himself in space, in the
force that impels through faith, through belief, in the
individual entity. As a Spirit entity. Hence not in a
Body in the Earth, but may come at will to him who
WILLS to be One with, and acts in Love to make
same possible.
For, He shall come as ye have seen Him go, in the
BODY He occupied in Galilee. The Body that He
formed, that was crucified on the cross, that rose from
the tomb, that walked by the sea, that appeared to
Simon, that appeared to Phillip, that appeared to "I,
even John."
(5749-4)

...who is the blessed and only Potentate, the King of Kings and the Lord of Lords.

I Timothy 6:15

He alone is each soul pattern. He ALONE is each soul pattern!

(2067-2)

For, ONE is the authority – even Him, who has bought the Life, the soul of each entity, with His own PERFECTED Way.

(2132-1)

We have the Gift of the Holy Spirit (which the world cannot receive).

We have the Gift of Grace.

We have our own special place reserved in Christ if we will accept it.

He will walk and talk with us, guide and direct us if we choose Him.

But He does not come unbidden.

For the Master, Jesus, even the CHRIST, is the pattern for every man in the Earth, whether he be gentile or Jew, Parthenian or Greek. For ALL have the pattern, whether they call on that name or not; but there is NO other NAME given under Heaven whereby men may be saved from themselves.

(3528-1)

OPEN the door of thy heart!

For He stands ready to enter, to those who will bid Him enter.

He comes not unbidden, but as ye seek, ye find; as ye knock it is opened.

(5749-10)

For know, as ye live and move and have thy being in
Him, so He is the supply – whether it be material, the
mental, the spiritual.
(1770-2)

...every soul must take Jesus with him if he would
succeed in ANY undertaking.
For He is FIRST in everything and thus the Savior of
the world.
(5083-2)

Life is an essence of the Father. The Christ, taking up
the Life of the man Jesus, becomes Life in glory; and
may be glorified in each atom of a physical Body that
attunes self to the consciousness and the WILL of the
Christ Spirit.
(5749-4)

What, then, will ye do with Jesus?
For He is the Way, He is the Light, He is the hope,
He IS ready. Will ye let Him into thy heart?
Or will ye keep Him afar or apart?
Will ye not eat of His Body, of the bread of Life?
Drink from that fountain that He builds in the Minds,
the hearts, the souls of those that seek to know Him
and His purposes with men, with the world!
For having overcome the world, He INDEED has it- as
it were- in the palm of His hand; and has entrusted to
you this world, because of His faith, His Love for you.
What will you do about Jesus and His trust IN YOU?
(254-95)

For ye have all been with Him from the beginnings
of the experiences of the separations, that ye might be
companions, as One with Him.
(1468-1)

CHAPTER X

THE SECOND COMING
OF JESUS

For God, who commanded the Light to shine out of
darkness, hath shined in our hearts, to give the Light
of the knowledge of the glory of God in the FACE of
Jesus Christ.

II Corinthians 4:6

In thy movements, then, let thy thoughts, thy purposes,
thy hopes, thy desires, ever be towards that of Light.
Not as Light of the sun, or even of the stars - for these
are but reflections of that GLORIOUS LIGHT, which
is in the Son of God – who is thy Light, thy Brother,
yea, thy Lord, thy GOD!

(2067-1)

But, if the heart is open, He will come and abide with
thee. And He in thee, as He in the Father, may know
the Truth that will make thee free indeed.

(1770-2)

Then again He may come in Body to claim His own.
Is He abroad today in the Earth?
Yea, in those that cry unto Him from every corner; …
for, He IS the Son of Light, of God, and is Holy before
Him. And He comes again in the hearts and souls and
Minds of those that seek to know His Ways.
…HE will come in the flesh, in the Earth, to call His
own by name.
(5749-5)

The Cayce Readings indicate that the Second Coming of Jesus
Christ is available, first in Spirit, and in the hearts and Minds of
those who seek Him.
He has been in close personal contact with those who love Him
since the Resurrection and Ascension.
Indeed, even before that, for there never was a time when there was
not the Christ who loves and cares for us all.

If ye call, I will hear. Even though ye be far away, even
though ye be covered with sin, if ye be washed in the
blood of the Lamb, ye may come back.
…He LIVES - and is at the right hand of God to make
intercession for YOU.
(5749-6)

Ye become aware of that consciousness, of that Christ
Spirit, of that Christ Consciousness as He gave – "Ye
abiding in me and I in the Father, WE – the Father, I
will COME and abide with thee."
(272-9)

For as the Heaven is His Throne and Earth is His
footstool, so may we at His feet learn, know, become
aware of, the knowledge of His Ways.
For He is not past finding out. For is God, the Father,
so far away that He answers our pleas, our prayers, as

from afar? Rather is His presence felt when we become aware of His force, His Power, His Love; the knowledge of His presence in our lives, our experiences, our undertakings in His name.
(262-95)

I go to prepare a place that where I am there ye may be also. I will come again and receive you unto myself.
(262-58)

Both Edgar Cayce and Gladys Davis Turner had personal communications and visions of Jesus Christ which were very real and meaningful to them.
Anyone who has ever had a personal experience with Jesus Christ and experienced the Love that He is, will be transformed and humbled by the Light.

There are several Readings that state, "The Lord will come, even as ye have seen Him go."

...there will again appear in the Earth that One through whom many will be called to meet those that are preparing the Way for His day in the Earth.
The Lord, then, will come, even as ye have seen Him go.
(262-49)

Gladys Davis Turner told me that she thought that the statement referred to our own personal relationships with Him from our experiences in Mind, soul, and Spirit, and also from former incarnations.
Those who had watched Him ascend into Heaven would see Him in the air. We have images in our soul consciousness of how we view Him and that is how He will appear to us.
I had a childhood dream of sitting under a tree next to Him and being one of the children blessed by Him. That image has returned to my Mind many times throughout this Lifetime. It has always been a memory to me of a real experience.

I also have had visions of seeing Him before the crucifixion when His hair was chopped off in places and His face was beaten.
When you see Him, face to face, in whatever manner He appears, you will know who He is.

> As ye have seen Him go, so will ye see Him come again. Thou wilt be among those in the Earth when He comes again.
> (3615-1)

> But ye shall receive Power, after that the Holy Ghost is come upon you; and ye shall be witnesses unto me both in Jerusalem, and in all Judea, and in Samaria, and unto the uttermost part of the Earth.
> And when He had spoken these things, while they beheld, He was taken up; and a cloud received Him out of their sight.
> And while they looked steadfastly toward Heaven as He went up, behold, two men stood by them in white apparel; which also said, "Ye men of Galilee, why stand ye gazing up into Heaven? This same Jesus, which is taken up from you into Heaven, shall so come in like manner as ye have seen Him go into Heaven."
> Acts 1:8-11

The Readings state that not one person knows the time when Jesus will return to Earth, except the Father.

> Q: He said He would come again. What about His Second Coming?

> A: The time no one knows. Even as He gave, not even the Son Himself, ONLY the Father. Not until His enemies - and the Earth – are wholly in subjection to His will, His Powers.
> (5749-2)

If we have to wait until the Earth and the enemies of Christ are in subjection to His will, I would say that is far into the future.

> Q: In Revelation 21:1, what is the meaning of "A new Heaven and a new Earth; for the first Heaven and the first Earth were passed away; and there was no more sea?"
>
> A: When the foundations of the Earth are broken up by those very disturbances.
> Can the Mind of man comprehend NO desire to sin, no purpose but that the glory of the Son may be manifested in his Life?
> Is this not a new Heaven, a new Earth?
> (281-37)
>
> Q: What is meant by "The day of the Lord is near at hand?"
>
> A: That as has been promised through the Prophets and the sages of old, the time – and half time - has been and is being fulfilled in this day and generation, and that soon there will again appear in the Earth that one through whom many will be called to meet those that are preparing the Way for His day in the Earth. The Lord, then, will come, even as ye have seen Him go.
>
> Q: How soon?
>
> A: When those that are His have made the Way clear, PASSABLE, for Him to come.
> (262-49)

There will be a thousand year reign of Jesus Christ on Earth with those souls, who have dedicated their lives to do Good and have accepted Him as Lord.

Then, as that coming into the world in the Second Coming – for He will come again and receive His own, who have prepared themselves through that belief in Him and acting in that manner; for the SPIRIT is abroad, and the time draws near, and there will be the reckoning of those even as in the first so in the last, and the last shall be first; for there is the Spirit abroad – He standeth near. He that hath eyes to see, let him see.

He that hath ears to hear, let him hear that music of the coming of the Lord of this vineyard, and art THOU ready to give account of that THOU hast done with thine own opportunity in the Earth as the sons of God, as the heirs and joint heirs of glory WITH the Son? Then make thine paths straight, for there must come an answering for that THOU hast done with thine Lord!

He will not tarry, for having overcome He shall appear even AS the Lord AND Master. Not as One born, but as One that returneth to His own, for He will walk and talk with men of every clime, and those that are faithful and just in their reckoning shall be caught up with Him to rule and to do judgment for a thousand years!

(364-7)

(Notice that Cayce says "caught up" indicating a higher dimension of consciousness.) During this period of time, Satan will be bound for a thousand years. This means that all those souls whose purpose is selfishness, self indulgence, and self glorification will be banished. They will not be allowed to incarnate.

The gates of reincarnation will be closed to them.

Evil influences will be banished from this era.

Cayce tells us to pray to be part of that number who will be in the Earth during that thousand year period.

The Millennium is that time when the material changes will occur. This seems to indicate that the new Fifth Root Race, with a more spiritual Body and a higher level of dimensional functioning, will be present.

> For the Lord Himself shall descend from Heaven with a shout, with the voice of the Archangel, and with the trump of God: And the dead in Christ shall rise first.
>
> Then we which are alive and remain shall be caught up together with them in the clouds, to meet the Lord in the air: And so shall we ever be with the Lord.
>
> I Thessalonians 4:16-17

> Now this I say, brethren, that flesh and blood cannot inherit the Kingdom of God; neither doth corruption inherit incorruption.
>
> Behold, I show you a mystery; we shall not all sleep, but we shall all be changed; in a moment, in the twinkling of an eye, at the last trump; for the trumpet shall sound, and the dead shall be raised incorruptible, and we shall be changed.
>
> For this corruptible must put on incorruption, and this mortal shall have put on immortality, then shall be brought to pass the saying that is written, "Death is swallowed up in victory."
>
> I Corinthians 15:50-54

Before the Second Coming of Christ, many changes will happen in the Earth. Cayce says that the poles will begin to shift in 2000 to 2001 which will cause climates to change and a NEW CYCLE to begin.

Q: What great change or the beginning of what change, if any, is to take place in the Earth in the year 2000 to 2001 A.D.?

A: When there is a shifting of the poles.
(826-8)

Lands will disappear. The east and west coasts will be changed. Los Angeles, then San Francisco and later New York City will disappear. Southern portions of Carolina and Georgia will disappear.

Portions of the now east coast of New York, or New York City itself, will in the main disappear.
This will be another generation, though, here; while the southern portions of Carolina, Georgia - these will disappear. This will be much sooner.
(1152-11)

Most of Japan will go into the sea. The Great Lakes will empty into the Gulf of Mexico.
Land will rise off the Atlantic and Pacific coasts of the U.S. Earthquakes and food shortages will cause mankind to return to the land to grow food.
Montana will be a main food supplier. Ohio, Virginia, Indiana, Illinois, Nebraska and parts of Canada will be safety lands. Europe will be changed in the twinkling of an eye.

As to the changes physical again: The Earth will be broken up in the western portion of America. The greater portion of Japan must go into the sea. The upper portion of Europe will be changed as in the twinkling of an eye.
Land will appear off the east coast of America.
There will be the upheavals in the Arctic and in the Antarctic that will make for the eruption of volcanos in the torrid areas, and there will be shifting then of the

poles – So that where there has been those of a frigid
or the semi-tropical will become the more tropical,
and moss and fern will grow.

And these will begin in those periods in '58 to '98,
when these will be proclaimed as the periods when
His Light will be seen again in the clouds.

(3976-15)

...the entrance of the Messiah in this period -1998.

(5748-5)

The poles have not shifted and the western coast of California has
not changed yet.

Jesus has not returned to set up His Kingdom on Earth.

However, we need to remember that all things happen in Spirit
before they manifest in the flesh.

1998 was given frequently as a very important year. I think that in
1998 the new era began in Spirit.

The Christ Light and presence became more available to us.
Children are being born with open memories and with a higher
level of spiritual understanding.

There are some people who think that the Fifth Root Race has
already begun.

Because major Earth changes have not happened as yet, we may
assume that God has extended the time for these things to occur.

In the early and middle 1970s, when a lot of people were storing
food and buying country property to prepare for the predicted
disasters, many of us were told that the time had been extended by
God. I was one that got that message.

I do not know how long the extension is for but that is up to the
Mercy of God.

Fifty or a hundred years is long to us but not to God who sees a
thousand years as but a day.

There is a Reading for a lady (who had been in Noah's Ark) which
mentions the destruction of the Earth by fire.

Will this entity again see such disaster occur in the Earth? Will she be among those who may be given directions as to how, where, the elect may be preserved for the replenishing again of the Earth?

> Remember, not by water – for it is the Mother of Life in the Earth – but rather by the elements, fire.
> (3653-1)

> But the day of the Lord will come as a thief in the night; in the which the Heavens shall pass away with a great noise, and the elements shall melt with fervent heat, the Earth also and the works that are therein shall be burned up.
> Seeing then that all these things shall be dissolved, what manner of persons, ought ye to be in all Holy conversation and Godliness, looking for and hasting unto the coming of the day of God, wherein the Heavens being on fire shall be dissolved, and the elements shall melt with fervent heat?
> Nevertheless we, according to His promise, look for new Heavens and a new Earth, wherein dwelleth righteousness.
> II Peter 3:10-13

> For the Lord will not always tarry. For He will come as a thief in the night. Are ye ready for His coming?
> (281-27)

Jesus cannot return until the world is in subjection to the Power of His will.
We have not made the Way passable for His return.

During Cayce's time it was asked if they were entering into a time to prepare for the Second Coming.
It was stated that they were entering a period of testing.

Q: Are we entering the period of preparation for His coming?

A: Entering the test period, rather.
(5749-2)

We all dislike the "end of the world" and "doomsday" type prophecies, but it seems that Earth changes and tribulations might have to occur to wake us up.

None of these things has to happen if mankind would rise up and become his Brother's keeper and treat all others as he wants to be treated in every circumstance.

We should manifest Love and kindness instead of hate and greed.

What happened to, "In God We Trust?"

Mankind needs to be ruled by the spiritual influences of the Love and nature of Christ, not the ego and animal influences of selfishness.

"Thou shall Love the Lord thy God with all thine heart, and thy neighbor as thyself."
This is the basis of ALL SPIRITUAL LAW!
(3976-14)

For many shall come in my name saying, I am Christ; and shall deceive many.

And ye shall hear of wars and rumors of wars; see that ye be not troubled; for all these things must come to pass, but the end is not yet.

For nation shall rise against nation, and Kingdom against Kingdom; and there shall be famines, and pestilences, and earthquakes, in divers places.

All these are the beginning of sorrows.
Matthew 24:5-8

Unless these days be shortened – as has been given – the very elect may be shaken, may tremble at the destruction, the littleness to which human Life is held in the ideas of groups or nations, or those purposes that have been set.

(3976-27)

These changes in the Earth will come to pass, for the times and half times are at an end, and there begin those periods for the readjustments.
For how hath He given?
"The righteous shall inherit the Earth."

(294-185)

As to the material changes that are to be as an omen, as a sign to those that this is shortly to come to pass – as has been given of old, the sun will be darkened, and the Earth will be broken up in divers places - and THEN shall be PROCLAIMED - through the spiritual interception in the hearts and Minds and souls of those that have sought His Way – that HIS star has appeared, and will point the Way for those that enter into the Holy of Holies in themselves.

(3976-15)

Before the thousand year reign of Christ with His followers, it is stated that Satan shall be bound.
Then it states that Satan will be loosed for a season.

Q: When Jesus the Christ comes the second time, will He set up His Kingdom on Earth and will it be an everlasting Kingdom?

A: Read His promises in that ye have written of His words, even as I gave. He shall rule for a thousand years. Then shall Satan be loosed again for a season.

(5749-4)

Both the Bible and Cayce seem to agree that there will be souls of the FIRST resurrection who will be with Christ for a thousand years, then the other souls who are bound and not allowed to incarnate will be given another chance. God is merciful beyond our comprehension.

> And I saw an Angel come down from Heaven, having the key of the bottomless pit and a great chain in his hand.
> And he laid hold on the Dragon, that old Serpent, which is the Devil, and Satan, and bound him a thousand years.
> And cast him into the bottomless pit, and shut him up, and set a seal upon him, that he should deceive the nations no more, till the thousand years should be fulfilled:
> And after that, he must be loosed a little season.
> And I saw Thrones, and they sat upon them, and judgment was given unto them: And I saw the souls of them that were beheaded for the witness of Jesus, and for the Word of God, and which had not worshipped the beast, neither his image, neither had received his mark upon their foreheads, or in their hands; and they lived and reigned with Christ a thousand years.
> But the rest of the dead lived not again until the thousand years were finished.
> This is the First Resurrection.
> Revelation 20:1-5

Q: What is the meaning of one thousand years that Satan is bound?

A: Is banished.
...those only that are in the Lord shall rule the Earth, and the period is as a thousand years.

> Thus is Satan bound, thus is Satan banished from the Earth. The desire to do evil is only of him.
>
> And when there are - as the symbols - those only whose desire and purpose of their heart is to glorify the Father, these will be those periods when this shall come to pass.
>
> Be YE ALL DETERMINED within thy Minds, thy hearts, thy purposes, to be of that number!
>
> (281-37)

The Bible is symbolic and literal but in parts must be spiritually discerned.

The Book of Revelation is symbolic but literal in places.

It is written in symbols to help those souls who SEEK to know and walk in a closer communion with the Christ, through deep spiritual meditation.

> For the visions, the experiences, the names, the churches, the places, the Dragons, the cities, all are but emblems of those forces that may war within the individual in its journey through the material, or from the entering into the material manifestation to the entering into the glory, or the awakening in the Spirit, in the inter-between, in the borderland, in the shadow.
>
> Hence we find, as the churches are named, they are as the forces that are known as the senses, that must be spiritualized by the will of the individual made One in the very activities in a material world.
>
> (281-16)

The Cayce material contains many Readings on the Book of Revelation which relate to the human Body with its psychic or glandular centers that need to be spiritualized (seven endocrine glands).

Cayce links the seven glands with the seven churches in Revelation (pituitary, pineal, thyroid, thymus, solar plexus, lyden, gonads to: Laodicea, Philadelphia, Sardis, Thyatira, Pergamos, Smyrna, Ephesus). During meditation the Life force energy called the Kundalini is raised from the lower centers of the gonads and the lyden center upward in the spine through nerve centers to the higher centers of pineal and pituitary.

> In the Body we find that which connects the pineal, the pituitary, the lyden, may be truly called the Silver Cord, or the Golden Cup that may be filled with a closer walk with that which is the creative essence in physical, mental, and spiritual Life; for the destruction wholly of either will make for the disintegration of the soul from its house of clay.
> (262-20)

Cayce tells us that true meditation loosens us from physical consciousness into the Universal Consciousness.

> Thus, an entity puts itself, through such an activity, into association or in conjunction with all it has EVER been or may be. For, it loosens the physical consciousness to the Universal Consciousness.
> (2475-1)

The flesh Body with its ego consciousness must be in subjection to the will of the soul in Spirit for One to be in God's will.
No one really knows what the thousand year or Millennium with the Fifth Root Race will be like.
But the righteous shall inherit the Earth.
He will come AGAIN in the FLESH, in the Earth to call His own by name.
He will come in His resurrected Body that He had in Galilee.

> Then again He may come in Body to claim His own.
> (5749-5)

...for He will walk and talk with men of every clime...
(364-7)

There will be no desire in mankind to commit sin. Man's motivation will be to glorify God.
There will be a reckoning in which those souls, chosen to be a part of this era, will have to give an account of all that they have done with the Lord.

> And when there are - as the symbols - those only whose desire and purpose of their heart is to glorify the Father, these will be those periods when this shall come to pass.
> (281-37)

> ...and those that are faithful and just in their reckoning shall be caught up with Him to rule and to do judgment for a thousand years!
> (364-7)

> ...those only that are in the Lord shall rule the Earth, and the period is as a thousand years.
> (281-37).

It was stated that the pyramid which contains the Hall of Records of creation and history of Christ will not be opened until the Fifth Root Race begins.

> ...NOT be passed until after a period of their regeneration in the Mount, or the Fifth Root Race begins.
> (5748-6)

(The Mount is often referred to as the "Holy of Holies" within). It was also stated that the selfish motivations in mankind must be eliminated before the opening of these sacred records.

...it will be necessary to wait until the full time has
come for the breaking up of much that has been in the
nature of selfish motives in the world.

(2329-3)

Cayce gave Readings for people who would be a part of the
Millennium.

Ye, too, may minister in those days when He will come
in the flesh, in the Earth, to call His own by name.

(5749-5)

Thou wilt be among those in the Earth when He
comes again.

(3615-1)

For, we shall see Him as He is. He will walk among
men. He will be in thy midst. Be thou, then, those that
will make His paths straight; for narrow is the Way yet
straight is the gate that leads to that knowledge that
may be had in Him.

(294-174)

...His promises are sure, that there may come that
Life in a manifested form that would BEGIN AGAIN
those of face to face may they speak with the Father
and with the Son.

(254-68)

There is a Reading that indicates that Edgar Cayce may return again
in the 1998 era with many of his followers from the Ra Ta period as
a liberator of the world.

...as this Priest may develop himself to be in that
position, to be in the capacity of a LIBERATOR of
the world in its relationships to individuals in those

> periods to come; for he must enter again at that
> period, or in 1998.
> (294-151)

He also had a dream of another incarnation in the year 2158 showing Nebraska being on the coast in which he recalled his Lifetime as Edgar Cayce.

> I had been born again in 2158 A.D. in Nebraska; the
> sea apparently covered all of the western part of the
> country, as the city where I lived was on the coast.
> (294-185)

Cayce tells us it is best to live every day as if we expected Jesus to come today.

> Live ye then, each soul, as though ye expected Him
> today. Then ye shall see Him as He is when ye live
> such a Life.
> (3011-3)

It will be revealed to those who are His, who love His coming, when He will appear. He calls His own by name. Those who reject Him will be passed over.

> And He will come again and again in the hearts, in
> the Minds, in the experiences of those that LOVE His
> coming.
> BUT those when they think on Him and know what
> His presence would mean and become FEARFUL,
> He passeth by -
> (1152-1)

> As to times, as to seasons, as to places, ALONE is it
> given to those who have named the NAME – and who

bear the mark of those of His calling and His election
in their bodies. To them it shall be given.
(3976-15)

I leave thee, but I will come again and receive as many
as ye have quickened through the manifesting in thy
Life the WILL of the Father in the Earth.
(262-58)

He comes unto His own.
Art thou His?
Have ye claimed Him?
Have ye put on the Christ?
(262-103)

CHAPTER XI

THE ANTI-CHRIST

Q: In what form does the Anti-Christ come, spoken of in Revelation?

A: In the Spirit of that opposed to that of the Spirit of Truth.
The fruits of the Spirit of the Christ are Love, joy, obedience, long-suffering, Brotherly Love, kindness. Against such there is no Law.
The Spirit of hate, the Anti-Christ, is contention, strife, fault-finding, lovers of self, lovers of praise.
Those are the Anti-Christ, and take possession of groups, masses, and show themselves even in the lives of men.
(281-16)

Q: Explain what is meant by those whose names are not written in the Book of Life?

A: Those not written are those who have climbed up some other Way...

... there are those who from the first – as he that is last to be bound – had the import to do evil. Then those who have followed closely after the flesh, or the indulgences of the emotions of the Body alone, without the considerations of others, without, other than self's own interests - as is shown by the beast that is loosened - these are they whose names are not written, and these are they who are easily led about by every wind that bloweth, unstable...not hot, not cold, but allowing today, tomorrow, the circumstance of the moment to sway - without purpose, without direction, without the Name.

(281-34)

Cayce did not like to personalize evil and made the statement that evil did not become manifested in matter but is rather of a mental and spiritual influence. This is not to say that there is not evil in the world but it comes through man's choices that are selfish.

Evil cannot come in unless allowed and invited in by man.

For, the Spirit of evil has not, did not become manifested in matter; only has it moved by or upon or through matter.

(5752-3)

We all have within us the Christ Light of Truth and a past history of patterns in rebellion.

A good example of how evil influences can work within a person who is seeking to manifest Truth, is Peter.

First, Peter was lead by the Spirit to know who Jesus really is.

He saith unto them, "But whom say ye that I am?" And Simon Peter answered and said, "Thou art the Christ, the Son of the living God." And Jesus answered and said unto him, "Blessed art thou, Simon Bar-jona: For flesh and blood hath

343

not revealed it unto thee but my Father which is in Heaven."

Matthew 16:15-17

Then, Peter was led by evil influences to persuade Jesus to evade the suffering and death that was to come.

> From that time forth began Jesus to show unto His disciples, how that He must go unto Jerusalem, and suffer many things of the elders and chief Priests and scribes, and be killed, and be raised again the third day. Then Peter took Him, and began to rebuke Him, saying, "Be it far from thee, Lord: This shall not be unto thee."
> But He turned, and said unto Peter, "Get thee behind me, Satan: Thou art an offense unto me: For thou savorest not the things that be of God, but those that be of men."
>
> Matthew 16:21-23

In Chapter III, The Fall of Celestial Beings, a lot about Good and Evil was mentioned.
There are influences that have been in Spirit since before Earth was created that seek to hinder the souls created by/in Christ.
There is spiritual wickedness in high places (fallen Angels).
Nevertheless, evil influences have no Power over us unless we give in to them by making self centered, self indulgent choices.

> For the Angels of Light only use material things for emblems, while the Angels of death use these as LURES that may carry men's souls away. For the Master gave, "There is a Way that seemeth right to the hearts of men, but the end thereof is death and confusion."
>
> (1159-1)

Edgar Cayce personally believed that Satan was an actual person, not just an evil influence.

> "We can try to delude ourselves by saying that there is NO evil; yet if we believe in the record laid down for us we must realize that Satan is abroad in the Earth, seeking to add to his side all who will listen to him."
> (A quote from Cayce's Bible class)

The following Reading indicates that Satan is either an Angel or a Son, perhaps both:

> Readest thou how the sons of God came together, and Satan came also?
> "Hast thou considered my servant? (Job)
> Hast thou seen his Ways?"
> And the answer, even from the EVIL force,
> "Put forth thy hand – touch him in those things that pertain to the satisfying of desire that is flesh, and he will curse thee to thy face."
> "He is in thine hand, but touch not his soul, touch not his soul!" (God speaking)
> So we see how that the coming into the Earth has been and is for the evolution or the evolving of the soul unto its awareness of the effect of all influences in its experience in the varied spheres of activity; and that only in HIM who was the Creator, the Maker, the experiencer of mortality and Spirit, and soul COULD this be overcome.
> (5749-5)

There is a Reading which states...

> ...as the Powers of evil are loosed for the correcting of many...
> (262-30)

There is another Reading that refers to Satan as a "wayward son."

> For the Law of the Lord is perfect and ye as a child of
> the divine may apply it to the works of thy Lord and
> Savior, or to His wayward son, Satan.
>> (3541-1)

> ...and apple trees don't produce peaches, neither does
> a son of Satan produce Saints.
> But ye are the son of the Almighty, the creative forces,
> even as Satan.
> Whose side are you on?
> Ye alone can determine. Will ye?
>> (4083-1)

How do we know the difference between Good and Evil ?
Cayce says to ask within, "What would Jesus do?"

> "What would Jesus have me do" regarding every
> question...this rather should be the question, rather
> than "What shall I do?"
>> (1326-1)

How do we take sides?
We determine whom we will serve by our choices.

> There is before thee this day Life and death, Good
> and Evil.
> These are the ever present warring influences within
> materiality.
> "...My Spirit beareth witness with thy Spirit as to
> whether ye be the Children of God or not."
> This becomes, then, that force, that influence for
> comparisons; as the entity meditates upon its own
> emotions, its own influences, these become very
> apparent within itself for comparisons.

> Do they bespeak of kindness, gentleness, patience, -
> that threshold upon which Godliness appears?
> Desire may be Godly or ungodly, dependent upon the
> purpose, the aim, the emotions aroused.
> Does it bring, then, self abstinence?
> Or does it bring self desire?
> Does it bring Love? Does it bring long-suffering? Is it
> gentle? Is it kind?
> Then, these be the judgments upon which the entity
> uses those influences upon the lives of others.
> (1947-3)

There are two influences available to all of us; Good and Evil, and we choose continually which influence we will manifest by our choices.
These spiritual conditions within battle and war against each other. The same forces are outside in the mental – spiritual realms seeking to influence us in our choices.

I remember the old cartoons in the 1940s. There would be a Devil with a pitch fork sitting on one shoulder of a person and an Angel with a halo on the other one, each urging us to choose its influence. This is still a continuing reality.

> For the material conditions, spiritual conditions, and
> the relations between each, show the two BATTLING
> conditions as exist in the world – called God and
> Christianity on one side, with flesh and the DEVIL
> on the other.
> (195-19)

Lucifer, Satan, or the Devil is a manifestation of evil influences personified.
Is he an actual individual person besides being an influence? Cayce personally thought that Satan was an individual as well as an influence for evil and the Readings agree.

> As there is, then, a personal Savior, there is a personal
> Devil.
> (262-52)

Jesus Christ is a personification of God in manifestation,
demonstrating the nature of Love and Goodness.

> It has been understood by most of those who have
> attained to a consciousness of the various presentations
> of Good and Evil in manifested forms, that the
> Prince of this world, Satan, Lucifer, the Devil—as a
> SOUL- made those necessities, of the consciousness
> in materiality; that man might – or that the soul
> might — become aware of its separation from the
> God-Force.
> Hence the continued warring that is ever present in
> materiality or in the FLESH, or the warring between
> those influences of Good and Evil.
> As the soul is then a portion of the divine, it must
> eventually return to that source from which, of which
> it is a part.
> Will THY name be written there?
> (262-89)

Lucifer, Satan, the Devil, is also called the son of perdition, the man
of sin, the Prince of this world, the Father of lies, the accuser of the
brethren, the Dragon, Serpent, beast, tormentor, false Prophet, et al.
The Spirit of the Anti-Christ is rebellion, disobedience, hate,
selfishness, self indulgence, self glorification, contention, strife, lies,
deception, the flesh/material over the Spirit, etc.
The seven deadly sins are: Envy, lust, pride, wrath, sloth, gluttony,
and greed.
The Readings say that this Spirit of the Anti-Christ takes over groups
and masses as well as individuals.
It is not our place to judge others but we need to have spiritual
discernment.

Judging is assuming the offices of God. God alone sees the heart and soul of each individual.

But we need to be able to discern Good from Evil to make correct choices in our lives for Good.

Think about all those souls who will be bound for a thousand years with the Satanic group because they made choices for selfishness not fully understanding the consequences.

One of the biggest flaws or deceptions in the New Age logic is, "There is NO EVIL."

This means no retribution or Karma.

Anything goes since there is no punishment or payment for actions.

Many think that the murderers and rapists go instantly back to God, as if all their deeds were acceptable. "After all, this is only a dream down here on Earth and not real," they say.

But our experiences are written and recorded and we will be held accountable for them.

According to the Readings, our consciousness must be pure enough and be like Christ to return to God.

We cannot return until we are FIT companions.

We were created in His image and we must conform to that image. Jesus Christ is the pattern of God's likeness which is written within us. That is what all the reincarnations are about, to give us opportunities to cleanse ourselves of pollutions and selfish patterns that would not fit in the creative Source of God which is all Light and Love.

This is why Jesus came, suffered, died, and resurrected, then ascended into Heaven to be the mediator for us to return through Him.

Without the knowledge of Good and Evil, we cannot choose correctly.

> ...as to whether it will be One with the Father or, even as the son of perdition, attempt to establish self in glory of self.
> (262-118)

Q: Explain John 17:12

"...and none of them is lost, but the son of perdition."

A: He had chosen rather to seek his OWN Ways and to deceive others into seeking to follow their own manner rather than that there should be credence or credit or loyalty or Love shown to that Source from which Life, consciousness or manifestations emanated. Hence that spoken of him that rebelled against the Throne of Heaven, and manifested in the flesh in the one who betrayed Him.

Then, all are sons of perdition – or allow that force to manifest through them – who deny Him, or who betray Him, or who present themselves to be one thing and - under Earthly environment or for personal gain, or for reasons of gratification – do otherwise; for they do but persecute, deny, betray Him.

(262-93)

The Anti-Christ is the force that denies the Christ Son and seeks to replace Him or to take His PLACE.

The Anti-Christ Source denies the Christ or that Jesus was Christ in the flesh. The divinity of Jesus is always fought against. The Anti-Christ goes to great lengths to discredit Jesus as the manifestation of Christ in the Earth.

To deny that there is a God or that there is a spiritual Source results in materialism and selfishness.

The Anti-Christ Source always assumes a position that he did not merit, claiming to be more than he is entitled to be. The Anti-Christ claims to be God or Christ rather than to serve the One God. The Anti-Christ never bows but instead sets himself up or one of his Angels as a substitute for Christ.

Self exaltation, self glorification and superiority are prime motivators of the Anti-Christ who wishes to deceive others into joining his side. "I am God or I am Christ" Lucifer proclaims, trying to steal a position that he did not earn.

We are meant to reflect the Light within us, to be channels of God in the Earth.

We are created to be One with God through Christ and to keep our own individuality so we can be companions.

We will never be the Whole but we can be our own individual portions of that Whole in Christ.

> For whom He did foreknow, He also did predestinate to be conformed to the image of His Son, that He might be the Firstborn among many brethren.
>
> Romans 8:29

> Who is a liar but he that denieth that Jesus is the Christ. He is Anti-Christ, that denieth the Father and the Son.
> Whosoever denieth the Son, the same hath not the Father...
>
> I John 2:22-23

> Beloved, BELIEVE NOT every Spirit, but try the Spirits whether they are of God; because many false Prophets are gone out into the world.
> Hereby know ye the Spirit of God; every Spirit that confesseth that Jesus Christ is come in the flesh is of God; and every Spirit that confesseth not that Jesus Christ is come in the flesh is not of God; and this is that SPIRIT of Anti-Christ, whereof ye have heard that it should come; and even now already is it in the world.
>
> I John 4:1-3

The Bible warned about false Prophets.

> Beware of false Prophets, which come to you in sheep's clothing, but inwardly they are ravening wolves.
>
> Matthew 7:15

Jesus told of the separation of Good from Evil in the scriptures.

> When the Son of Man shall come in His glory, and all the Holy Angels with Him, then He shall sit upon the Throne of His glory. And before Him shall be gathered all nations: And He shall separate them one from another, as a shepherd divideth his sheep from the goats.
> Matthew 25:31-32

He also gave the parable of the wheat and the tares.

> Let both grow together until the harvest; and in the time of harvest I will say to the reapers, gather ye together first the tares, and bind them in bundles to burn them:
> But gather the wheat into my barn.
> Matthew 13:30

He recognized that there are those who are serving Satan (self) instead of God even though they may be in high positions in the world.

> For false Christs and false Prophets shall rise, and shall shew signs and wonders, to seduce, if it were possible, even the elect.
> Mark 13:22

Jesus spoke very strongly and directly to the important religious figures during His Lifetime but those leaders did not really know God personally.

> ...If God were your Father, ye would love me; for I proceeded forth and came from God; neither came I of myself, but He sent me.
> Why do ye not understand my speech?

Even because ye cannot hear my word.
Ye are of your Father, the Devil, and the lusts of your Father ye will do. He was a murderer from the beginning, and abode not in the Truth, because there is no Truth in him. When he speaketh a lie, he speaketh of his own; for he is a liar and the Father of it.
And because I tell you the Truth, ye believe me not.
Which of you convinceth me of sin?
And if I say the Truth, why do ye not believe me?
He that is of God heareth God's words; ye therefore hear them not, because ye are not of God.
John 8:42-47

Just because we are in the world does not mean we have to join forces with the Prince of this world. The scripture below told us to be in the world but not of it.

Love not the world, neither the things that are in the world.
I John 2:15

The people who worship the animal - beastly nature over their spiritual nature have submerged the Light within by choices not in God's will. These are the souls led by the Anti-Christ Spirit.
Those souls who are bound for a thousand years then loosed again indicates that they can incarnate again and then will have an opportunity never available to them before.
I think this scripture may refer to Christians who were deluded into believing the Anti-Christ's lies and were taken over by evil influences.
There will be a new Body-type (Fifth Root Race) and a Christ – centered world of Peaceful, loving people to help them make higher choices.
These clean birth channels will create a world without greed or strife or selfishness which will help those souls led by the Anti-Christ

Joan Clarke

Spirit to remember who they are in Spirit. No soul will be lost unless they will it.
How long is "loosed for a season" going to be?
A thousand years or more?

Christian fundamentalists believe the Book of Revelation is to be taken literally and expect Satan to manifest in the Earth as a man. Satan will sit in the Temple of God as if he were God, exalting himself. Traditional Christians understand the temple to be a physical temple in Jerusalem that must be rebuilt or a church as yet unidentified.
It may be literal. With the big self image that Lucifer seems to have, it would be logical that he would want to be seen in the flesh personified.

> Let no man deceive you by any means; for that day shall not come, except there be a falling away first, and that man of sin be revealed, the son of perdition; who opposeth and exalteth himself above all that is called God, or that is worshipped; so that he as God sitteth in the Temple of God, shewing himself that he is God.
> II Thessalonians 2:3-4

The Cayce material does not confirm this version but does see groups and individuals controlled by the Anti-Christ Spirit.
Jesus said, "Destroy this temple, and in three days I will raise it up." (See John 2:19.) They did not realize that He meant His Body as the temple, not some physical structure.
The Anti-Christ as Satan is seen as an individual in Spirit as well as an influence for evil. But there are a few Readings about Judas that may indicate that he was a part of the Anti-Christ group incarnating in the Earth.

> Hence that spoken of him that rebelled against the Throne of Heaven, and manifested in the flesh in the one who betrayed Him.
> (262-93)

354

I was involved in the Charismatic Movement throughout most of the 1970s.

There are various doctrines about the Great Tribulation, the Rapture, Armageddon, and the Second Coming of Jesus Christ.

I had several very clear inner directions (visions, dreams, direct voice) that said the details of ALL of these concepts are incorrect.

It will happen differently from what any of us expect (including me).

These theories by the churches are deducted from an intellectual viewpoint and not spiritually discerned.

Most of these ideas are taken from a literal translation of the Bible instead of symbolic as intended.

The Great Tribulation is thought to occur before the Second Coming of Jesus Christ.

It is stated to be a period of seven years of great persecution for those who follow Christ.

> For then shall be Great Tribulation, such as was not since the beginning of the world to this time, no, nor ever shall be.
> And except those days be shortened, there should no flesh be saved; but for the elect's sake those days shall be shortened.
> Matthew 24:21-22

The Tribulation timetable is based on the prophecies of Daniel.

Different religions have various views and interpretations of how this will occur. Some groups believe that they will be taken out (the Rapture) before the Tribulation begins and others believe it will happen in the middle or end of the seven years. Then some believe the Tribulation already occurred in 70 A.D. when the temple in Jerusalem was destroyed by the Romans.

The Rapture is a concept based on the scripture quoted earlier about the return of Jesus to gather His Saints and their being "caught up together to meet the Lord in the air."

> For the Lord Himself shall descend from Heaven with
> a shout, with the voice of the Archangel and with the
> trump of God; and the dead in Christ shall rise first;
> then we which are alive and remain shall be caught up
> together with them in the clouds to meet the Lord in
> the air; and so shall we ever be with the Lord.
>> 1 Thessalonians 4:16-17

The Rapture has been taught since the 1700s.
The idea of Christ coming after the Tribulation is based on the
Scripture below.

> Immediately AFTER the Tribulation of those days
> shall the sun be darkened, and the moon shall not give
> her Light, and the stars shall fall from Heaven, and
> the Powers of the Heavens shall be shaken; and then
> shall appear the Son of Man in Heaven; and then shall
> all the tribes of the Earth mourn, and they shall see
> the Son of Man coming in the clouds of Heaven with
> Power and great glory.
> And He shall send His Angels with a great sound of
> a trumpet, and they shall gather together His elect
> from the four winds, from one end of Heaven to the
> other.
>> Matthew 24:29-31
>> (also found in Mark 13:24-27 & Luke 21:25-27)

The Tribulation period is when the Anti-Christ rules and the Mark
of the Beast is established in which no one can buy or sell without a
mark of 666 on the forehead or hand.
The Cayce material does not state clearly if this will be an actual
event but it does discuss those who bear the Mark of the Beast.

> Q: Is this the period of the Great Tribulation spoken
> of in Revelation?…

A: The Great Tribulation and periods of Tribulation are the experiences of every soul, every entity. They arise from INFLUENCES created by man through activity in the sphere of any sojourn. Man may become, with the people of the universe, ruler of any of the various spheres through which the soul passes in its experiences. Hence, as the cycles pass, as the cycles are passing, when there IS come a time, a period of readjusting in the spheres (as well as the little Earth, the little soul) – seek then, as known, to present self spotless before that Throne; even as ALL are commanded to be circumspect, in thought, in act, to that which is held by self as that necessary for the closer walk with Him.

In that manner only may each atom (as man is an atom, or corpuscle in the Body of the Father) become a helpmeet with Him in bringing that to pass that all may be One with Him.

   (281-16)

Q: Explain the symbol of the 2nd beast with two horns, having the Power to perform miracles. Revelation 13.

A: As has been given by Him, the Power as attained by the study that has been shown in the first portions is to be applied, or may be applied unworthily – as is shown by the beast with two Ways, two horns. Then here, how hath it been given? One Lord, One faith, One God, One baptism, One Way! Yet in the experiences as ye watch about you there are constantly shown the influences by the very forces of the beast with the double-mindedness, as showing wonders in the Earth yet they must come even as He hath given, "Though ye may have done this or that, though ye may have healed the sick, though ye may have cast

Joan Clarke

out Demons in my name, I know ye not; for ye have
followed rather as the beast of self-aggrandizement,
self-indulgence, self-glorification," even as the beast
shown here.

(281-34)

Those who have the Mark of the Beast are those who join with the
work of organizations and groups that are not directed by God.

Q: What is meant by the Mark of the Beast in the
right hand or forehead?

A: These are as signs or symbols of this or that grouping,
or of the organizations that become as a part of the
vows or obligations to those who have joined in with
the WORK of the beast.
Hence the warning that if these come to mean more
in the experience they stand as that which condemns,
rather than that which is the helpful experience.
For having the MARK of the Beast and the MARK of
the Lamb becomes the DIFFERENCE between the
consciousness of the indwelling presence of the Christ
and the hoped for yet not seen or known.

(281-34)

Simply put, it is the same old principles of Good and Evil, those that
serve self and indulgences. Those who glorify themselves are taking
the Mark of the Beast within and gathering together without. Those
who serve Christ and are washed in the blood of the Lamb belong
to Him and serve God.

The Battle of Armageddon is a war between the forces of Good and
Evil. Armageddon is when the Messiah, Jesus Christ, returns and
destroys the rule of Satan on Earth. It is usually seen as happening
before the reign of Christ.
Satan will be put in the bottomless pit for 1000 years.

Some see the Battle of Armageddon to occur after the 1000 year period when Satan is loosed for a season.

The Cayce Readings indicated that Armageddon is a battle in Spirit between hosts of Angels of Light and those Angels who serve the darkness. They war against souls coming into the Earth and leaving the Earth as well.

The Angels of Light are protecting the souls from those Angels of darkness who are seeking to harm or prevent them from entering.

This war will last 1000 years the Readings state; it is not clear if it means during the reign of Peace or Millennium or if it is at a later time after Satan is loosed for a season or even before the return of Christ.

It does not make sense that if Satan is bound and has no influence that evil forces would still be hindering souls in Spirit but not in Earth during the reign of Peace.

It is supposed to be a time of a "new Heaven" as well as a "new Earth." It seems more logical that they would be warring for those souls who were bound with Satan but who seek another chance in incarnating as they come back into the Earth (unless it is referring to the period just before the Christ returns).

At some point in time, there will be a final decision in which the fate of Lucifer or Satan, his Angels, and those souls who sided with him, will forever be decided.

That will be the "final Judgment Day."

It seems reasonable to think that this will be AFTER the 1000 year reign of Peace after which Satan will be loosed for a season; then AFTER that season is over, the end will come.

> Q: If the Armageddon is foretold in the Great Pyramid, please give a description of it...
>
> A: Not in what is left there.
> IT WILL BE AS A THOUSAND YEARS, WITH THE FIGHTING IN THE AIR, and – as has been

- BETWEEN THOSE RETURNING TO AND
THOSE LEAVING THE EARTH.
(5748-6)

...and those that in the inmost recesses of themselves
awaken to the spiritual Truths that are to be given,
and those places that have acted in the capacity of
teachers among men, the rottenness of those that have
ministered in places will be brought to Light, and
turmoils and strifes shall enter.

And, as there is the wavering of those that would enter
as emissaries, as teachers, from the Throne of Life,
the Throne of Light, the Throne of Immortality, and
wage war in the air with those of darkness, then know
ye that Armageddon is at hand. For with the great
numbers of the gathering of the HOSTS of those that
have HINDERED and would make stumbling blocks
for man and his weaknesses, they shall wage WAR
with the Spirits of Light that come into the Earth for
this awakening; that have been and are being called
by those of the sons of men into the service of the
living God.

For He, as ye have been told, is not the God of
the dead, not the God of those that have forsaken
Him, but those that love His coming, that love His
associations among men - the God of the LIVING,
the God of Life!

For, He IS Life.
(3976-15)

My direction back in the 1970s was that none of us has the proper
understanding of all of these events that are to come. I guess we as
humans cannot help but try to figure things out.

It would be best to keep an open Mind but stay centered in Christ.

What did Cayce say about Heaven and Hell?

The "final Judgment Day" has NOT come so these decisions will
not be made until some point in the future.
In the meantime, we make our own Heaven and Hell according to
our choices.
In the spiritual planes there are many dimensions of consciousness
and we enter the realms we earn and deserve according to what we
have built by our choices in materiality and in other dimensions
of consciousness. There are all these different planetary levels of
awareness available to us to grow in Truth.

> Heaven is that place, that awareness where the soul
> – with all its attributes, its Mind, its Body – becomes
> aware of being in the presence of the creative forces or
> One with same. That is Heaven.
> (262-88)

> ...but the Kingdom of the Father or the Kingdom of
> Heaven is within! Why? Because our Mind, the Son,
> is within us.
> (1567-2)

> For you grow to Heaven, you don't go to Heaven.
> (3409-1)

Death of the physical Body is just a transition into another awareness
of Universal Consciousness that is non-flesh. When we die, we lose
our conscious human Mind and our unconscious Mind becomes
the conscious Mind of the soul.
Our individual soul is our Body containing all that we are and have
been.

> And with error entered that as called DEATH, which
> is only a transition – or through God's other door –
> into that realm where the entity has builded, in its
> manifestations as related to the knowledge and activity
> respecting the Law of the universal influence.

361

...Death in the material plane is passing through the outer door into a consciousness in the material activities that partakes of what the entity, or soul, has done with its spiritual Truth in its manifestations...
(5749-3)

When the Body physical lays aside the the material Body, that in the physical called SOUL becomes the BODY of the entity, and that called the superconscious the consciousness of the entity, as the subconscious is to the physical Body. The subconscious the Mind or intellect of the Body.
(900-304)

During the Readings on the Book of Revelation, a question was asked if we were to be punished by fire and brimstone.

For, each soul is a portion of creation – and builds that in a portion of its experience that it, through its physical-mental or spiritual-mental, has builded for itself. And each entity's Heaven or Hell must, through SOME experience, be that which it has builded for itself.
Is thy Hell one that is filled with fire and brimstone?
But know, each and every soul is tried so as by fire; purified, purged; for He, though He were the Son, learned obedience through the things which He suffered.
Ye also are KNOWN even as ye do, and have done.
(281-16)

Does fire burn the soul or the physical Body?
Yet, self may cast self into a fire element by doing that the soul knows to be wrong!
(5753-1)

...He broke the bonds of death, overcame Hell and the grave, and rose in a newness of Life; that ye - here and now - may know that Peace in these troubled times.
(3976-27)

From what may ANYONE be saved?
Only from themselves!
That is, their individual Hell, they dig it with their own desires!
(262-40)

Does this mean there is no Hell?
I think not, because the Readings agree with the Bible and state that Hell was made ready for Satan and his Angels.

Hell was prepared for Satan and his Angels, yet God has not WILLED that any soul should perish!
(900-20)

And the Angels which kept not their first estate, but left their own habitation, He hath reserved in everlasting chains under darkness unto the judgment of the great day.
Jude:6

Is this a final destiny for Satan and those souls who have refused to accept Christ?
The Bible and the Readings seem to indicate that it is, but there is a lot of time left before the final end so who knows what can happen in the future?

Another controversial subject is about the fallen Angels.
Since very early times there have been people who taught and believed that some of these fallen Angels incarnated in flesh on the Earth.

The goals of these beings are corruption, dominion, lust, and Power. Some sources claim that the sons of Belial in Atlantis were fallen Angels.

Is it possible for an Angel to incarnate in flesh?

As stated earlier in this book, Cayce never gave a Reading for anyone who was said to have been an Angel. But there are Readings for individuals who have Guides that were used in the capacity of Angels who have at one time lived in Earth as a human entity (See Page 303 re Demetrius.)

Cayce described the fall of the sons of God in the beginning as the fall of celestial beings who were similar to Angels.

The Cayce material makes a difference between the creations of sons and Angels. However, some individuals who have been on the Earth have completed their cycle of incarnations and are of the Saint realm and serve in ways that are protective like Angels. These are the true ascended souls who work for Christ. They do not set themselves up as Masters who think themselves superior to Christ.

The Readings stress to not be concerned with the name of any of these messengers God uses but to concentrate on the message. We need to glorify the Creator, not the messenger whom God sends.

A true messenger or Angel of Light will never seek to create a personal relationship with humans or personify themselves.

Lucifer, who is an Angel, is called Satan on the Earth and a "wayward son."

Here the Angel, Satan, is being called a son.

> But ye are the son of the Almighty, the creative forces, even as Satan.
> (4083-1)

Then we are told that we each have a Guardian Angel before the Throne of Heaven and that our self is that Angel.

> Q: Is it through the Guardian Angel that God speaks to the individual?

A: Ever through that influence or force as He has
given, "Ye abide in me and I in thee, as the Father
abideth in me, so may we make our abode with thee."
Then, as the Guardian influence or Angel is ever
before the Face of the Father, through same may that
influence ever speak – but only by the command of or
attunement to that which is thy ideal.
What then is thy ideal?
In WHOM have ye believed, as well as in what have
ye believed? Is that in which thou hast believed able
to keep ever before thee that thou committest unto
Him?
YES- through thy Angel, through thy SELF that IS
the Angel – does the self speak with thy ideal!
(1646-1)

A man is told that he may meet in the flesh some of the White
Brotherhood which is a group of very anointed spiritual beings who
seek to help mankind.
Some of the Holy Saints who have lived on Earth are described
as being similar to the Angels and are members of the White
Brotherhood.

Q: Is it likely that I will meet any of the Brothers in
the flesh, as Mr. Cayce has done, in this incarnation?
(White Brotherhood)

A: Ye may meet many. For, oft doth man entertain
Angels unawares.

Q: What can I do further to become more serviceable
to the Brotherhood and my fellow man?

A: Purifying, dedicating, consecrating self and purpose
in the Master – the ONE Master - Him.
(3011-3)

I prayed for years asking God what the purpose of all this incarnating and Life on Earth is all about.

Then one day over forty years ago, Jesus Christ spoke to me in a voice and said, "To teach the Angels a lesson."

I am still not sure exactly what it meant but I have my own interpretation of the meaning.

The interesting thing is that a few years later I met a woman who had a Gift of prophecy.

This woman did not have a Cayce or New Age background but had a regular fundamentalist Bible education as a Minister.

She had asked the same question and received the exact same direction.

I felt that her hearing the very same words that I did was a confirmation that it was indeed of God.

This woman is someone who heard from Jesus Christ daily and has had many dreams and visions that I have seen come true over the years.

Lucifer rebelled in Heaven and he and a third of the Angels were cast out. The Angels were cast out instead of being destroyed as their rebellion had to fully manifest to demonstrate forever the results of their disobedience and sin of selfishness and self glorification. Then, the forces of evil were loosed for the correction of many.

How else could we learn the difference between God's will and selfish will or Good and Evil?

By their fruits we shall know them when they are grown into full manifestation.

> ...that the Prince of this world, Satan, Lucifer, the Devil – as a SOUL – made those necessities, of the consciousness in materiality; that man might – or that the soul might- become aware of its separation from the God-Force.
>
> Hence the continued warring that is ever present in materiality or in the flesh, or the warring - as it is termed – between those influences of Good and Evil.
>
> (262-89)

Lucifer is described as a soul. But there is no Reading that mentions that he has ever incarnated in flesh.

I personally think that some of the fallen Angels did manifest in flesh and are still here.

One of the issues of the rebellion in Heaven was that the Angels wanted the position that Christ had and the sons were to have. They wanted to be sons, too.

Perhaps they have been given that opportunity.

Nevertheless, I do not think that it is a good idea to go around thinking we are all Angels. Isn't being a son as a portion of Christ in God enough?

Remember that self glorification was part of the fall and is one of the fruits of the Anti-Christ Spirit.

But we still have the potential to be as Gods in Christ.

> I have said, Ye are Gods; and all of you are children of the Most High.
> Psalm 82:6

> For, as the Master gave, "Ye ARE Gods," if ye will use His force of desire and will in His Kingdom, but NOT thine own.
> (262-64)

> For, ye ARE Gods! But you are becoming Devils or real Gods!
> (281-30)

> For ONLY in man is there the existence of the soul that is not just universal, but individual; capable of becoming as a God, as One with the creative forces.
> (1587-1)

> Thus as ye apply Brotherly Love, patience, long suffering, gentleness – in thy dealings with thy fellow

man - ye may commune with the Holy Saints that are
as Angels before the Throne of God.
(3617-1)

Another controversial subject that needs to be mentioned is spiritual
Guides and Masters.
The Readings warned about going to outside influences for guidance
and recommended that we go within directly to the Throne of Grace
through the ONE Master, Jesus Christ. However, many celestial
beings as Angels and highly developed entities are often used as
messengers by God.
Often loved ones that are departed can be sent to us. Then we all
have our personal Guardian Angels.
There are loving beings who serve God that also seek to help us.
Mediumship as such and spiritualism is frowned upon in the
Readings as not the best form of communication for guidance
except for closure and Peace about loved ones who have died.
However, it does occur at times in the Readings themselves.
The Archangel Michael was a frequent visitor to the Readings and
gave many messages and prayers.
There are Readings for individuals who had an Angel as a Guide
who was also one used by God in many other capacities besides for
this entity.

Q: Who is giving this information?

A: That same that stood in the position for the entity as
a Guide and an aide, and that one who may be termed
the Guardian of this entity's activities – Demetrius…

Q: What is Demetrius at present?

A: The Body's Guardian Angel. As he stood and
reasoned with Paul, again as he stood as the aide to
Paul in the Spirit world, this entity in attune with that
as was given by this entity as the messenger in Egypt

- for Demetrius there, again, the Brother and aide in the flesh.
(311-6)

The Cayce Readings were said to come from his own higher self, the unconscious Minds of those seeking or from the Akashic Records of an individual rather than that of a Guide. Cayce was able to access the Christ within himself and the Christ without.

In a few of the Readings a mysterious Source, that of an Angel named Halaliel appeared and offered to be their Guide.

> COME, my children! Ye no doubt have gained from the comment this day a new initiate has spoken in or through this channel. (Edgar Cayce);
> Halaliel, that was with those in the beginning who WARRED with those that had separated themselves and became as naught.
> (262-56)

> Q: Who is Halaliel?

> A: One in and with whose courts Ariel fought when there was the rebellion in Heaven.
> Now, where is Heaven? Where is Ariel and who was he? A companion of Lucifer or Satan, and one that made for the disputing of the influences in the experiences of Adam in the Garden.
> (262-57)

The Cayce group rejected the offer by Halaliel as they felt that they should stick with the Christ as Guide since Jesus Christ was over all the Angels being a part of the Godhead. Why accept anyone lower when they could be guided by the Throne of Grace itself?
The Readings agreed later that they had made the right choice.

> He is to be the Master, the Christ, sufficient unto every soul, the MAKER, the CREATOR of all that is in this sphere! The LORD of all! Let Him send whom He would for the development, but rather prepare thine own Body, thine own soul, for that meeting with Him.
> (254-71)

This seemed to be the way to determine if a Guide were acceptable. If it were directed by Christ, it will NOT deny Him and will be coming in His name. These others are only as Lights along the Way. The Truth is only in Him, Jesus Christ. We were told to "Try the Spirits."

> TRY ye the Spirits. TRY ye the aspects; they that acknowledge that He, the Christ is come in the flesh are of the Spirit of Truth.
> (922-1)

> Better turn it into spirituality rather than an "ism". The divine is within self.
> Hear the voice within, NOT the Tempter from without.
> (5018-1)

> And if He chooses a director or Guide to walk with thee day by day, well; but why walk with a disciple when ye may walk with the Master?
> (2441-2)

> Q: How can I discern the helpful entities or forces from those forces that would do me harm?

> A: In each experience ASK that they acknowledge the Life, the death, the Resurrection of Jesus, the Christ.

They that answer only as in the affirmative; otherwise, "Get thee behind me, I will have no part with thee.
Through His name only will I ACCEPT direction."
(422-1)

...as the Master gave; the children of this world are wise in their own conceit; again, that the children of this world are wise even unto those that are the Children of Light.
(262-93)

The above Reading also states that the Children of Light are considered as babes by the worldly wise.

There are instances in the Readings when a certain Guide was acceptable and other times warnings were given that they were not. Just because a person dies does not make them enlightened. Most of those in the borderland need our help and are not any more developed than we are.

Those that climb up some other Way are called thieves and robbers. This scripture is quoted a lot in the Readings. It is therefore possible to attain awareness without earning it or having it given by God.
I think that psychedelic drugs are an illegal Way to enter into higher spiritual realms. (Just ask anyone who went through the LSD drug culture in the 1960s.)
There are many drugs now available that can be a method of being able to tune into other levels of realities and dimensions one has not merited.
The psychic centers can be forced open by drugs and other influences, even fasting and meditation.
The Angels of death use material things to lure souls away from God.

> While the material things exist, yet to thee and to thine own Life they be emblematical experience.
>
> For the Angels of Light only use material things for emblems, while the Angels of death use these as to lures that may carry men's souls away.
>
> (1159-1)

Many individuals incarnate as a group and it is similar to a cosmic or spiritual family.

Edgar Cayce seemed to continually meet the same individuals over and over in most of his Lifetimes.

When his Twin–Soul was not in the incarnation with him, she was influencing and helping from the other side.

There are special circumstances when Guides are a part of our soul group and beneficial.

Individual Guides as a rule were not recommended, as the One Guide for all is within.

> If ye seek individual Guides – these we would NOT give as that best to be entertained.
>
> (2251-1)

> Q: In view of the WARNING in my Life Reading about NOT using psychics to my undoing, is there any danger to me in such a venture?
>
> A: IF self is constantly surrounded with that purpose, that desire to fulfill that He would have thee do, it is well. IF it is to lend self for those that are unnamed, or having a name below, beyond or between HIS NAME, not so well.
>
> (1058-5)

> Q: How may I be given a Master for spiritual guidance?

A: Read that as has been given as to WHO IS thy Master! There should be only ONE!

For, as He hath given. "If ye love me, ye will keep my commandments, and I AND the Father will come and abide with thee."

Seekest thou some other Way?

Hast thou not accepted Him as the Way?

Analyze thyself. Take thought, and act.

For there is no other name given under Heaven whereby men, or women, may be saved.

(1947-7)

There are impostors and seducing Spirits that seek to lead us away from God.

They are very experienced at their jobs and can cause much confusion.

Those who have not made spiritual commitments are the ones most susceptible to deceptions.

It is important that we make our commitment to Truth, for one day we shall all stand before the judgment bar.

Regardless of spiritual belief or religious affiliation, we can all agree in the ideal of a loving God whom we can serve and we can seek to make wherever we are a better place for all, loving and helping others who come into our lives.

For, as has been given, when the last trumpet is sounded and the VOICE shall say time is to be NO more, then may the record of each soul become fully known to all that have hidden themselves in that which has been left as the approach of soul to its Maker. For, all shall stand before that judgment bar, before the Lamb, before Him who has created the Heavens and the Earth and set them in their varied realms of activity, and given the Earth to the souls, His brethren, His companions, that they might enter

> there and - in the activities of their consciousness to
> the action of individuals one to another – show forth
> that which makes for the acceptance or rejection of
> that which is their approach to Him.
>
> (585-2)

One more controversial subject...
When we return back to God, do we keep our individuality or can
we be dissolved back into the Oneness???
This is our own personal choice.
It is the will of God for us to keep our individuality as souls and still
be One with Him, but we can choose to be blotted out.

> The soul is a portion of the Whole, with that
> companionship of the subsconscious or unconscious
> forces (the Mind of the soul), with its spiritual
> companion that makes the individual entity as a
> portion of the Whole, with the will that makes it so,
> and knowing itself to be a portion of the Whole yet
> NOT the Whole, yet retaining its IDENTITY in the
> Whole...
>
> (1924-1)

> ...to be One with the creative forces from which every
> entity emerges in the beginning.
> ...Not to be LOST wholly in the Oneness of the
> Father, but with the abilities to know self to be One
> with – yet of – the Father.
>
> (283-4)

> For, Life is of the Creator – and it may only be changed,
> it CANNOT be ended or destroyed.
> It can ONLY return from whence it came.
>
> (497-1)

The soul cannot be destroyed but it can be dissolved back into its Source if it banishes itself or chooses Ways that lead to nothingness and self annihilation.
It will not know itself to be itself anymore.
This is like putting the pancake back into the batter and it is dissolved again into its original ingredients.

> Q: Is it the destiny of every spiritual entity to eventually become One with God?
>
> A: Unless that entity wills its BANISHMENT.
> As is given with man, in the Giving of the soul, the will, wherewith to manifest in the entity, whether spiritual, whether material.
> With that, the entity, either spiritual or physical may banish itself.
> Again a compliance with Law; as has been given.
> As in destiny, meaning a Law, compliance with a Law, destined to be subject, or BEING the Law. The destruction of some destined to the contribution to the destruction of such Law.
> (900-20)

So the entity or the soul or One Body, that is separated and has its abilities for Life and activity and movement in its various spheres, is as the atom in the universe; that may make or MAR that which will create with the Creator the purpose, the need to which it has been appointed. Or it may turn empty handed, and indeed – as has been given- to OUTER DARKNESS.
(633-2)

As a corpuscle in the Body of God, ye are free willed
- and thus a co-creator with God...

> An individual entity's experience must be finished before the entity may either be BLOTTED OUT or come into full Brotherhood...
> (3003-1)

It makes no sense to return the original energy or Life force of God within us back to the Source at the expense of the destruction of the soul individuality.
The Whole purpose of souls and manifestations in the first place was about companionship.
How can God be companionable with a nonentity or nothingness?
It is not God's will for any soul to perish.
To blot out the soul's individual self is defeating the purpose of creation.
What parent wants to destroy its own child or turn it back into what it was before it was created?
It seems to be a clever deception or a trap of the Dark Forces to kill souls.
It is what I call the "Second Death" or final death.

Remember the Angel Ariel who was with the Lucifer group.

> Where is Ariel, and who was he?
> A companion of Lucifer or Satan, and one that made for the disputing of the influences in the experiences of Adam in the Garden.
> (262-57)

The Angels of death are real evil influences!!!

> No urge exceeds the will of the individual entity, that Gift from and of the creative forces that separates man, even the Son of Man, from the rest of creation. Thus it is made to be ever as One with the Father, knowing itself to be itself and yet One with the Father, never losing its identity.

For, to lose its identity is death indeed, separation from the creative force.

The soul may never be lost, for it returns to the One force, but knows not itself to be itself anymore.

(3357-1)

An ideal means that to which the entity may, itself, ever look up, knowing itself to be gradually becoming a portion, but NEVER may it be the Whole.

...at an At-Onement with same, a portion of same, but NEVER the Whole.

(256-2)

Why do you think Jesus said, "No man cometh unto the Father except by me?"

Jesus saith unto him, "I am the Way, the Truth, and the Life: No man cometh unto the Father, but by me.

If ye had known me, ye should have known my Father also: And from henceforth ye know Him, and have seen Him."

Philip saith unto Him, "Lord shew us the Father, and it sufficeth us."

Jesus saith unto him, "Have I been so long time with you, and yet hast thou not known me, Philip? He that hath seen me hath seen the Father; and how sayest thou then, shew us the Father?

Believest thou not that I am in the Father, and the Father in me? The words that I speak unto you I speak not of myself: But the Father that dwelleth in me, He doeth the works.

Believe me that I am in the Father and the Father in me: Or else believe me for the works' sake."

John 14:6-11

He cannot hear thy petition. Why? Because there
has another entered with thee into thy chamber, thy
closet, and He thy God - that answers prayer, that
FORGIVES through His Son – is shut out.
In His name, then, ONLY; for, as He gave, "They that
climb up some other Way are thieves and robbers."
(262-77)

Me ye have known, and the Way ye know, for I am the
Way, the Truth, and the Light.
Had ye NOT known me ye would NOT have known
the Father, but seeing me, IN ME ye see the Father also.
(137-123)

Abide in me, and I in you. As the branch cannot bear
fruit of itself, except it abide in the vine; no more can
ye, except ye abide in me.
John 15:4

God desired companionship and created only One Son, the Christ.
The Son is in the bosom or center of the Father and is the part or
portion of God that manifests.
All souls and universes are created IN the Christ Son.
That is our ONE Source. There is only ONE soul, the Christ. The
Christ Light gives Life to every individual being that lives. He that
lives in Christ lives in the Father as well.

...remember it has been given that the purpose of the
heart is to know YOURSELF to BE yourself and yet
ONE with God even as Jesus, even as is represented in
God the Father, Christ the Son, and the Holy Spirit;
each KNOWING THEMSELVES to be themselves
yet ONE!
(281-37)

Follow in that Way, for my yoke is easy and my burden
is Light, for in me is Life, and the water of Life, for I
am the vine, and ye are the branches. He that dwelleth
in me dwelleth in the Father also.
   (853-1)

Ye abiding in me and I in the Father, WE - the Father,
I – will COME and abide with thee.
   (272-9)

Jesus is not very popular in our culture today.
Jesus is not politically correct.
Yet we who know Him, behold Him as the Face of the Father.

For indeed He is the Creator. He indeed is the Maker
of all that doth appear.
For all Power in Heaven and in Earth has been given
unto His keeping…
   (1499-1)

He, the Son was in the Earth-Earthy even as we – and
yet is of the Godhead.
Then Mind, as He, was the Word - and dwelt among
men; and WE BEHELD HIM AS THE FACE OF
THE FATHER.
   (1567-2)

What, then, will you do with Jesus?
   (254-95)

ABOUT THE AUTHOR

Joan Clarke was born June 9, 1938 in Norfolk, VA and died on September 11, 2009 in Edenton, NC. She knew as a child that she would become a writer. Her lifelong imagination and story-telling are renowned within her family circle. After marriages, four children, and seven grandchildren, Joan Clarke has written two books, both unique and spiritually oriented. Joan's failing health in her last few years of life prompted her to finally finish writing what she had begun many years earlier. She attributed her years of studying both the Edgar Cayce Readings and the Bible to her ability to tie them together in her final book. This book is a tribute to Jesus Christ Himself.

To quote the author herself, she stated:
"I have been a student of the Edgar Cayce Readings for over 40 years. Every day I learn something new or see a concept in more depth. Living by the Readings has been a great blessing to me on the physical, mental, and spiritual levels. Every day I apply the principles from the Cayce Readings in my life from the dietary rules and home remedies to dream interpretation and revelations of Creation and the Christ.

I was fortunate to have known Gladys Davis Turner, who was a great inspiration to me and who shared a lot of her experiences with me. I feel blessed to have known Hugh Lynn Cayce as he was an expert on the Readings in every subject.

I also lived at A.R.E. in the winter of 1966 until June of 1967 in the south dorm of the old building. I did private research for Paula and Edward Fitzgerald who wrote plays based on the Readings. I researched the Readings for Col. Frank Adams to add to a book of poetry by Lydia Clark Markum."